ANTISEMITISM

ANTISEMITISM

WHAT EVERYONE NEEDS TO KNOW®

DAVID HARRIS

OXFORD
UNIVERSITY PRESS

OXFORD
UNIVERSITY PRESS

Oxford University Press is a department of the University of Oxford. It furthers the University's objective of excellence in research, scholarship, and education by publishing worldwide. Oxford is a registered trade mark of Oxford University Press in the UK and certain other countries.

"What Everyone Needs to Know®" is a registered trademark of Oxford University Press.

Published in the United States of America by Oxford University Press
198 Madison Avenue, New York, NY 10016, United States of America.

CIP data is on file at the Library of Congress

ISBN 978–0–19–780067–6 (pbk.)
ISBN 978–0–19–780066–9 (hbk.)

DOI: 10.1093/wentk/9780197800669.001.0001

Paperback printed by Integrated Books International, United States of America
Hardback printed by Bridgeport National Bindery, Inc., United States of America

The manufacturer's authorized representative in the EU for product safety is Oxford University Press España S.A., Parque Empresarial San Fernando de Henares, Avenida de Castilla, 2 – 28830 Madrid (www.oup.es/en or product.safety@oup.com). OUP España S.A. also acts as importer into Spain of products made by the manufacturer.

To my Libyan-born wife, Jou Jou, and to the memory of my Soviet-born mother, Nelly, and Hungarian-born father, Eric, each of whom faced real-world, life-threatening antisemitism and, miraculously, survived.

I'm sorry, but I don't want to be an emperor. That's not my business. I don't want to rule or conquer anyone. I should like to help everyone—if possible—Jew, Gentile—black man—white. We all want to help one another. Human beings are like that. We want to live by each other's happiness—not by each other's misery. We don't want to hate and despise one another. In this world there is room for everyone. And the good earth is rich and can provide for everyone. The way of life can be free and beautiful, but we have lost the way.

—Charlie Chaplin, *The Great Dictator*, 1940

CONTENTS

ACKNOWLEDGMENTS

In the fall of 2023, I received an unexpected phone call. It came from Nancy Toff, who identified herself as a vice president and executive editor of Oxford University Press.

She asked if, in light of growing antisemitism, I might be interested in writing a book on the topic aimed for a wide audience. I was beyond honored, much as I was distressed by the need for such a book at this time.

Nancy has since retired after a distinguished, decades-long career in publishing, but not before getting me started, sharing her incredible experience, and offering a remarkably steady navigational hand.

She turned over this project to Angela Chnapko, a fellow executive editor at OUP. How fortunate I was! Angela is exceptionally capable at what she does, and the manuscript has been improved in countless ways, while my many questions along the way were always answered so ably and graciously.

In other words, without Nancy and Angela, there simply would have been no book. My heartfelt and everlasting gratitude goes to both.

And I had another stroke of luck. When it came to the production phase of this book, I was assigned to Rajeswari Srinivasan. Not only was Raji impressively capable and professional, but also always accessible and supportive.

I was assisted in the long journey of writing this volume by a remarkable young woman, Martha Kashti, a graduate of the University of Oxford. I had come to know her through our shared interest in the important work of the Institute for the Study of Global Antisemitism and Policy (ISGAP).

Martha was there every step of the way, with her enthusiasm, can-do spirit, talent, and personal commitment to the project. From research to technology to sounding board, she was an integral part of the entire process, and I could not be more admiring and appreciative.

Speaking of ISGAP, its founding and visionary leader, Dr. Charles Small, a world-class scholar on antisemitism, was an inspiration for my work. He helped me understand the intellectual underpinnings of what many have called the world's oldest and most enduring social disease.

Finally, my family played a significant role in the writing of this book. My late parents were victims of frenzied antisemitism—my mother, Nelly, first from the Bolsheviks, then from the Nazis; my father, Eric, from the Nazis. My wife, Giulietta, experienced brutal Jew-hatred in her native Libya.

I wanted to understand the sources of this deep, deadly, and obsessive hatred that directly affected the three people closest to me, not to mention countless millions more. I also sought to help others to do so as well.

I earnestly hope this book will contribute to that goal, ensuring that our three sons, their wives, and our eight grandchildren can live in a world safe for Jews—and for all people of goodwill.

AN AGE-OLD HATRED

Antisemitism is among the world's oldest, most enduring forms of virulent hatred. Indeed, some observers argue it is the oldest. Tragically, it has been an all-too-frequent factor in the millennia-long development of Western civilization.

Antisemitism has ebbed and flowed like a mutating malignancy into new forms and variations and proven stubbornly resilient. It has caused untold harm to Jews and Jewish communities throughout the centuries in which antisemites define the Jew as the enemy of all that is good and decent. The deicide charge, blood libels, inquisitions, ghettos, expulsions, pales of settlement, pogroms, forced conversions, discriminatory laws, and, most catastrophically, the Holocaust were the result.

At its heart, antisemitism has two distinguishing features. First, it is an elaborate conspiracy theory. It ascribes to Jews, a tiny percentage of the world's population, extraordinary powers of evil intent and behavior—from plagues to economic depressions, from war to revolution. Second, it is an irrational and contradictory belief system. Jews are variously seen as capitalists and communists, White and non-White, manipulative insiders and unassimilable outsiders.

History teaches that antisemitism is a disease which begins with the Jews but does not end with them. Once antisemitism is unleashed, it knows no bounds and can attack the very fabric of society, making the Jewish people, some would say, the early warning system. This deadly strain of hatred often turns against other minority groups as well, not to mention foundational democratic values, beginning with equal rights and equal protection before the law. Therefore, antisemitism should be viewed as a universal human rights issue of importance to all, and not solely as a Jewish or Israeli concern.

In the 21st century, antisemitism is once again resurgent after several postwar decades when it appeared, at least in Western democratic societies, to be in remission. In recent years, the FBI has reported that well over half of all religiously motivated hate crimes in the United States targeted Jews, even though Jews comprise just over 2% of the population.[1] This led the Biden administration to launch the National Strategy to Combat Antisemitism in 2023, the first time in U.S. history such a nationwide effort was established. The 27-member European Union had announced its own strategy two years earlier, while urging member states to develop national action plans and appoint special envoys to monitor and combat antisemitism.

Why is there a rise in antisemitism just decades after the Holocaust and when so many countries, institutions, and leaders have declared "Never again"? Are there multiple sources of antisemitism today? How relevant is the perception of Israel, the one Jewish-majority nation, to an understanding of contemporary antisemitism? How has the explosion of social media contributed to the rise in Jew-hatred? As the Holocaust recedes in memory, and survivors and eyewitnesses are fewer among us, does this change the discourse? And, against the backdrop of age-old antisemitism, what are the possible responses that have a chance of succeeding? Is there any conceivable "Pfizer vaccine" to cure the world, once and for all, of this deadly pathology?

1. U.S. Department of Justice, "2022 FBI Hate Crimes Statistics," October 2023, https://www.justice.gov/crs/highlights/2022-hate-crime-statistics.

It is striking how little understood antisemitism, including the term itself, still is. This extends quite widely to political leaders, educational authorities, law enforcement and the judiciary, civic groups, and media outlets. Polls have also shown how knowledge of the Holocaust, which was widely considered to be a firewall against the resurgence of antisemitism, is declining, notwithstanding ongoing attention to the topic in education, museums and memorials, and culture.

There have been excellent scholarly studies of antisemitism from a historical perspective, largely geared to a specialized readership. However, this book, intended for a wider audience, sets the stage with a look back in time, then focuses on antisemitism in its various contemporary guises.

1

WHAT IS ANTISEMITISM?

A key to understanding antisemitism is defining it. Yet this has not always proved as simple as it might seem for a social pathology in existence for millennia. First, the term "antisemitism" itself, sometimes hyphenated, came into use only in the late 19th century. Why then? What preceded it? In the 21st century, there have been attempts to create a standardized definition, most notably by the intergovernmental International Holocaust Remembrance Alliance (IHRA), which also seeks to take into account anti-Zionism as a key element of contemporary antisemitism. What exactly is this definition? Has it been universally accepted? And what are the practical implications of such an effort to create a standardized understanding of the term?

What is antisemitism in plain speech?

Above all, antisemitism is an enduring and infinitely adaptable conspiracy theory.

It ascribes to Jews, as a group, malevolent characteristics and aims. Even if historical circumstances should change over time, those essential characteristics and aims do not.

Thus, for hardcore antisemites who seek off-the-shelf answers for the world's calamities, the Jews offer a convenient, one-size-fits-all answer. Jews are evil incarnate. They are the devil incarnate. They are Satan incarnate. They are the anti-Christ.

According to this worldview, or, more precisely, demonology, the Jews are always plotting, scheming, deceiving, cheating, undermining, sabotaging, or manipulating. They are at any moment conspiring with Masons, Bolsheviks, globalists, cosmopolitans, Black people, even Nazis to undermine the established order and gain power. They are clannishly out for themselves at the expense of others, seeking political and economic control, starting wars for their own benefit, spreading diseases to the non-Jewish population, pursuing other nefarious aims to weaken and dominate society at large (Figure 1.1). How else, then, to explain their ability to achieve "disproportionate influence" in key sectors of society, be it in prewar Germany or contemporary America, other than by their treachery?

To those who malevolently seek explanation, justification, or distraction, such trigger words as "Jew," "Yid," "Hebrew," or, in the modern era, "Zionist" or "Israeli" can offer an irresistible temptation, with the foreknowledge that there is likely to be a ready-made audience that picks up the charge and runs with it. After all, how many people have been conditioned to believe any and all accusations against the Jewish people and, since 1948, the Jewish state?

And to match the wicked intentions, Jews must be depicted accordingly: caricatured, demonized, vulgarized. They need to be portrayed as short, hunched, ghoulish, gnarled, hook-nosed, beady-eyed, secretive, avaricious, sinister, mysterious, animalistic, donkey-eared, spidery, ratlike, blubbery, or otherwise physically repulsive and subhuman.

Because of the Jews' alleged perfidy, they merit no understanding, much less sympathy. Whatever tragedies befall them are fully deserved. After all, should there be any other fate for unadulterated wickedness?

And if, after the Holocaust, antisemitism got a "bad" name among those who thought the gas chambers and crematoria

1re Année — N 16 | Paris et Départements, le Numéro : 10 Centimes | Samedi 28 Octobre 1893

LA LIBRE PAROLE

ILLUSTRÉE

La France aux Français !

RÉDACTION 14 Boulevard Montmartre | Directeur : EDOUARD DRUMONT | ADMINISTRATION 14, boulevard Montmartre

LEUR PATRIE.

Figure 1.1 An 1893 cover of *La Libre Parole*, a notoriously antisemitic newspaper published by Edouard Drumont in France, depicting a grotesque, power-hungry Jew straddling a globe. The two-word caption underneath says, "Their homeland."

"Leur Patrie (Libre Parole illustrée, 1893-10-28)," *GetArchive*, https://timelessmoon.getarchive.net/amp/media/leur-patrie-libre-parole-illustree-1893-10-28-cbe190.

were a step too far, then the rebirth of Israel offered a new outlet, according to some observers, including Michal Cotler-Wunsh, Israel's special envoy for combating antisemitism.

According to this view, the evil is shifted from the individual Jew to the Jewish nation, together with the projection of every imaginable sin, from genocide to ethnic cleansing, war crimes to child murder. Yet, at the same time, proponents insist that such accusations are anti-Israel, not antisemitic, even as they are transparently transferable tropes from long-held antisemitic beliefs and have no relation to the truth.

At heart, then, antisemitism is an irrational, intractable set of views about an entire group of people. Facts alone are unlikely to cure the disease. As the Irish author Jonathan Swift wrote centuries ago, "You cannot reason a person out of a position he did not reason himself into in the first place."[1]

When was the term "antisemitism" first used? What words were used to describe the phenomenon before this term was coined?

In 1879, German anti-Jewish journalist Wilhelm Marr coined *Antisemitismus* to mean hatred of the Jewish "race." His definition shifted the discourse, defining Jew-hatred as racial and not, as in previous centuries, primarily religious. Over time, the term has become the overarching definition to encompass hostility and hatred of Jews.

However, even prior to the 19th century, there were other linguistic manifestations of the phenomenon. Perhaps best known is William Shakespeare's Shylock in *The Merchant of Venice* (1598), who is portrayed as greedy, bloodthirsty, and utterly revolting. The name Shylock became synonymous with these vile traits over the ensuing centuries.

1. Good Reads, "Quotable Quote," accessed April 14, 2025, https://www.goodreads.com/quotes/9838985-you-cannot-reason-a-person-out-of-a-position-he.

Shylock's character demands a pound of flesh for a debt owed to him, even after the debtor, Antonio, offers to pay him twice the amount. In other words, Shylock's wickedness knows no limits.

Jews have been consistently accused of bloodthirstiness (perhaps most famously in the blood libel, the false allegation that Jews need the blood of non-Jews for ritual purposes). The earliest references to blood libel are found in the Hellenistic writings of Apion in the second century BCE. The first charge of blood libel in Europe during the Middle Ages was made by William of Norwich in 1144. In this case, the Jews of Norwich in England were charged with ritual murder after the body of a young boy was discovered in the woods. They were alleged to have "bought a Christian child [the 'boy-martyr' William] before Easter and tortured him with all the tortures wherewith our Lord was tortured, and on Long Friday hanged him on a rood in hatred of our Lord."[2]

Accusations of blood libel continue to the present. Israel is accused of "stealing organs" from Palestinians killed in Gaza or, in the words of Britain's Baroness Tonge, harvesting organs of earthquake victims in Haiti while allegedly assisting on the ground. She has also claimed that "child murder" is a preferred "ritual" for Israel, with babies being a "favorite target."[3]

Jews have also been classified as inhuman. To return to *The Merchant of Venice*, Shylock is described as both "the very devil incarnate" and a "cut-throat dog." At once, alas, the Jew is both all-powerful (the devil) and not quite human (a dog), to be at once feared and despised.

2. U.S. Holocaust Memorial Museum, "Blood Libel,": *Holocaust Encyclopedia*, accessed April 14, 2025, https://encyclopedia.ushmm.org/content/en/article/blood-libel.
3. Simon Rocker, "Tonge: Investigate IDF Stealing Organs in Haiti," *Jewish Chronicle*, February 11, 2010, https://www.thejc.com/news/tonge-investigate-idf-stealing-organs-in-haiti-xpfhpt5z.

Why is the word sometimes hyphenated and sometimes not?

There exists a debate around the spelling of the term "antisemitism." Should it be hyphenated?

The word "Semitic" was first used by German historians in the 18th century to group together languages of Middle Eastern origin with linguistic similarities. However, there is no such thing as a Semitic nation or shared heritage of a "Semitic people." Some, claiming to be of Semitic origin themselves, may use the term to fend off accusations of antisemitism.

With the advent of biological constructions of race in the mid-19th century, the concept of the Semite was developed as a racial category. This racial classification of Jews culminated in the Nazi ideology of the Jew as a Semitic race, "lesser than" the "pure" Aryan White race. The racialization of Jews is a phenomenon imposed on Jews rather than a self-identity embraced by a majority of Jews. In fact, the notion of Jews forming "one race" flies in the face of the multitude of groups who identify as Jews, from dark-skinned African, African American, and Yemeni Jews to light-skinned Jews from Europe.

Thus the etymological merger of the term "anti-Semitism," forming one, unhyphenated word; the term "antisemitism" seeks to confine its scope to Jew-hatred.

What is Zionism?

Zionism is the widely held belief among Jews that they have the right, as a people, to self-determination and sovereignty in the Jewish ancestral homeland. As it is phrased in "Hatikvah," Israel's national anthem, "To be a free people in our own land, the land of Zion and Jerusalem," Zionism refers to the millennia-old biblical, spiritual, metaphysical, and geographic link between a people and a land. According to this viewpoint, the denial of such a fundamental right is inherently antisemitic.

Others, however, assert that anti-Zionism is merely a criticism of the political ideology of Zionism and not an attack on the Jewish people. Those who take this view may also note that some Jews do not associate with the ideology of Zionism, including the ultra-Orthodox and anti-Zionist Neturei Karta, who "pray for the peaceful dismantlement of the state of Israel," believing that a Jewish state can come about only through divine action, not as a secular project.[4]

The heated debate about anti-Zionism as antisemitism is discussed further in Chapter 6.

Is there an accepted definition of antisemitism today?

In short, no. There are currently three definitions of antisemitism in circulation. Formally adopted in 2016, the working definition by the IHRA, an intergovernmental body of 35 member countries and 10 observer nations, is the most widely accepted:[5]

> Antisemitism is a certain perception of Jews, which may be expressed as hatred toward Jews. Rhetorical and physical manifestations of antisemitism are directed toward Jewish or non-Jewish individuals and/or their property, toward Jewish community institutions and religious facilities.
>
> To guide IHRA in its work, the following examples may serve as illustrations:
>
> Manifestations might include the targeting of the state of Israel, conceived as a Jewish collectivity. However, criticism of Israel similar to that leveled against any other country cannot be regarded as antisemitic. Antisemitism frequently charges Jews with conspiring to harm

4. Anti-Defamation League, "Neturei Karta," accessed April 14, 2025, https://www.adl.org/resources/backgrounder/neturei-karta.
5. International Holocaust Remembrance Alliance, "Working Definition of Antisemitism," accessed April 14, 2025, https://holocaustremembrance.com/resources/working-definition-antisemitism.

humanity, and it is often used to blame Jews for "why things go wrong." It is expressed in speech, writing, visual forms and action, and employs sinister stereotypes and negative character traits.

Contemporary examples of antisemitism in public life, the media, schools, the workplace, and in the religious sphere could, taking into account the overall context, include, but are not limited to:

1. Calling for, aiding, or justifying the killing or harming of Jews in the name of a radical ideology or an extremist view of religion.
2. Making mendacious, dehumanizing, demonizing, or stereotypical allegations about Jews as such or the power of Jews as collective—such as, especially but not exclusively, the myth about a world Jewish conspiracy or of Jews controlling the media, economy, government or other societal institutions.
3. Accusing Jews as a people of being responsible for real or imagined wrongdoing committed by a single Jewish person or group, or even for acts committed by non-Jews.
4. Denying the fact, scope, mechanisms (e.g. gas chambers) or intentionality of the genocide of the Jewish people at the hands of National Socialist Germany and its supporters and accomplices during World War II (the Holocaust).
5. Accusing the Jews as a people, or Israel as a state, of inventing or exaggerating the Holocaust.
6. Accusing Jewish citizens of being more loyal to Israel, or to the alleged priorities of Jews worldwide, than to the interests of their own nations.
7. Denying the Jewish people their right to self-determination, e.g., by claiming that the existence of a State of Israel is a racist endeavor.

> 8. Applying double standards by requiring of it a behavior not expected or demanded of any other democratic nation.
> 9. Using the symbols and images associated with classic antisemitism (e.g., claims of Jews killing Jesus or blood libel) to characterize Israel or Israelis.
> 10. Drawing comparisons of contemporary Israeli policy to that of the Nazis.
> 11. Holding Jews collectively responsible for actions of the state of Israel.
>
> Antisemitic acts are criminal when they are so defined by law (for example, denial of the Holocaust or distribution of antisemitic materials in some countries).
>
> Criminal acts are antisemitic when the targets of attacks, whether they are people or property—such as buildings, schools, places of worship and cemeteries—are selected because they are, or are perceived to be, Jewish or linked to Jews.
>
> Antisemitic discrimination is the denial to Jews of opportunities or services available to others and is illegal in many countries.

According to the IHRA website, 43 UN member states have adopted or endorsed this working definition of antisemitism. A wide range of regional, state, and local governments have done the same. According to the Combat Antisemitism Movement, 38 states in the United States have embraced this working definition. So, too, have many universities.[6] In the

6. Combat Antisemitism Movement, "CAM Information Hub Database of IHRA Antisemitism Definition Adoptions by US States," June 23, 2023, https://combatantisemitism.org/government-and-policy/cam-information-hub-database-of-ihra-antisemitism-definition-adoptions-by-us-states-2/.

On August 7, 2024, New Hampshire adopted the definition, bringing the total number of states to 38.

United Kingdom, for example, at least 119 universities have accepted the IHRA definition, including the University of Oxford and the University of Cambridge.

A further definition of antisemitism, which seeks to narrow the IHRA focus, especially with respect to anti-Israel and anti-Zionist behavior deemed to be antisemitic, is known as the Jerusalem Declaration on Antisemitism (JDA).[7] As of 2024, this definition has garnered 350 individual signatories.

A third definition of antisemitism is known as the NEXUS Document.[8] Like the Jerusalem Declaration on Antisemitism, this was also meant to limit the IHRA definition with respect to Israel, though not as narrowly. Nonetheless, critics of the NEXUS definition argue that it permits double standards against Israel to go unchallenged. The definition states that "treating Israel differently than other countries is not prima facie proof of antisemitism." However, supporters of the IHRA definition argue that treating Israel (the lone Jewish-majority state) differently than any other country is inherently antisemitic.

Notably, in the first U.S. federal strategy to combat antisemitism in 2022, the White House cited both IHRA and NEXUS in its plan, though not JDA, while placing more emphasis on IHRA.

Are there any other words used to describe "antisemitism"?

Yes. Other terms to describe antisemitism are "Jew-hatred," "Judeophobia," and "anti-Judaism."

7. JDA, "The Jerusalem Declaration on Antisemitism," accessed April 14, 2025, https://jerusalemdeclaration.org/.
8. NEXUS, "The Nexus Document," accessed April 14, 2025, https://nexusproject.us/the-nexus-document/.

If antisemitism is referred to as the world's oldest hatred, what were some of its earliest manifestations?

In the Greco-Roman period, Jewish resistance to the dominant polytheistic belief system resulted in early manifestations of antisemitism. During this time, many Jews refused to worship emperors as gods or to embrace a wide set of deities. For Jews, there was only one god, and that god did not take the form of a human being on earth, much less stone, brick, clay, or wooden renderings. As a result, Jews were seen as stubborn, disloyal, and untrustworthy.[9]

In the Christian era, Jews were held responsible for the crucifixion of Jesus Christ, the son of God. The destruction of the Temple by the Romans in 70 CE and the exile of the Jewish people were seen as just punishments for their sins and refusal to accept Christianity, deemed to be the superseding, replacement faith.

Jews were early dissenters. More often than not, they refused to go along with the status quo or majority, whether it was ruler worship, idol worship, polytheism, or, later, the two other monotheistic religions, Christianity and Islam, that emerged from Judaism and were meant to leapfrog it theologically. And Jews were early revolutionaries who introduced new concepts of human equality, morality, law, justice, and compassion that threatened the existing order.

After all, if there was only one God who was universal and unseen, that undercut the self-proclaimed divinity of rulers. Declaring that all human beings were created in the image of that God introduced the concept of human equality, anathema to the deeply stratified worlds at the time. And if there was a set of commandments governing human behavior and distinguishing between good and evil, that directly challenged the authority and edicts of those in charge. All along, the Jewish

9. Michael Berenbaum, "Anti-Semitism," *Britannica*, last updated April 11, 2025, https://www.britannica.com/topic/anti-Semitism.

core stubbornly clung to their faith, rituals, and laws, come what may. And given half a chance, they also succeeded in the workplace, triggering anger, envy, and resentment. Each of these strands contributed to the foundation of anti-Judaism and, as it was later called, antisemitism.

At its heart, is antisemitism a set of conspiracy theories?

Yes, antisemitism, at its heart, is a never-ending set of conspiracy theories, ascribing to Jews extraordinary power, malevolence, and imagination. Here are some examples.

Medieval Blood Libel: The term "blood libel" refers to the false allegation that Jews used the blood of non-Jewish, usually Christian, children for ritual purposes. The blood libel myth burgeoned in Europe in the 12th century, following the First Crusade. Christians chose to believe that not only did Jews want to kill them but also that they craved the "superior" blood of Christians.

In the medieval period, the blood libel was perhaps best illustrated in literature by the renowned 14th-century English author and poet Geoffrey Chaucer. In his most famous work, *The Canterbury Tales*, he includes *The Prioress' Tale*. A Christian child walks through a Jewish ghetto while singing a religious song. The Jews murder him. Even after his death, the child, blessed by the Virgin Mary, continues to sing, while the Jews are put to death. Literary scholars debate to this day whether Chaucer was intentionally antisemitic, indeed if he had ever had any contact with Jews, as no Jews lived in England for three centuries after their expulsion in 1290. Whatever the case, here was another illustration of alleged Jewish wickedness and perfidy, embedded in the canon of Western civilization for more than six centuries.

The accusations continued. In the modern era, Menachem Mendel Beilis was tried in tsarist Russia for allegedly killing and mutilating the body of a 13-year-old Christian boy for ritualistic purposes, triggering an outpouring of antisemitism, followed by imprisonment, a trial, and eventual exoneration. A fictionalized account of the ordeal, *The Fixer*, was written by Bernard Malamud and published in 1966.

In the 21st century, the Israeli government accused the BBC of perpetrating a "modern blood libel" in its coverage of an alleged Israeli strike on the al-Ahli Hospital in Gaza and claim of hundreds of fatalities. Subsequent investigations revealed the strike occurred due to an errant Palestinian Islamic Jihad missile.

The Dreyfus Affair: Alfred Dreyfus was a captain in the French army and a Jew. In 1894, he was wrongly accused of passing military secrets to the German embassy in Paris and convicted of treason. It took 12 years, during which Dreyfus endured harsh punishment, before he was finally exonerated and reinstated in the armed forces. The case divided France and exposed the wide chasm between liberal, secular, and republican forces and antisemitic, reactionary, and monarchist elements, and drew such prominent individuals as the writer Émile Zola, who accused the prosecutors of blatant antisemitism.

One of the journalists covering the case was Theodor Herzl, a Hungarian-born Jew writing for *Neue Freie Presse*, a Vienna-based newspaper. Witnessing the trial and the depth of antisemitism against a Jew who, on the surface, was fully integrated into French life and an officer in the French army helped convince Herzl that, in the end, Jews would never be fully accepted and protected as minorities, even in self-declared liberal societies. He believed this trial was evidence of the urgent need for a Jewish state and Jews' control over their own destiny. Indeed, in 1896 his book *Der Judenstaat* (*The Jewish State*) was published, a seminal event in the evolution of modern Zionist thought.

The Protocols of the Elders of Zion: *The Protocols of the Elders of Zion* is an antisemitic forgery, a concoction of the Russian secret police, published in Russia in 1905 as an appendix to *The Great in the Small: The Coming of the Anti-Christ and the Rule of*

Satan on Earth. It has 24 chapters, or protocols, which are allegedly minutes from secret planning meetings of Jewish leaders to rule the world by manipulating the economy, controlling the media, and fostering religious conflict.

By the 1920s the document was being circulated across Europe, the United States, South America, and Japan. An Arabic translation first appeared in the 1920s and continues to surface to the present day, including in citations by Hamas to justify attacks against Israel. And in 2002, Egypt's government-sponsored television channel aired a miniseries based on the *Protocols* during the Muslim holy month of Ramadan, which is peak time for the viewing audience. The extent of the damage done to the Jewish people by the *Protocols* for more than a century cannot be overstated.

Nazi Theories (Jewish Bolshevism, World War I, Genocide): Hitler frequently referred to the *Protocols* as evidence of the myth that "Jewish Bolsheviks" were conspiring to control the world. The *Protocols* subsequently played an important role in Nazi propaganda. The Nazi Party published at least 23 editions between 1919 and 1939, and the conspiratorial document was used widely in schools to indoctrinate youth.[10]

Jewish Bolshevism is an antisemitic conspiracy theory which claims that the Russian Revolution (1917) was a Jewish plot, falsely asserting Jewish domination of the Soviet Union—for starters, Lenin and Stalin were not Jews—and international communism. This theory was then used by the Nazis as a rationale for the German invasion of the USSR in 1941 and was one of the many justifications employed by the Nazis for the murder of 6 million Jews. Communist figures of Jewish descent, including Leon Trotsky, were cited to "prove" the "natural" attraction of Jews to communism.

10. U.S. Holocaust Memorial Museum, "Protocols of the Elders of Zion," *Holocaust Encyclopedia,* accessed April 14, 2025, https://encyclopedia.ushmm.org/content/en/article/protocols-of-the-elders-of-zion.

Further, the "stab-in-the-back" legend blamed the Jews for Germany and Austria's defeat in World War I. Indeed, the theory accused internal traitors—primarily Jews and communists—of working for foreign interests against Germany and Austria. In truth, Jews had served their country loyally in the war and, in fact, did so disproportionately to their numbers in the population.

The word "genocide" entered the linguistic lexicon in response to the Holocaust. Polish Jewish lawyer Raphael Lemkin coined the term in an effort to describe Nazi policies of systematic mass murder.[11] However, while the Nazis were carrying out this unprecedented annihilation, they actually accused their victims of the very crime. Indeed, a popular conspiracy theory was that Jews were planning mass murder against Nazi Germany. Nazi propaganda relied on a self-published book, *Germany Must Perish!*, written by an obscure American Jewish businessman, Theodore N. Kaufman, as proof of the Jews' genocidal intent.[12]

Doctors' Plot (1953): The Doctors' Plot was a Soviet state-sponsored conspiracy theory alleging that Soviet medical experts plotted to murder leading government and party officials. In 1953, nine doctors serving Soviet leaders—at least six of whom were Jewish—were arrested and charged with attempted murder and poisoning. Moreover, the doctors were accused of being employed by U.S. and British intelligence services, in addition to serving the interests of international Jewry. The Soviet press reported that all the doctors confessed their guilt. This saga drew on classical antisemitic tropes, including Jewish omnipotence, malevolence, disloyalty, and

11. U.S. Holocaust Memorial Museum, "What Is Genocide?," *Holocaust Encyclopedia*, accessed April 14, 2025, https://encyclopedia.ushmm.org/content/en/article/what-is-genocide.
12. U.S. Holocaust Memorial Museum, "Nazi Propaganda Poster Claiming American Jews Want to Exterminate the German People," accessed April 14, 2025, https://collections.ushmm.org/search/catalog/irn3770.

international connections. In 1956, Soviet leader Nikita Khrushchev admitted that Stalin had ordered the confessions to be forcibly extracted as a pretext to start a new purge and mass deportation of Soviet Jews to Birobidzhan, a remote region in eastern Russia that Stalin saw as a place to concentrate the Jewish population. Only Stalin's death in 1953 upended the plan.

9/11: Following the September 11, 2001, terror attacks by al-Qaeda, conspiracy theories that accused the Jews of being the masterminds, or puppeteers, abounded.

Allegations that the Mossad, Israel's intelligence agency, was behind the attacks quickly circulated. According to the Anti-Defamation League, the most common "proof" cited was the false claim that five Israeli Mossad agents were arrested on 9/11 by police who observed them filming and celebrating the attack.[13] A further charge was that Jewish neoconservatives plotted with members of the Bush administration to benefit Israel and create a pretext to invade Iraq for geopolitical and socioeconomic profit.

The familiar tropes and themes of Jewish power and manipulation anchored the theories surrounding 9/11, as Jews were accused of placing blame on Muslims and thereby deflecting blame from themselves.

Perhaps the most widely circulated antisemitic lie about 9/11 was that Jews or Israelis were forewarned of the attack and chose not to inform the U.S. government. This myth claimed that 4,000 Jews who worked in the World Trade Center were alerted by Israeli intelligence to avoid showing up for work on the devastating day. In a similar vein, the antisemitic trope of "Jewish lightning" surfaced. This trope, alluding to the stereotype of Jewish greed (in this case, the act of burning down a

13. Anti-Defamation League, "Antisemitic Conspiracies about 9/11 Endure 20 Years Later," accessed April 14, 2025, https://www.adl.org/resources/report/antisemitic-conspiracies-about-911-endure-20-years-later.

building to collect insurance money), was used against Jewish businessmen who had financial investments in the World Trade Center.

COVID Pandemic: A more recent antisemitic conspiracy theory is that COVID was a Jewish plot and that vaccines were invented by Jews to poison the population. A 2020 survey conducted by the University of Oxford revealed that one in five Britons believed that Jews created the virus for their own financial gain.[14] Another conspiracy theory was that the pandemic was spread by the Rothschild family, a name largely synonymous with Jewishness and that surfaces endlessly in antisemitic tropes, to increase global vaccine intake (to control the population and restrict civil rights).

A third conspiracy theory was advanced by Robert F. Kennedy Jr., a presidential candidate until August 2024, who, at a New York gathering, asserted, "Covid-19. There is an argument that it is ethnically targeted. Covid-19 attacks certain races disproportionately. Covid-19 is targeted to attack Caucasians and Black people. The people who are most immune are Ashkenazi Jews and Chinese."[15]

Money: Many conspiracy theories involving Jews focus on money: "Jews seek the money of non-Jews," "Jews control the U.S. Federal Reserve," "Jews get rich at the expense of others," "Jews manipulate global markets," and more. Sometimes the Rothschild name is invoked, or "globalists," "usurers," or "East Coast elites," or some other thinly veiled reference that unmistakably points the finger at Jews. Once again, these tropes, which ascribe malicious, malevolent motives to an entire group of people and their centuries-long

14. World Jewish Congress, "Conspiracy Myths," accessed April 14, 2025, https://www.worldjewishcongress.org/en/conspiracy-myths/jews-as-creators-of-the-covid-19-pandemic.
15. *New York Times*, "Robert F. Kennedy Jr. Airs Bigoted New Covid Conspiracy Theory about Jews and Chinese," July 15, 2023.

history, highlighted by figures like Shakespeare's Shylock, practically assure a ready-made audience prepared to believe the latest outlandish theory. Moreover, a vulgar and repulsive phrase, "to Jew someone down," meaning to negotiate a lower price, exists in the English language, as if Jews possess an innate, seemingly unscrupulous need to get a better deal, once again linking Jews and money. At one and the same time, then, Jews are seen as insatiably greedy and compulsively stingy.

In sum, conspiracy theorists are not limited to the extreme right or extreme left or to a physical or temporal location. They particularly flourish amid social or economic turmoil, providing instant explanations and convenient scapegoats.

How does one explain all the strikingly contradictory tropes—such as Jews as the embodiment of both capitalism and communism—used by antisemites?

Antisemitic beliefs are infinitely elastic, contradictory, durable, and conspiratorial. Antisemitism has no logic. There is no rational thought process behind antisemitism. Rather, it is based on an attribution to Jews of collective, irrational, and eternal evil.

Jews are deemed communists and Bolsheviks. Conversely, Jews are also seen as symbols and purveyors of global capitalism. They have been accused of being the ultimate insiders and, at the same time, irredeemable outsiders. And Jews have been accused, simultaneously, of "poisoning" White people and of being exemplars of White privilege.

Why have Jews been blamed throughout history for bringing antisemitism upon themselves?

The phenomenon of "victim blaming" is certainly not unique to antisemitism. Rapists may blame their victims for the clothing they wear. In another universe, Moscow blamed Poland, the first victim nation, for starting World War II, even as the Soviet army invaded Poland on September 17, 1939. The concept also applies to antisemitism. One definition of "victim blaming" reads, "Blaming the victim is a phenomenon in which victims of crimes or tragedies are held accountable for what happened to them."[16] By blaming Jews for causing their own antisemitism, the perpetrator is absolved of responsibility and the fault is deflected onto the victim. This does not mean to suggest, however, that individual Jews cannot be engaged in antisemitic acts out of identification with groups hostile to the larger Jewish community or other motivating factors.

As the Kaufman case illustrated, one of the most striking examples of blaming Jews for their victimhood was Hitler's repeated claims that they were planning a war against Germany, not the other way around. On January 30, 1939, for example, he declared: "If the international finance Jewry inside and outside Europe should succeed in plunging the nations once more into a world war, the result will be not the Bolshevization of the earth and thus the victory of Jewry, but the annihilation of the Jewish race in Europe."[17] He never needed hard evidence to support his outlandish claim. There was none.

Another noteworthy example is contained in a quote—"The Germans will never forgive the Jews for Auschwitz"—which is attributed to Zvi Rex, an Israeli psychoanalyst. In other words, Jews gave the Germans a bad name by revealing the depths of barbarism to which they descended in perpetrating the

16. Kendra Cherry, "Why Does Blaming the Victim Happen?," *verywellmind*, November 29, 2023, https://www.verywellmind.com/why-do-people-blame-the-victim-2795911.
17. Yad Vashem, "Extract from the Speech by Adolf Hitler, January 30, 1939," accessed April 14, 2025, https://www.yadvashem.org/docs/extract-from-hitler-speech.html.

Holocaust. By being a permanent reminder, in effect a mirror held up to Germany, the Jews could not be forgiven.

Are there some notable quotes about antisemitism which help shed light on the social disease?

> Who has made us Jews different from all other people? Who has allowed us to suffer so terribly up until now? It is God who has made us as we are, but it will be God, too, who will raise us up again. Who knows? It might even be our religion from which the world and all peoples learn good, and for that reason and only that reason do we suffer. We can never become just Netherlanders, or just English or representatives of any country for that matter. We will always remain Jews, but we want to, too.
>
> (Anne Frank)[18]

> Anti-Semitism can take many forms, from a mocking contemptuous ill-will to murderous pogroms. It can be met within the marketplace and in the Academy of Sciences, in the soul of an old man and in the games children play in the yard. Anti-Semitism is always a means rather than an end; it is a measure of the contradictions yet to be resolved. It is a mirror for the failings of individuals, social structures and state systems. Tell me what you accuse the Jews of, I'll tell you what you are guilty of. . . . Anti-Semitism is also an expression of a lack of talent, an inability to win a contest on equal terms—in science, in commerce, in craftsmanship or in painting. States look to the imaginary intrigues of World Jewry for explanations of their own failure.
>
> (Vasily Grossman) [19]

18. Julie Nathan, "Anne Frank on Antisemitism," *Times of Israel*, July 1, 2015, https://blogs.timesofisrael.com/anne-frank-on-antisemitism/.
19. Douglas Murray, "The Pathology of anti-Semitism," *The Spectator*, April 29, 2023, https://www.spectator.co.uk/article/what-the-left-doesnt-understand-about-anti-semitism/.

We have honestly endeavored to merge ourselves in the social life of surrounding communities and to preserve only the faith of our fathers. We are not permitted to do so. In vain we are loyal patriots.

(Theodor Herzl)[20]

The mark of Cain is stamped upon our foreheads. Across the centuries, our brother Abel was lain in blood which we drew, and shed tears we caused by forgetting Thy love. Forgive us, Lord, for the curse we falsely attributed to their name as Jews. Forgive us for crucifying Thee a second time in their flesh. For we knew not what we did.

(Pope John XXIII)[21]

My people were brought to America in chains. Your people were driven here to escape the chains fashioned for them in Europe. Our unity is born of our common struggle for centuries, not only to rid ourselves of bondage, but to make oppression of any people by others an impossibility.

(Martin Luther King Jr.)[22]

Each era has its antisemitism. Antisemitism is a famously shape-shifting virus. Sometimes in the past people hated Jews for their religion. Then you couldn't hate people for their religion, so you hated them for their race. Then when you weren't allowed to hate people for their race, you could hate the Jews for having and defending a state. This is the eternal challenge for the Jews. It's their challenge to be hated for being poor and for being rich. For being integrated and for not integrating. For being

20. Theodor Herzl, "The Jewish State (1896)," https://history.hanover.edu/courses/excerpts/261herz.html.
21. Good Reads, "Quotable Quote," accessed April 14, 2025, https://www.goodreads.com/quotes/106953-the-mark-of-cain-is-stamped-upon-our-foreheads-across.
22. Martin Luther King Jr., quoted in "American Jewish Congress (AJC)," Stanford University, accessed June 2, 2025, https://kinginstitute.stanford.edu/american-jewish-congress-ajc.

> stateless—remember "rootless cosmopolitans"—and also to be hated for having a state.
>
> (Douglas Murray)[23]

> [The Jew] has made a marvellous fight in this world, in all the ages; and has done it with his hands tied behind him. He could be vain of himself, and be excused for it. The Egyptian, the Babylonian, and the Persian rose, filled the planet with sound and splendor, then faded to dream-stuff and passed away; the Greek and the Roman followed, and made a vast noise, and they are gone; other peoples have sprung up and held their torch high for a time, but it burned out, and they sit in twilight now, or have vanished. The Jew saw them all, beat them all, and is now what he always was, exhibiting no decadence, no infirmities of age, no weakening of his parts, no slowing of his energies, no dulling of his alert and aggressive mind. All things are mortal but the Jew; all other forces pass, but he remains. What is the secret of his immortality?
>
> (Mark Twain)[24]

Why are Jews sometimes referred to as "the canary in the coal mine"?

For miners, having a canary along in the coal mine was a matter of life and death. If carbon monoxide, which is odorless and colorless, was present, the canary would feel it well before the miner, in fact dying as an alert to the miner to get out immediately.

Jews have often been cast by the world in essentially the same role as the canary. When antisemitism rises and Jews'

23. La règle du jeu (Revue RDJ), "L'Europe contre l'antisémitisme," Facebook, June 6, 2024, https://www.facebook.com/share/v/9mhDxv4R32qamWPG/?mibextid=UalRPS.
24. Mark Twain, "Concerning the Jews—The Essay," Ohr Somayach International, accessed April 14, 2025, https://ohr.edu/judaism/concern/concerna.htm.

anxiety level grows, it is a warning sign that something bigger and broader is amiss. It may first affect Jews, but left unchecked it will threaten society as a whole, be it other minorities, respect for human dignity, or broader democratic values.

Some Jews, however, reject the description of the canary in the coal mine not because it is inaccurate but because they say they are unwilling to continue to die from society's poisonous carbon monoxide, in this case antisemitism, so that others might have the chance to live.

What is the "dual loyalty" accusation?

Historically, it is the accusation that Jews cannot be trusted to be loyal to their country of residence because their only perceived loyalty is to themselves and their "insatiable quest" for "domination" and "control."

Jews were accused of poisoning the wells and spreading plagues and pandemics in the medieval period in Europe. Dreyfus was falsely charged with treason in France on the grounds of giving military secrets to Germany. Jews in Germany were alleged by Hitler to have aided the enemy in World War I. Jews in communist countries were hauled before kangaroo courts on the grounds of aiding "international Zionism" and other alleged acts of disloyalty. Since the rebirth of Israel in 1948, some accuse Jews in the diaspora of greater loyalty to the Jewish state than to the nation in which they live.

Jews have time and again shown their deep loyalty to their country, including the United States. If they weren't loyal, why would they continue to live there proudly when they have other choices, including Israel? Why would polls repeatedly show that Jews vote in American elections based on a wide range of issues, with Israel-related concerns being one of many but infrequently the driving force? And why would Jews serve in the armed forces or run for office on platforms dealing with the economy, taxes, environment, social issues, education, and the like?

True, most American Jews support a strong U.S.-Israel bilateral relationship, but why should that be news? For the same reasons of history, affinity, family, or faith, Irish Americans support a close link with Ireland, as do Korean Americans with South Korea, Indian Americans with India, Arab Americans with the Arab world, Hellenic Americans with Greece and Cyprus, and American Catholics with the Holy See.

But to single out Jews and question their trustworthiness, motives, or loyalty—or to harp on one shameful case in 75 years of an American Jew, Jonathan Pollard, convicted of spying for Israel—is once again to treat Jews differently than all others and hold them to a different standard of behavior. In the words of historian and former U.S. special envoy to monitor and combat antisemitism Deborah Lipstadt: "People were willing to believe it [charges of dual loyalty], even though the evidence from the very outset was shaky, because it made sense to them. They had been so exposed to this stereotype, it had become so much the pivot point and the central element of antisemitism that Jews have other loyalties, that it seemed like it must be true, and they were ready to believe the worst."[25]

25. World Jewish Congress, "The Myth of Dual Loyalty," April 14, 2025, https://www.worldjewishcongress.org/en/conspiracy-myths/the-myth-of-dual-loyalty.

2

ANTISEMITISM IN THE CHRISTIAN WORLD

It is impossible to understand the longevity, durability, and reach of antisemitism without considering its central role in Christian theology and dogma over nearly two millennia, at least until the Catholic Church's historic decision in 1965, at the Second Vatican Council, to end the deicide charge. That false accusation, claiming Jews were to be held eternally responsible for the death of Jesus, resulted in catastrophic consequences for the Jewish people. How did antisemitism manifest in the Catholic Church over the centuries, including, importantly, during the Holocaust? What was the aftermath of the 1965 decision? How have other modern-day Christian denominations, for example, the Lutheran Church, dealt with their own centuries-long hostility to Jews and Judaism? And what about evangelical Christians, whose eschatological beliefs have created a complex relationship with Jews?

What was the deicide charge? When did it first appear?

The deicide charge is the accusation that Jews crucified Jesus, the son of God, the Messiah, and the central figure in the Christian faith. It largely stems from a highly questionable sentence in the Gospel of Matthew 27:24–25, "His blood be on us, and on our children," also known as the blood curse. The impact of this accusation on the development of Western civilization, and on the fate of the Jewish people, cannot be overstated. It is almost beyond description.

In the modern era, the Catholic Church and many non-Catholic Christian theologians have repudiated the interpretation of these nine words as justification for the persecution of Jews. Rowan Williams, Archbishop of Canterbury from 2002 to 2012, wrote:

> The evangelist's bitterness at the schism within God's people that continues in his own day, his impatience with the refusal of the Jewish majority to accept the preaching of Jesus, overflows into this symbolic self-denunciation by "the people." It is all too likely that his first readers heard it as a corporate acknowledgement of guilt by the Jewish nation, and that they connected it, as do other New Testament writers, with the devastation of the nation and its sacred place in the terrible disasters of AD 70, when the Romans destroyed the Temple and along with it the last vestiges of independent power for the people. Read at this level, it can only make the contemporary Christian think of all the centuries in which Jewish guilt formed so significant a part of Christian self-understanding, and of the nightmare which was made possible by this in the twentieth century.[1]

From the time Catholicism first took root up until the eve of World War II, was its attitude toward Jews and Judaism consistent?

Former priest James Carroll's comprehensive history of the attitudes and policies of the Catholic Church since its

1. Rowan Williams, *Christ on Trial: How the Gospel Unsettles Our Judgment* (William B. Eerdmans, 2003), 32.

inception, *Constantine's Sword*, tells a powerful and immensely painful story.

While the church on occasion had its champions of moderation toward Judaism and the Jewish people, the overall storyline could perhaps best be summed up by this paragraph from his book: "For hundreds of years, popes had defined their power in terms of their sovereignty over Jews, and for nearly two thousand years Catholic theology had projected almost every affirmation of the Church against the negative screen of a detested Judaism. Here was the Church's first, and permanent, mistake . . . a refutation of the core idea, expressed in various ways, that the Church is a 'perfect society,' that as Bride of Christ it is spotless, that the claim to infallibility in matters of faith and morals is more than wishful thinking or rank denial."[2]

In essence, the Catholic Church held Jews collectively and eternally responsible for the death of Jesus (until the revolutionary doctrine of the Vatican Council in 1965, which is discussed in the next section); condemned Jews to eternal damnation and wandering; despised Jews for their refusal to accept Christianity as the true faith; attempted to convince Jews of the Church's intellectual superiority, as exemplified by the "Trial of the Talmud" in 1240; sought to isolate Jews from the rest of the population and demonize them and their beliefs; attempted to convert Jews whenever possible, including, as a telling example, the kidnaping, baptism, and separation of Edgardo Mortara, age six, from his Jewish family in Bologna in 1858; accused Jews of an endless array of sins, including abducting Christian children for religious rituals and starting deadly plagues among the Christian population; denied Jews access to certain trades and professions; and, most ominously, at times justified the outright murder of Jews through the Inquisition and blood libels.

2. James Carroll, *Constantine's Sword* (Mariner Books, 2002), 551.

As one tiny but revealing story, there is a small church in Rome, San Gregorio della Divina Pietà, adjacent to the Great Synagogue (built in 1904), which itself is located in what was the designated ghetto for Jews. Under papal orders, the ghetto's gates were locked every night to keep the Jews in. This lasted from 1555 to 1870, when Italy was united as a country and the controlling Papal States lost their sovereign powers. Every Shabbat (Sabbath) until 1870, the Vatican compelled the Jews to attend church services. Many Jews stuffed their ears with wax to avoid listening or tried to sleep. In the church, overseers checked Jews' ears and used long wooden poles to ensure they stayed awake. Why this Catholic obsession? Because of Jewish "stubbornness" and "blindness" in refusing to acknowledge that Christianity, the "new revelation," displaced and perfected the "old," superseded Judaism.

What is "Nostra Aetate"? Why is it so important in the history of Catholic-Jewish relations?

On October 28, 1965, the Second Vatican Council adopted a groundbreaking statement titled "Nostra Aetate" ("In Our Time"), which sought to define the church's relationship with other faiths.

The fourth section focused on Jews. Its major elements included ending the age-old deicide charge against the Jewish people and affirming the religious ties between Catholics and Jews. It also called, for the first time, for launching a dialogue and greater theological understanding between the two faiths. Here is an excerpt:

> Sounding the depths of the mystery which is the church, this sacred council remembers the spiritual ties which link the people of the new covenant to the stock of Abraham . . . .

> Since Christians and Jews have such a common spiritual heritage, this sacred council wishes to encourage and further mutual understanding and appreciation. This can be achieved, especially, by way of biblical and theological enquiry and through friendly discussions.
>
> Even though the Jewish authorities and those who followed their lead pressed for the death of Christ (see John 19:6), neither all Jews indiscriminately at that time, nor Jews today, can be charged with the crimes committed during his passion. It is true that the church is the new people of God, yet the Jews should not be spoken of as rejected or accursed as if this followed from holy scripture. Consequently, all must take care, lest in catechizing or in preaching the word of God, they teach anything which is not in accord with the truth of the Gospel message or the spirit of Christ.
>
> Indeed, the church reproves every form of persecution against whomsoever it may be directed. Remembering, then, its common heritage with the Jews and moved not by any political consideration, but solely by the religious motivation of Christian charity, it deplores all hatreds, persecutions, displays of antisemitism directed against the Jews at any time or from any source.[3]

The importance of these words cannot be overstated. The deicide accusation—the claim that all Jews were responsible, in perpetuity, for the crucifixion of Jesus, the son of God—was a principal cause of antisemitism for nearly two millennia. For the Jews, it resulted in untold suffering, persecution, prejudice, and violence.

3. Phil Jenkins, trans., "The Church and the Jews: German Bishops' Conference, Bonn 1980," Boston College, accessed April 14, 2025, https://www.bc.edu/content/dam/files/research_sites/cjl/texts/cjrelations/resources/documents/catholic/german_church_jews.html.

The years following the adoption of "Nostra Aetate" witnessed a veritable revolution in Catholic-Jewish relations, including an active role by the Vatican in combating antisemitism. For example, in 1986 Pope John Paul II became the first pope to visit a synagogue. On that occasion, he said words never before heard from a Catholic pontiff: "The Jewish religion is not 'extrinsic' to us, but in a certain way is 'intrinsic' to our own religion. With Judaism, therefore, we have a relationship which we do not have with any other religion. You are our dearly beloved brothers, and in a certain way, it could be said that you are our elder brothers."[4]

More recently, on February 2, 2024, Pope Francis wrote a letter addressed to "My Jewish brothers and sisters in Israel." He said:

> The path that the Church has walked with you, the ancient people of the covenant, rejects every form of anti-Judaism and anti-Semitism, unequivocally condemning manifestations of hatred toward Jews and Judaism as a sin against God . . . .
>
> Together with you, we Catholics are very concerned about the terrible increase in attacks against Jews around the world. We had hoped that "never again" would be a refrain heard by the new generations, yet now we see that the path ahead requires ever closer collaboration to eradicate these phenomena.[5]

4. Linda Bordoni, "35 Years since Pope St John Paul II's Historic Visit to Rome's Synagogue," *Vatican News*, April 13, 2021, https://www.vaticannews.va/en/pope/news/2021-04/st-john-paul-ii-rome-synagogue-visit-jewish-catholic-anniversary.html.
5. Cindy Wooden, "Pope, in Letter to Jews in Israel, Condemns Antisemitism as a Sin," U.S. Conference of Catholic Bishops, February 3, 2024, https://www.usccb.org/news/2024/pope-letter-jews-israel-condemns-antisemitism-sin.

While residual antisemitism can still be found in corners of the Catholic world, the era of friendship and cooperation ushered in by the promulgation of "Nostra Aetate" in 1965 was a dramatic turning point in confronting the most enduring source of antisemitism in history.

What was the attitude of the Catholic Church during the Holocaust?

For decades, there has been a major dispute surrounding this question. On the one hand, in 1964, Pope Paul VI defended the record of his wartime predecessor, Pius XII: "Suspicions and accusations have clouded the memory of this great Pope. . . . Anyone who like us had the chance to meet him in person will know that this soul is worthy of our admiration; they know how sensitive he was, how compassionate he was toward human suffering, how courageous he was and how gentle his heart was. Those who came to him with tears in their eyes at the end of the war, to thank him for saving their lives, are also aware of this."[6] And in 1998 the Vatican's declaration "We Remember: A Reflection on the Shoah" noted, "Pius XII, in his very first Encyclical, *Summi Pontificatus*, of 20 October 1939, worried against theories which denied the unity of the human race and against the deification of the State, all of which he saw as leading to a real 'hour of darkness.'"[7] This groundbreaking statement on the Shoah—and, to its credit, to ensure uniqueness the Vatican used the Hebrew word, *Shoah*, rather

6. "Paul VI's Trip to the Holy Land 50 Years Ago Marked the Dawn of Papal Visits," *La Stampa*, May 23, 2014, https://www.lastampa.it/vatican-insider/en/2014/05/23/news/paul-vi-s-trip-to-the-holy-land-50-years-ago-marked-the-dawn-of-papal-visits-1.35756969/.
7. Dicastery for Promoting Christian Unity, "We Remember: A Reflection on the Shoah," accessed April 14, 2025, http://www.christianunity.va/content/unitacristiani/en/commissione-per-i-rapporti-religiosi-con-l-ebraismo/commissione-per-i-rapporti-religiosi-con-l-ebraismo-crre/documenti-della-commissione/en1.html.

than "Holocaust," a word of Greek origin that translates as "a burnt sacrifice to God" and could be applied in various other situations—was welcomed by a number of Jewish leaders, including Rabbi A. James Rudin, a longtime pioneer in interfaith dialogue. At the same time, he noted, "Missing is a sign that the church is taking responsibility for having helped to create a climate, through anti-Jewish teachings, in which lethal anti-Semitism could flourish."[8]

Despite this shortcoming, the declaration did acknowledge, "The fact that the Shoah took place in Europe, that is, in countries of long-standing Christian civilizations, raises the question of the relations between the Nazi persecution and the attitudes down the centuries of Christians towards Jews. . . . We deeply regret the errors and failures of those sons and daughters of the Church." In stark contrast, James Carroll argued: "But the failure of Pius XII to pass the decisive moral test of the 20th century undercuts this hierarchy (of truth, i.e., Christian faith is over other faiths: Roman Catholicism is over other Christian faiths; and the pope is supreme over Roman Catholics, infallible in matters of 'faith and morals'), and any meaningful claim to papal infallibility, which is why his failure (during the Holocaust) must be denied at all costs."[9]

David Kertzer, professor at Brown University and author of *The Pope at War*, based on his work in Vatican archives that were opened to researchers in 2020, agreed with Carroll's conclusion on the record of Pius XII. He noted that the pontiff failed to speak out and that he put protection of the Church at every step ahead of "courageous moral leadership." Kertzer

8. Gustav Niebuhr, "A Vatican Peace Offering Reopens War Wounds," *New York Times*, March 29, 1998.
9. James Carroll, "The Pope's Big Holocaust Lie," *Daily Beast*, December 23, 2009, https://www.thedailybeast.com/the-popes-big-holocaust-lie.

concluded, "As a moral leader, Pius XII must be judged as a failure."[10]

The debate over the Vatican's role in the war and regarding the Holocaust continues to the present. That said, to their eternal credit, some individual Catholic churches, monasteries and convents, and local leaders during the war courageously sought to assist imperiled Jews.

As Protestant denominations emerged, what were their attitudes toward Jews, and how have these evolved over the centuries?

The Protestant Reformation began in the 16th century. One of its best-known figures was Martin Luther, a German theologian.

Originally, he was quite sympathetic to the Jews because of their rejection of the Catholic Church. But when he realized that Jews were not prepared to embrace his doctrine either, embodied in his *95 Theses* written in 1517, he became a virulent antisemite.

In 1543, he published *On the Jews and Their Lies*, in which he wrote that the Jews are "miserable, blind and senseless people" and "thieves and robbers," and that synagogues are "a den of devils." He urged that "rabbis be forbidden to teach on pain of loss of life and limb. For they have justly forfeited the right to such an office by holding the poor Jews captive with the saying of Moses in which he commands them to obey their teachers."[11]

Luther died in 1546, but his antisemitism lived on for centuries in the church that bore his name and that took root in northern and central Europe and, later, the United States

10. Jason Berry, "Historian's New Book Highlights Pius XII's Moral Failures," *National Catholic Reporter*, July 2, 2022, https://www.ncronline.org/news/opinion/historians-new-book-highlights-pius-xiis-moral-failures.
11. Jewish Virtual Library, "Anti-Semitism: Martin Luther—'The Jews and Their Lies' (1543)," accessed April 14, 2025, https://www.jewishvirtuallibrary.org/martin-luther-quot-the-jews-and-their-lies-quot.

and elsewhere. Indeed, some German Lutherans invoked his antisemitic tropes in supporting the Nazi regime.

Several decades after the end of World War II, the Lutheran Church embarked on a process of self-examination, culminating, in 1994, in "Declaration to the Jewish Community" by the Evangelical Lutheran Church in America in association with the Lutheran World Federation. The final words were:

> In concert with the Lutheran World Federation, we particularly deplore the appropriation of Luther's words by modem anti-Semites for the teaching of hatred toward Judaism or toward the Jewish people. Grieving the complicity of our own tradition within this history of hatred, moreover, we express our urgent desire to live out our faith in Jesus Christ with love and respect for the Jewish people. We recognize in anti-Semitism a contradiction and an affront to the Gospel, a violation of our hope and calling, and we pledge this church to oppose the deadly working of such bigotry, both within our own circles and in the society around us. Finally, we pray for the continued blessing of the Blessed One upon the increasing cooperation and understanding between Lutheran Christians and the Jewish community.[12]

Elsewhere in the Christian world, the Anglican Church has an official state status in England, and its supreme governor has been the reigning monarch since the 16th century. In 2019, the church issued *God's Unfailing Word*, which acknowledged the church's role in nurturing "a fertile seed-bed for murderous antisemitism."

12. Evangelical Lutheran Church in America, "A Declaration of the Evangelical Lutheran Church in America to the Jewish Community" (1994), https://resources.elca.org/wp-content/uploads/Guidelines_For_Lutheran_Jewish_Relations_1998.pdf.

The introduction sets forth the historical context:

> [Attention must be paid] to the persecution and prejudice experienced by Jewish people through history, the responsibility held by Christians for that and its persistence in the contemporary context. In a contribution to a report published in 2016, Archbishop Justin Welby likened antisemitism to a virus that may appear dormant but can all too easily be activated in all kinds of contexts, including churches. In commenting on the specific challenges facing the Church in seeking to eradicate it, he identified theology as a vital issue: "It is a shameful truth that, through its theological teachings, the Church, which should have offered an antidote, compounded the spread of this virus."[13]

God's Unfailing Word also admitted that two Anglican cathedrals, in Norwich and Lincoln, were linked to blood libels which, "originating in England, became the catalyst for the murder of many Jews in this country and across Europe, especially in pogroms at Eastertide."

While this document was a milestone, Jewish leadership in England noted with regret its failure to "reject the efforts of those Christians . . . who as part of their faithful mission dedicate themselves to the purposeful and specific targeting of Jews for conversion to Christianity."

By contrast, four years earlier the Vatican had issued "The Gifts and Calling of God Are Irrevocable," in which it affirmed for the first time that "the Catholic Church neither conducts nor supports any specific institutional mission work directed

13. Church of England, Faith and Order Commission, *God's Unfailing Word: Theological and Practical Perspectives on Christian-Jewish Relations,* 2019, https://www.churchofengland.org/sites/default/files/2019-11/godsunfailingwordweb.pdf.

towards Jews," thus ending what Carroll described as the centuries-long "Christian (i.e., Catholic) obsession with Jewish conversion."[14]

The moral reckonings by the various churches were late in coming. The Jewish suffering—for the Roman, not Jewish, crucifixion, and for refusing to renounce their own faith and adopt Christianity—was incalculable. Yet, starting in the mid-1960s in the Catholic Church, followed by various Protestant denominations, two of which were cited here, an entirely new chapter in Christian-Jewish relations unfolded.

What is replacement theology, also known as supersessionism?

It is the belief, in essence, that Christianity has replaced or superseded Judaism and represents the new, and eternal, covenantal relationship with God, overtaking the Mosaic or, more broadly, Jewish covenant with God.

Drawing from this core belief, those who subscribe to it may see the Hebrew Bible as the "Old" Testament and the Christian Bible as the "New" Testament. They might regard Jews as believers in an "incomplete" faith, whose only recourse is to convert and join the "completed" faith, Christianity. If not, according to this view, Jews will either land in hell or face an apocalypse when the Second Coming of Jesus occurs.

While these beliefs have existed among a wide spectrum of Christian denominations and believers, others strenuously reject them, believing that Jews and Christians are umbilically linked theologically, that Christianity would not have emerged

14. Dicastery for Promoting Christian Unity, "The Gifts and the Calling of God Are Irrevocable (Rom 11:29)," accessed April 14, 2025, http://www.christianunity.va/content/unitacristiani/en/commissione-per-i-rapporti-religiosi-con-l-ebraismo/commissione-per-i-rapporti-religiosi-con-l-ebraismo-crre/documenti-della-commissione/en.html.

but for Judaism, that the Jewish covenant with God is eternal, that disparaging Jews and Judaism has led to unspeakable atrocities in the name of a loving (and Jewish) Jesus, and that there is no place for a sense of religious "triumphalism," however deep their own faith may be.

In Islam there is also a widespread belief that the religion, born in the seventh century CE, has surpassed both Judaism and Christianity in the infallibility and inerrancy of its teachings. Indeed, according to this view, it is the final revelation of God. Thus, while the other two monotheistic religions are to be respected, that should not be confused with putting them on equal footing or according non-Muslims full rights and protections. Hence proselytizing non-Muslims continues to be a goal of many Muslims, while in a number of Muslim-majority nations, religious minorities, be they Christian, Hindu, Buddhist, Jewish, Baha'i, Zoroastrian, Sikh, Ahmadi, Yazidi, or other, have not fared well.

By contrast, Judaism as a faith has not yielded to those who assert it has been replaced, or overtaken, by newer monotheistic faiths and their most venerated leaders, Jesus and Muhammad, nor do its foremost religious and scholarly figures devote serious time and effort today in seeking to delegitimize those religions. Moreover, unlike both Christianity and Islam, Judaism does not actively seek converts; even those eager to enter the faith must pursue a lengthy process of study and come before a rabbinic court that has jurisdiction in these matters.

How did the Christian world react to the rebirth of Israel as a sovereign nation in 1948, and in the years since?

The concern of the Christian world was directed to the 1947 United Nations Partition Plan, which proposed an Arab state, a Jewish state, and a separate status for Jerusalem. Since holy sites—sacred to Christians, Jews, and Muslims—were in Jerusalem, a *corpus separatum* was envisioned for the city. It would be under neither Jewish nor Arab administration. But the Arab world categorically rejected the partition plan.

By and large, the mainstream Christian world had difficulty accepting the rebirth of Israel as a nation in 1948. It meant not only acknowledging Jewish sovereignty over some Christian holy sites but, even more, grappling with the return, one might say, of the Jewish people to a central place in history as a sovereign nation.

It took 16 years before a pontiff traveled to Israel. Pope Paul VI visited the "Holy Land" in January 1964, but, while it was a pathbreaking visit, he never referred to it as Israel. And the Holy See did not formally recognize the State of Israel until 1993, with the signing of the Fundamental Agreement that established diplomatic relations with the Jewish state. Indeed, the Holy See was the last government on the European continent, following Spain and Greece, to do so.

However, Pope John Paul II's historic five-day pilgrimage to Israel in March 2000 ushered in a new chapter in the relationship between the Vatican and Israel, as the pontiff called for peace, blessed Israel, and apologized for sins committed by Christians against Jews. That trip, in turn, led to a steadier, sturdier link, with more frequent contact and mechanisms in place to address any difficult issues that could arise.

Do evangelical Christians believe that Jews must be converted or else are doomed to eternal damnation?

The evangelical-Jewish relationship is complicated and multifaceted. At times, it is fraught with misunderstanding and mistrust. And given the fact that there is considerable diversity within both faith traditions—more than either side might sometimes appreciate—generalizations, while tempting, do a disservice to reality.

For some Jews, any reference to evangelicals evokes thoughts of attempted conversion and damnation in hell for those who do not accept their beliefs. It also evokes an eschatology—an end-of-days doctrine—that views Israel and the Jewish people as a stepping stone to the battle of Armageddon, after which the faithful will be transported to heaven and those who have refused conversion will face a holocaust.

Evangelizing—a word that originates in Greek and means "spreading or sharing the good news"—is an integral part of evangelical faith. Each evangelical has to have a personal, "born again" experience to bring Jesus into their lives and cannot do so by inherited faith alone. Thus evangelicals aim to encourage others to follow the same path. And yes, some evangelicals might well see Jews as "incomplete" unless they accept Jesus into their lives, and, further, may view Christianity as superseding or displacing Judaism, even as the Hebrew Bible is an essential and inerrant part of their religious foundation.

Yet there is more to the story. Not all Jews mistrust evangelicals or question their motives, as Christian Zionists, for supporting Israel and showing up in large numbers whenever the Jewish state is under threat. Instead, these Jews view them as valued allies, while mainline Protestant congregations, such as the Episcopal and Presbyterian churches, have been seen as turning against Israel, influenced in part by their own congregations in the Arab Middle East.

Not all evangelicals want to proselytize among Jews or believe Jews are consigned to hell if they do not "complete" the spiritual journey. Rather, they acknowledge God's covenant with the Jewish people and believe it to be eternal.

To illustrate the divide among evangelicals, the late Billy Graham, arguably America's best-known evangelical leader in the 20th century, wrote on conversion in *Christianity Today* in 1973. This was the same year, incidentally, that he used the pejorative term "Synagogue of Satan" with President Richard Nixon in describing some Jews. Graham said, "I believe God has always had a special relationship with the Jewish people, as St. Paul suggests in the Book of Romans. In my evangelistic efforts, I have never felt called to single out the Jews as Jews nor to single out any other particular groups, cultural, ethnic or religious."[15]

On the other hand, Dallas-based pastor Robert Jeffress, one of the most prominent evangelical leaders in the early 21st century, declared in a televised interview in 2010, "Not only do religions like Mormonism, Islam, Judaism, Hinduism—not only do they lead people away from the true God, they lead people to an eternity of separation from God in hell. Hell is going to be filled with good religious people who have rejected the truth of Christ."[16]

How are Jews viewed in predominantly non-monotheistic societies?

Historically, two major countries that never experienced serious bouts of antisemitism are China and India. To the contrary, though tiny in number, Jewish communities in both countries generally lived securely and at peace with their neighbors. Why?

A major explanatory factor is that Christianity and Islam were not dominant religions in the spiritual tapestry of China and India. Other faiths, non-monotheistic in makeup,

15. Holly Lebowitz Rossi, "Billy Graham Leaves a Positive Interfaith Legacy, with a Few Blemishes," *Salt Lake Tribune*, February 21, 2018, https://www.sltrib.com/religion/2018/02/21/billy-graham-leaves-a-positive-interfaith-legacy-with-a-few-blemishes/; Gerald Zelizer, "How Should Jews Remember Rev. Billy Graham?," Jewish Telegraphic Agency, February 21, 2018, https://www.jta.org/2018/02/21/ny/how-should-jews-remember-rev-billy-graham.
16. Matthew Haag, "Robert Jeffress, Pastor Who Said Jews Are Going to Hell, Led Prayer at Jerusalem Embassy," *New York Times*, May 14, 2018, https://www.nytimes.com/2018/05/14/world/middleeast/robert-jeffress-embassy-jerusalem-us.html.

such as Buddhism, Confucianism, Hinduism, and Taoism, prevailed.

There is no real doctrinal competition or rivalry between Judaism and these Asian religions. They evolved in different ways and spaces, and they are not vying with each other for what might be called spiritual superiority, as Christianity and Islam are with one another and both with Judaism, the "mother" of the monotheistic religions. They are not challenging one another for God's ultimate approval, nor are they threatened, theologically or intellectually, by the others' existence. Moreover, as Judaism is not a proselytizing faith, it never sought new adherents, unlike Christianity and Islam, and therefore never attempted to alter the existing religious landscapes.

That said, there was a terrorist attack targeting the Chabad House in Mumbai in 2008. The rabbi, his pregnant wife, and four others were killed. It was one of several deadly assaults across the city in a four-day shooting spree. The perpetrators were from a jihadist group, Lashkar-e-Taiba, housed in neighboring Pakistan.

And speaking of Pakistan, in any discussion of contemporary antisemitism, the murder of *Wall Street Journal* journalist Daniel Pearl in 2002 must be noted. Before his throat was slit by jihadists in Karachi, he expressed 11 words, recorded by his kidnappers: "My father is Jewish. My mother is Jewish. I am Jewish." Unmistakably, he was killed because he was a Jew, a proud Jew. His murderers reportedly "celebrated" by praying in the direction of Mecca.[17]

Meanwhile, though China has traditionally shown respect for the Jewish people and Israel, for geopolitical reasons it has become increasingly close to Iran and Hamas, both of which

17. Asra Q. Nomani, "'I Am Jewish.' Everything Has Changed. And Nothing Has Changed," *Jewish Journal*, October 10, 2023, https://jewishjournal.com/commentary/columnist/363691/i-am-jewish-everything-has-changed-and-nothing-has-changed/.

openly call for the destruction of Israel and demonize the Jewish people. A headline in the *Washington Post* summarized the new challenge: "Fueling online antisemitism is China's new tool against the West."[18]

18. Josh Rogin, "Fueling Online Antisemitism Is China's New Tool against the West," *Washington Post*, January 8, 2024, https://www.washingtonpost.com/opinions/2024/01/08/china-antisemitism-online-tool-west-gaza/. See also Jeremy B. Merrill, Aaron Schaffer, and Naomi Nix, "A Firehose of Antisemitic Disinformation from China Is Pointing at Two Republican Legislators," *Washington Post*, October 10, 2024, https://www.washingtonpost.com/technology/2024/10/10/us-elections-china-influence-x/.

3

ANTISEMITISM IN THE ISLAMIC WORLD

Most scholarly attention has been focused on the place of Jews in the Christian-dominated world. However, Jews and Jewish communities have interacted with the Muslim world since Islam emerged in the Arabian Peninsula as a new faith in the seventh century CE. What does Muslim scripture say about Jews? Does Islam view Judaism as an authentic religion? What status was accorded to Jews in Muslim-majority societies? Were there periods of coexistence and equality? Were there periods of persecution? What was the impact on Jewish communities in the Muslim world of Israel's rebirth in 1948? How significant a factor is antisemitism in Muslim teaching and preaching in the present day?

Are Jews and Judaism mentioned in the Koran and other Muslim holy texts? If so, how are they portrayed?

This is a complicated question, which does not prevent some from seeking either to romanticize or to demonize the Koran, the Hadith (Islamic oral tradition), and other Islamic religious sources when it comes to Jews. The truth is that these interpreters are cherry-picking citations to prove a point. In reality, there are both positive and negative references aplenty.

On the one hand, Jews, alongside Christians, are seen as "People of the Book" (Ahl Al-Dhimma), whose belief in one

God predated the advent of Islam and who therefore are deserving of respect. The Islamic tradition venerates Jewish figures, including Moses, and it recognizes Abraham as the father of both Judaism and Islam. Indeed, the Koran mentions Israelites more than 40 times and affirms the link between the Jewish people and the land.[1] Moreover, there are many similarities in beliefs, rituals, and practices between Judaism and Islam, far more than either faith has with Christianity. Indeed, Judaism and Islam might be described as both religious and civilizational, insofar as they encompass (often overlapping) daily beliefs and behaviors far beyond Christian obligations. And many Muslims have Arabized names of biblical Jews, such as Suleyman (Solomon), Daoud (David), Yusef (Joseph), Sara (Sarah), and Yaqub (Jacob).

On the other hand, dating back to the seventh century, Muhammad, as the messenger of God, and local Jewish tribes were in conflict. Moreover, as with Christianity, Jews by and large failed to embrace the new faith emerging in the Arabian Peninsula, which triggered enduring hostility between the two religions. In the centuries that followed, Judaism was never put on an equal footing with Islam. Far from it.

Even as Judaism was meant to be respected as a monotheistic faith, some Muslim clergy referred to the Jews, and still do, as the "descendants of apes and pigs" for their alleged "disobedience." Jews were made to wear clothing identifying themselves as Jews, pay a special tax, and face certain restrictions.

But the Muslim world, in contrast to the Christian world, treated Jews, generally speaking, with more tolerance and less violence, at least until the 19th century. As Jonathan Spyer of the Jerusalem Institute for Strategy and Security noted, unlike

1. The term "Bani Israel," which translates to English as "the children [or descendants] of Israel," is mentioned more than 40 times in the Koran.

University of Michigan Library, "The Koran," accessed April 14, 2025, https://quod.lib.umich.edu/cgi/k/koran/koran-idx?type=simple&q1=Israel&size=Fi.

the Christian world, Muslims looked down on Jews as weak and contemptible but did not, at the same time, fear the Jews and their supposed demonic powers.

It was in the 19th century that European notions of antisemitism arrived in the Arab world. This led to the first reported blood libel case, in Damascus in 1840, in which some Christians and Muslims participated in the arrest, torture, and murder of a number of Jews. Later, translations of odious antisemitic tracts, such as *The Protocols of the Elders of Zion* and *Mein Kampf*, appeared. This period coincided with European colonialism in the Middle East and North Africa, the weakening of the Ottoman Empire, and, eventually, Israel's establishment and its defeat of five Arab armies in the process. How to explain this dramatic decline in the power and prestige of the Arab and Islamic worlds? One way was to blame Jews and Zionists—names used almost interchangeably—and ascribe to them previously unspoken powers of evil, connivance, and conspiracy.

What does the term "golden age" refer to in Spain?

In the year 711 CE, the Moors—Muslims from North Africa—conquered what we today call Spain, replacing the ruling Visigoths, who were Christian, with Islamic governance.

What followed was termed La Convivencia, a centuries-long period of coexistence and harmony for the three faiths—Muslims, Christians, and Jews. In other words, it was seen as a golden age during which Muslims ruled but respected the other two faiths and allowed them to flourish.

There is controversy among historians about the degree to which this description is accurate. Some insist that tolerance for Christians and Jews should not be equated with full equality and rights, and must not overlook the eruptions of intolerance and violence, most notably the anti-Jewish massacre in Granada in 1066. According to this view, Jews and Christians were always subject to certain restrictions that served as reminders of their unequal status, so the era, which lasted approximately four centuries, should not be overly romanticized.

Maria Rosa Menocal,[2] a professor at Yale University and author of the book *The Ornament of the World: How Muslims, Jews and Christians Created a Culture of Tolerance in Medieval Spain*, argued that new levels of interfaith tolerance and respect were achieved. By contrast, the late Bernard Lewis, professor at Princeton University and author of numerous studies on Islam and the Middle East, asserted, "The golden age of equal rights in Spain was a myth, and belief in it was a result, more than a cause, of Jewish sympathy for Islam. The myth was invented by Jews in nineteenth-century Europe as a reproach to Christians."[3]

That said, two points appear beyond dispute. First, given the limited alternatives at the time, Jews generally fared better during this era of Muslim rule in Al-Andalus, as Spain was called at the time, than under Christian rule elsewhere in Europe. Second, it was a period of extraordinary Jewish scholarship and creativity, both secular and religious. Jews made big strides in science, medicine, and mathematics, translated important works to and from the languages of the day, created magnificent poetry and song (often in Ladino, a Judeo-Spanish language) that survive to the present, held important positions in government, and contributed significantly to the richness of Jewish thought.

Second, when Catholic monarchs returned to power in the 15th century, the culmination of La Reconquista, they issued the Alhambra Decree on March 31, 1492, which ushered in the Spanish Inquisition. Forced to flee due to the decree (which was not formally rescinded until 1968), many Jews found a welcome refuge in the Ottoman Empire, principally Turkey and the Balkan lands, which were also under Muslim rule.

2. Maria Rosa Menocal, *The Ornament of the World: How Muslims, Jews and Christians Created a Culture of Tolerance in Medieval Spain* (Little, Brown and Company, 2002).
3. Bernard Lewis, *Islam in History: Ideas, People, and Events in the Middle East* (Open Court, 1993).

When did the yellow star first appear in the Muslim world?

The yellow star is often solely associated with the enforced Nazi policy during the Holocaust, whereby Jews were compelled to wear a yellow Star of David, usually emblazoned with the word *Jude* (Jew, in German).

However, the yellow star first appeared in the Muslim world as early as the eighth century CE. Jews and Christians, living under Shari'a law as People of the Book, were generally able to practice their religion and receive state protection. Nevertheless, Muslim rulers wished these groups to retain an identifiable distinctiveness, and they enforced upon them a code of conduct and a special tax, known as *jizya*.

As a result, Jews were forced to wear something to designate their identity. For example, under Caliph Haroun al-Rashid (807 CE), Jews in Baghdad were obligated to wear yellow belts or fringes, and during the reign of Caliph al-Mutawakkil (847–61) Jews wore a patch in the shape of a donkey. In 1005, Jews in Egypt were ordered to wear bells on their clothes.

If there were 850,000 Jews living in the Muslim world in 1948, why are there so few today?

An estimated 850,000 Jews were living in North Africa and the Middle East, including Iran and Afghanistan, in 1948, the year of Israel's rebirth. Many of the communities were ancient, dating back centuries, if not millennia, and often predating the advent of Islam in the seventh century.

Today, there are only a few thousand Jews left in this vast region, essentially remnant communities in Morocco, Tunisia, Turkey, and Iran. Once large populations have dwindled, though the atmosphere in, say, Morocco for Jews today is far more welcoming and open than it is in Iran.

At the same time, there is a growing Jewish community in the United Arab Emirates, with a thriving religious life, as well as a tiny community in Bahrain that has long enjoyed safety and protection. Indeed, a member of the Bahraini Jewish community, Houda Nonoo, was the country's ambassador to the United States from 2008 to 2013, a first in the Arab world.

The bulk of the Jews fled the Muslim world. They experienced persecution and discrimination prior to 1948, which only intensified afterward, when Arab societies tended to view local Jews as "extensions" or "surrogates" for the Jewish state.

Libya offers a revealing case study. Jews have reportedly lived on what is today Libyan territory since the Roman era, 2,000 years ago. Thus they predated the conquering seventh-century Arab Muslims by hundreds of years. In 1951, Libya became an independent country and adopted a constitution which guaranteed rights for all, but by then the vast majority of the nation's 39,000 Jews had left. Either they were drawn by the chance to live in Israel or they left out of fear of what would happen once the ruling British abandoned Libya.

The 4,000 to 5,000 Jews who stayed quickly discovered that their constitutional rights were enshrined on paper but not in practice. Jews were barred from certain professions, had difficulty obtaining a Libyan passport, could not own a business without a Muslim partner, and had no legal recourse in the face of bias.

By 1967, the remaining Jews were gone, except for the dozens murdered in pogroms, similar to the earlier deadly attacks on Jews in 1945 and 1948. As of 2024 there are no Jews left in Libya, nor any museum or monument acknowledging their long presence, nor any teaching module in the schools mentioning the Jewish dimension of Libyan history.

Libya is not an exception for the Jews. Other countries in which Jews experienced similar fates after 1948 include Algeria, Egypt, Sudan, Iraq, Syria, Yemen, Lebanon, and Afghanistan.

Some voices in the Arab world seek to deflect criticism and blame Israel for this vast exodus, arguing that it deliberately caused panic and fear in Jewish communities to encourage immigration. But the reality is that Jews in North Africa and the Middle East largely lived as second-class citizens in nondemocratic societies. While there were examples of cooperation and social interaction, Jews were always reminded they were not equal citizens with equal rights but lived at the whim of the nondemocratic leaders and majority societies.

Unlike the experience of Palestinians, the Jews did not become multigenerational refugees but quickly resettled in Israel, Europe, North America, Latin America, or Australia. Thus little is heard nowadays about their experiences, hence the name given to them as the "forgotten refugees" of the Arab-Israeli conflict.

Are the Iranian regime and its nonstate proxies—Hamas, Hezbollah, and Houthis—antisemitic?

Yes. Antisemitism is at the core of their political outlook and theology, beginning with the Iranian revolutionary regime, which took power in 1979. (Prior to 1979, Iran and Israel enjoyed strong bilateral ties, and the large Jewish community in Iran, dramatically diminished after 1979, felt quite safe and secure.)

Their goal, repeatedly and unambiguously stated, is an end to Israel—not a negotiated peace nor a two-state solution. Rather, the aim is to erase Israel from the map of the Middle East. By seeking to deny the Jewish people the right to self-determination and pursuing an ambitious arms program, including weapons of mass destruction, they have made clear that annihilation of a state of 9.5 million people, which they adamantly refuse to call by its rightful name, Israel, is on their agenda. And they wish to garner support in the larger Muslim world by demonstrating that, unlike Arab armies defeated by Israel in previous wars, they can achieve the goal and plant their flag in Al-Quds (Jerusalem).

Similar to Soviet leaders in the 1970s and 1980s, Iranian leaders interchange "Jews" and "Zionists," even as they occasionally claim they are not antisemitic, only anti-Zionist.

Their hatred and contempt of Jews, though, come through clearly. As Reuel Marc Gerecht and Ray Takeyh noted in a *Wall Street Journal* op-ed, "At least three generations of radical Iranian clerics have viewed Israel as illegitimate, usurping sacred Islamic lands in the name of a pernicious ideology advanced by history's most devilish and stubborn people. Using the language of French Marxism, they call Israel a Western 'colonial-settler state,' and they believe Jews guide American imperialism in the Middle East. In this struggle between good and evil, Muslims have a religious obligation to resist Israel and global Jewry."[4]

Apropos "global Jewry," in 1994 Iran masterminded the bombing of the AMIA building in Buenos Aires, the central address of the Jewish community in the city. Eighty-five people were killed and 300 injured. Five Iranians and one Hezbollah operative were identified as suspects by Argentine authorities, and INTERPOL issued red notices for their arrest. One of the five Iranians, Ahmad Vahidi, was Iran's minister of interior in 2024. None has been detained, though the Hezbollah suspect, Imad Mughniyeh, was killed in Syria in 2008 "in a joint CIA-Mossad operation," according to the *Wall Street Journal*.[5] This was not the only Iranian terrorist plot against Jews worldwide, but it was the most deadly. (For more information, see Chapter 9.)

At home, Iran has played host to David Duke, a far-right antisemite from the United States, who attended a conference promoting Holocaust denial in Tehran in 2006, which also included the "Holocaust Cartoon Competition."

While a match-up between a revolutionary Iranian regime and a former leader of the Ku Klux Klan may seem improbable

4. Reuel Marc Gerecht and Ray Takeyh, "The Real Reason Iran Hates Israel," *Wall Street Journal*, November 27, 2023, https://www.wsj.com/articles/the-real-reason-iran-hates-israel-anti-semitism-gaza-4f7ad96e.
5. Sune Engel Rasmussen, "How Israel Killed a Ghost," *Wall Street Journal*, August 18, 2024, https://www.wsj.com/world/middle-east/how-israel-killed-a-ghost-73e6db68.

on its face, it reveals the odd alliances formed across the far-right, far-left, and jihadist spectrum. What brings these figures together is a shared hatred of Jews and the aim of eradicating Israel, denying the Holocaust, and harming Jewish communities around the world.

The same mindset applies to Iran's proxies in the region, including Hamas, Hezbollah, and the Houthis.

The 1988 founding Hamas Charter in Gaza included these words, attributed to the Prophet Muhammad: "The Day of Judgment will not come about until Moslems fight Jews and kill them. Then, the Jews will hide behind rocks and trees, and the rocks and trees will cry out: 'O Moslem, there is a Jew hiding behind me, come and kill him.'"[6] In a similar spirit, the late Lebanon-based Hezbollah secretary-general Hassan Nasrallah said in 2002, in a recorded speech:

> Among the signs . . . and signals which guide us, in the Islamic prophecies and not only in the Jewish prophecies, is that this State [of Israel] will be established, and that the Jews will gather from all parts of the world into occupied Palestine, not in order to bring about the anti-Christ and the end of the world, but rather that Allah the Glorified and Most High wants to save you from having to go to the ends of the world, for they have gathered in one place—they have gathered in one place—and there the final and decisive battle will take place.[7]

Not to be outdone, the Houthis in Yemen, another Iranian proxy, proclaim these words on their flag: "Allah is great, death to the USA, death to Israel, curse the Jews, victory to

6. Avalon Project, "Hamas Covenant 1988," Yale University, August 18, 1988, https://avalon.law.yale.edu/20th_century/hamas.asp.
7. Yair Rosenberg, "Did Netanyahu Put Anti-Semitic Words in Hezbollah's Mouth?," *Tablet Magazine*, March 9, 2015, https://www.tabletmag.com/sections/news/articles/did-netanyahu-put-anti-semitic-words-in-hezbollahs-mouth.

Islam." Houthi leaders regularly invoke the forged *Protocols of the Elders of Zion* as the alleged clarion call of Jews in the 21st century, and even go so far as to cite Hitler, as the Middle East Media Research Institute reported in October 2023: "In one post from October 29, [Hezam] Al-Asad [a Houthi leader] shared a picture of Adolf Hitler, with text reading 'I could have killed all the Jews in the world, but I left some of them alive so that [the] world would know why I killed them.' Commenting on the image, Al-Asad asked in Arabic and Hebrew: 'Did he have a point of view? Was he right?'"[8]

In other words, hardcore antisemitism, whether drawn from modern or medieval sources, is intrinsic to the mindset and outlook of the Iranian regime and its proxies in the region. They view Jews, Zionists, and Israelis interchangeably and regard all as their implacable enemy. Israel must be destroyed because it has "no right" to "occupy" Muslim land, and the Jews are the centuries-long enemy of Islam and its founder, Prophet Muhammad.

What is the Muslim Brotherhood, and how does it view Jews?

The slogan of the Muslim Brotherhood is "Allah is our objective. The Prophet is our leader. The Qur'an is our law. Jihad is our way. Dying in the way of Allah is our highest hope."

The Ikhwan al-Muslimeen, or Muslim Brotherhood, is a pan-Islamist organization and ideology founded by Hassan al-Banna in Egypt in 1928. It was the world's first Islamist group and, in many ways, gave birth to most, if not all, subsequent Islamist and jihadist groups, including Hamas.

8. Middle East Media Research Institute, "Yemen's Ansar Allah Movement (Houthis) Promotes Antisemitism between Attacks on Israel," December 6, 2023, footnote removed, https://www.memri.org/jttm/yemens-ansar-allah-movement-houthis-promotes-antisemitism-between-attacks-israel.

Al-Banna, an admirer of Hitler, *Mein Kampf*, and the Nazi regime in Germany, told the *New York Times* in 1948, the year before his death, "We will never accept the Jewish state."[9]

Arguably its most influential thinker was Sayyid Qutb, an Egyptian who died in 1966. In a review of *The Antisemitic Origins of Islamist Violence*, a book authored by Evin Ismail, the reviewer, Daniel Ben-Ami, notes, "Qutb's outlook still provides the core of Islamist ideology. In his view, Muslims had suffered from the machinations of Jews and double dealing since the inception of Islam in the year 600. Jews had waged constant war against the Ummah (the Muslim community of believers) as part of their conspiratorial drive to dominate the world. The survival of Islam from this perspective depended on waging a religious war—in which killing was morally sanctioned—to defeat the cosmic evil of the Jews."[10]

When Mohamed Morsi became president of Egypt in 2012, the world witnessed a longtime adherent of the Muslim Brotherhood leading the Arab world's most populous nation and a country that had had a peace treaty with Israel since 1979. Anwar Sadat, the Egyptian president who signed the treaty and received a Nobel Peace Prize, was assassinated by the Muslim Brotherhood in Egypt in 1981. Morsi's record of antisemitism, his interchanging of "Zionists" and "Jews," and his unwillingness to back down despite the pleas of Western leaders, including German chancellor Angela Merkel, were all on display.

Among Morsi's most striking quotes while active in the Muslim Brotherhood, he said that Jews are "the descendants of apes and pigs" and that Egyptians must "nurse our children and grandchildren on hatred for them: for Zionists, for Jews.

9. "Terrorism: Muslim Brotherhood," *Jewish Virtual Library*, https://www.jewishvirtuallibrary.org/the-muslim-brotherhood.
10. Daniel Ben-Ami, "Book Review: The Antisemitic Origins of Islamist Violence: A Study of the Muslim Brotherhood and Islamic State," *Fathom Journal*, May 2023, https://fathomjournal.org/book-review-the-antisemitic-origins-of-islamist-violence-a-study-of-the-muslim-brotherhood-and-islamic-state/.

They must be breast-fed hatred. The hatred must go on for God and as a form of worshipping him." He referred to Zionists as "Draculas" and "vampires." "They have been fanning the flames of civil strife wherever they were throughout their history. They are hostile by nature." As Egypt's president, Morsi never retracted these statements, only saying, from time to time, that they were taken out of context or misunderstood.[11]

Yusuf al-Qaradawi was one of the most influential Islamic leaders in the world until his death in 2022. He was the author of 120 books, and his regular shows on Qatar-sponsored Al-Jazeera television attracted tens of millions of viewers. He was a spiritual guide of the Muslim Brotherhood, and his views on Jews were unambiguous. For example, on January 28, 2009, he declared, "I will shoot Allah's enemies, the Jews, and they will throw a bomb at me, and thus, I will seal my life with martyrdom." And two days later: "Throughout history, Allah has imposed upon the [Jews] people who would punish them for their corruption. The last punishment was carried out by Hitler. By means of all the things he did to them—even though they exaggerated this issue—he managed to put them in their place. This was divine punishment for them. Allah willing, the next time will be at the hand of the believers [Muslims]."[12] In other words, he called on his many followers to complete the genocidal work of Hitler and the Nazi regime.

As of 2024, the Muslim Brotherhood is banned in several Arab countries, including Egypt, Saudi Arabia, and the United

11. David Kirkpatrick, "Egyptian Court Rejects Verdict against Mubarak," *New York Times*, January 14, 2013, https://www.nytimes.com/2013/01/14/world/middleeast/egyptian-court-grants-hosni-mubarak-a-new-trial.html.
12. Middle East Media Research Institute, "Sheik Yousuf Al-Qaradhawi: Allah Imposed Hitler upon the Jews to Punish Them—'Allah Willing, the Next Time Will Be at the Hand of the Believers,'" January 28, 2009, https://www.memri.org/tv/sheik-yousuf-al-qaradhawi-allah-imposed-hitler-upon-jews-punish-them-allah-willing-next-time-will.

Arab Emirates, because of its threat to the existing order and support for radical interpretations of Islam. Efforts to ban it in some Western countries, including the United States, have not been successful, except in Austria, which took the step in 2021.

Are there Muslim-majority countries today where Jews live freely and securely?

In a number of nations, the Jewish community—often centuries if not millennia old—has vanished. From Afghanistan to Algeria, Sudan to Syria, Iraq to Yemen, Egypt to Lebanon, the Jewish presence is essentially gone.

As widely reported in the media, until 2005 there were just two Jews remaining in Kabul, Afghanistan's capital, and they did not get along. One died in 2005, and the other emigrated 16 years later. That brought an end to a community believed to be at least 1,000 years old, with as many as 40,000 Jews at its zenith.

In Iran and Turkey, there are still Jewish communities and communal institutions, but their numbers are greatly diminished from their peak, and they face restrictions. In Iran, any identification with Israel is forbidden. To the contrary, pressure is regularly brought to bear on the estimated 8,000 Jews to demonstrate their loyalty and patriotism by denouncing Israel and Zionism. In Turkey, the community is active but must be acutely sensitive to the long shadow of the country's leader, President Recep Tayyip Erdoğan, reportedly a sympathizer of the Muslim Brotherhood, whose deep-seated hostility to Israel erupts periodically. The number of Jews has dwindled, from a high of 100,000 to approximately 14,000 in 2024.

On a brighter note, Bahrain, Morocco, Sudan, and the United Arab Emirates all reached normalization agreements with Israel, known as the Abraham Accords, in 2020. They were brokered by the Trump administration and tripled the number of Arab nations at peace with the Jewish state. Moreover, despite occasional challenges, the Jewish communities in Bahrain, Morocco, and the United Arab Emirates appear quite secure.

Actually, the Jewish community in the United Arab Emirates is growing due to expatriates settling from elsewhere. Several rabbis are actively leading congregations. Plus, the United Arab Emirates has taken the lead in the Arab Middle East in teaching about the Holocaust, as well as in fostering interfaith dialogue and cooperation among the three Abrahamic religions. The community in Bahrain numbers no more than 50, but it lives undisturbed and well-integrated. And in Morocco, the remnant of Jews left from a once vast community benefits from good relations with King Mohammed VI and his government, a bilateral connection with Israel, and growing curiosity within the country about its extensive Jewish history.

There is also a small community in Tunisia, a fraction of a much larger population that left in anticipation of, then in the wake of, Tunisia's independence from French rule in 1956. A prominent feature of the Jewish presence is the synagogue known as El Ghriba, on the island of Djerba, home to about 1,300 Jews. It is believed to be the world's oldest standing Jewish house of worship, dating back as far as 2,500 years, and continues to be the site of annual pilgrimages, particularly for Jews of North African origin. At least three times, though, in 1985, 2002, and 2023, the synagogue was the target of deadly jihadist attacks. While Tunisia is often cited as one of the more forward-looking countries in the Arab world, between 2013 and 2017 it had, per capita, the highest number of foreign fighters in the ranks of ISIS in Iraq and Syria.

Another part of the Muslim-majority world is often overlooked in discussions about the state of Jewish communities: Central Asia and the former Soviet republics. While the majority of Jews emigrated during the Soviet and immediate post-Soviet period from Azerbaijan, Kazakhstan, Tajikistan, Turkmenistan, and Uzbekistan, those who stayed have, by and large, been able to participate actively in resurgent Jewish life.

Azerbaijan is a particularly good example. Overwhelmingly Shiite Muslim and bordering Iran, it has maintained strong ties with Israel, despite periodic Iranian efforts to sabotage the link, and it celebrates a robust Jewish life in Baku and Quba, while encouraging cooperative relations between Muslim and Jewish leaders.

And a word about Kurdistan, the semi-autonomous northern third of Iraq. Unlike the central government in Iraq, the Kurds provided a receptive home for Jews, as well as a temporary haven for Jews fleeing Arab antisemitism and seeking a new start in the West. While there is no Jewish community in Kurdistan today, the attitude toward Jews is markedly different, and far more positive, than in the rest of Iraq, much less in neighboring Iran.

Is there any polling data on attitudes toward Jews in the Muslim world?

Yes. In 2019, the Pew Research Center published data on Muslim views of Jews in seven countries.[13] In Jordan, 100% of those surveyed had an unfavorable view of Jews; in Lebanon, 99%; in Egypt, 98%; in Morocco, 88%; in Indonesia, 76%; in Pakistan, 74%; and in Turkey, 60%.

In a previous Pew study, conducted in 2005, the findings were essentially the same: "Throughout the Muslim world, opinions of Jews are highly unfavorable. Dislike of Jews is universal in Jordan and Lebanon, with 99% of the publics in both countries saying they have a very unfavorable view of Jews (the remaining 1% in Jordan takes a 'somewhat unfavorable' view, while in Lebanon 1% offer no response). Similarly, 76%

13. Lisa Katz, "Muslim Views of Jews," *Learn Religions*, February 10, 2019, https://www.learnreligions.com/muslim-views-of-jews-2076073.

of Indonesians, 74% of Pakistanis, and 60% of Turks have an unfavorable opinion of Jews."[14] It is important to stress that, in both surveys, these questions were about Jews, not Israelis.

The polls also measured attitudes toward Jews in several European countries, which will be detailed elsewhere. For the moment, the lowest unfavorable number in the Muslim world, in Turkey in 2019, was more than 20 points higher than the highest unfavorable number surveyed in Europe, which was in Greece.

14. Pew Research Center, "How Muslims and Westerners See Each Other," July 14, 2005, https://www.pewresearch.org/global/2005/07/14/i-how-muslims-and-westerners-see-each-other/.

4

ANTISEMITISM AS A RACIAL PHENOMENON

With the development of technological and scientific innovations in the late 19th century, including notions of human biology and genetics, "race" became an increasing focus of attention. More or less in tandem, the dominant form of antisemitism shifted from religious to racial and to notions of the "purity" of the nation. Jews were no longer primarily perceived as a religious group, but rather a fixed "race." As a consequence, the conversion of an individual Jew to Christianity could not change their racial "Jewishness," which would never be "pure." This racialized ideology of the Jew poisoning the "superior" White, Aryan race and nation ultimately led to the genocidal ideology framing the Holocaust.

What is the relationship between racial antisemitism and antisemitism more generally?

Antisemitism can be largely broken down into three phases. First, there was a religious phase, followed by a racialized phase, and, in the contemporary context, Jews are attacked as a state, often with racialized overtones.

In the Christian phase of antisemitism, Jews were perceived largely as being "blinded by evil" for not accepting the Christian notion of the Messiah. By not accepting it, Jews were cutting themselves off from personal redemption and, collectively, hindering the advent of world redemption. Thus the solution must be to convert them forcefully, drive them out, or, in some cases, destroy them.

When societies began shifting methods of classification in the 19th and 20th centuries, from religion to science or from the supernatural to the natural, pseudo-scientific notions of race and ethnicity emerged. Jews were now to be perceived in some places as foreign, corrupting elements. As a consequence, the purity of the race and nation had to be saved from Jewish impurity. Unlike the Christian phase, where Jews had an "out"—they could convert—the race-based ideology allowed no escape from innate and immutable racial characteristics and qualities. The Jews had to be either removed or eliminated.

Following the Holocaust, racist and Christian notions of antisemitism started to become taboo in mainstream Western societies. But, like a shape-shifting virus, antisemitism began to focus instead on the one and only Jewish-majority state, Israel, which was reborn in 1948, including accusations of "racism" and "apartheid."

How does the concept of racial identity in the United States impact notions of Jewish people as a race?

In the United States, the notion of race is primarily judged by the color of one's skin. However, as previously noted, the Jewish people are comprised of different "racial" groups.

The notion of race was used by Hitler and the Nazi Party to classify the Jews as "subhuman." Nazi ideology additionally utilized social Darwinist theories of the 19th century, which postulated that distinctive characteristics were passed on genetically, to formulate notions of race.

Also intrinsic to social Darwinism was the concept of the "survival of the fittest." The Nazi interpretation included notions of expanding the "fittest" (i.e., Aryan) race both genetically and geographically (through a policy of *Lebensraum*, "living space"). The Nazis believed they had an obligation to target the "inferior" races, including Jews, as well as Slavs, so-called Asiatics (peoples of Soviet Central Asia and the Muslim populations of the Caucasus region), Roma, people with disabilities, and Africans.

Apropos Africans, a number of whom served in the French army at the time, Joel Kotek, professor of political science at the Free University of Brussels, has collected cartoons from Nazi magazines that depict Jews and Black people scheming together to control the West. Black people are portrayed as sub-human, degenerate, predatory and a threat, through miscegenation, to the purity of the European bloodline. Of course, these were quite similar tropes to Nazi characterizations of Jews.

Despite Nazi belief, there existed no scientific methodology to classify Jews as a racial group. Indeed, in 1934 the Nazis widely featured, including on a magazine cover, the photo of a baby girl to highlight "the perfect example of the Aryan race to further Nazi philosophy." It turns out the girl was Hessy Levinsons, born to Jewish parents (Figure 4.1)![1]

In a similar vein, the *Berliner Tageblatt* published a wartime photo of Werner Goldberg, who was described as "the ideal German soldier" ("der ideale deutsche Soldat"). His photograph was used in Nazi recruitment propaganda in 1939 (Figure 4.2).[2] Goldberg's father, Albert Goldberg, was born Jewish in the German city of Königsberg.

Since many German Jews had assimilated into the cultural and social fabric of Germany, the Nazis relied on citizenship laws, which were passed in September 1935 and known as the Nuremberg Race Laws (Figure 4.3). A Jew was defined

1. Terrence McCoy, "The 'Perfect' Aryan Child Was Actually Jewish," *Washington Post*, July 7, 2014, https://www.washingtonpost.com/news/morning-mix/wp/2014/07/07/the-perfect-aryan-child-the-nazis-used-in-propaganda-was-actually-jewish/.
2. Ira Moskowitz, "Caught in the Middle, Part-Jewish Germans Served in Nazi Army," *Haaretz*, April 21, 2006, https://www.haaretz.com/caught-in-the-middle-part-jewish-germans-served-in-nazi-army-1.185805.

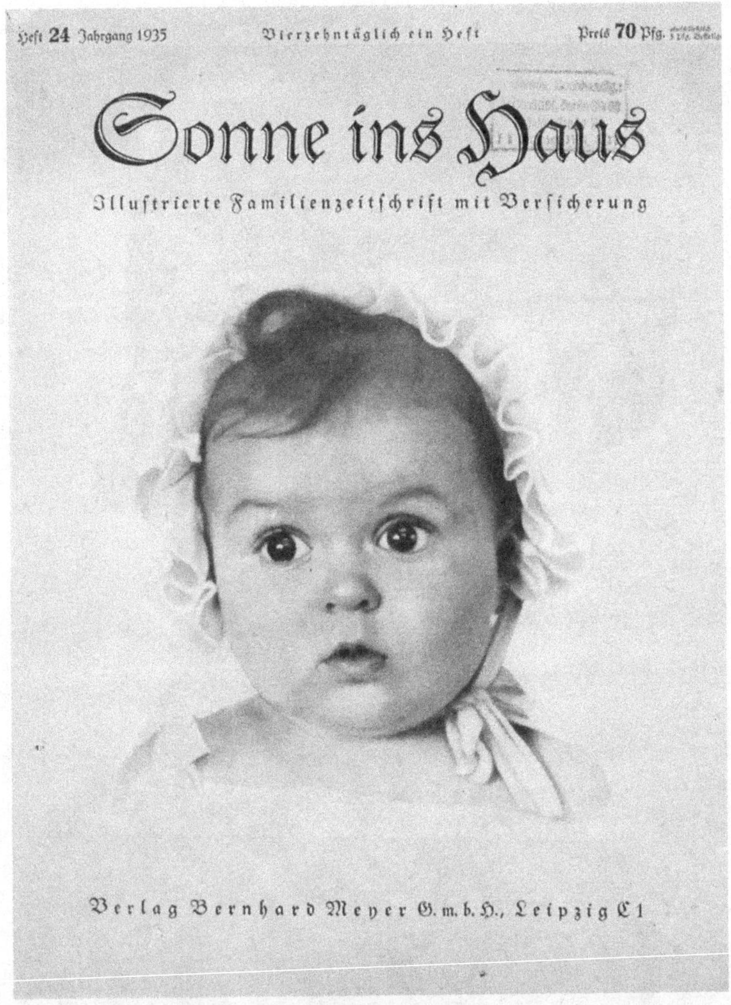

Figure 4.1 A Nazi German birthday card featuring a photograph of Hessy Levinsons, winner of the most beautiful Aryan baby contest (1935) who, in reality, was the daughter of Jewish parents. Source: U.S. Holocaust Memorial Museum, "A Birthday Card Featuring the Picture of Hessy Levinsons, Winner of the Most Beautiful Aryan Baby Contest," accessed April 21, 2025, https://collections.ushmm.org/search/catalog/pa1051800.

And Koops, "How German Comrades Really Talked About the War," *Historiek*, October 20, 2019, https://historiek.net/hoe-duitse-kameraden-echt-over-de-oorlog-spraken/42923/.

Figure 4.2 Werner Goldberg, depicted in Nazi propaganda as "the ideal German soldier," was, in fact, the son of a German-born Jew.

And Koops, "How German Comrades Really Talked About the War," *Historiek*, October 20, 2019, https://historiek.net/hoe-duitse-kameraden-echt-over-de-oorlog-spraken/42923/.

Figure 4.3 A visual representation of how the Nazis classified someone as racially Jewish, or *Mischlinge*, according to the Nuremberg Laws (1935).

Source: U.S. Holocaust Memorial Museum, "The Nuremberg Race Laws," accessed April 21, 2025, https://encyclopedia.ushmm.org/content/en/article/the-nuremberg-race-laws.

as someone with three or more grandparents who were born into the Jewish religious community. Under the law, Jews in Germany were no longer citizens, but instead "subjects" of the state. These laws defined people as Jewish who did not even regard themselves as Jews, due to their conversion to Christianity or to their secular beliefs. The laws also classified those who were considered "mixed-race" (*Mischlinge*) as those with only one or two grandparents born into the Jewish religious community. Despite initially being identified as "racial" Germans, as Nazi legislation expanded, the classification of *Mischlinge* Jews as such shrank accordingly.

In the contemporary era, ideas of racial classification may differ between the Jewish community and other groups, including the African American population. A person who is white-skinned, as some Jews are, may, ipso facto, be seen as a beneficiary of "White privilege."

Perhaps that is why Whoopi Goldberg, a popular African American actress and television personality, classified Jewish victims of the Holocaust as White. On a television show in 2022, Goldberg argued that the genocide was "not about race" but was instead about "man's inhumanity to man." She insisted that it involved "two White groups of people."

To clarify her argument, Goldberg explained that, in her experience, race is something "I can see": "If the [Ku Klux] Klan is coming down the street with a Jewish friend . . . I'm gonna run. But if my friend decides not to run, they'll get passed by most times, because you can't tell who's Jewish."[3]

However, to her credit, Goldberg eventually retracted her claim, saying that the Holocaust "is indeed about race because Hitler and the Nazis considered Jews to be an inferior race."[4] What she had also earlier failed to take into account is that

3. Gabe Friedman, "'The View' Holocaust Controversy: Are Jews White? Is Whoopi Goldberg Jewish?," *Times of Israel*, February 3, 2022, https://www.timesofisrael.com/the-view-holocaust-controversy-are-jews-white-is-whoopi-goldberg-jewish/.
4. Friedman, "'The View' Holocaust Controversy".

often, yes, one can indeed tell who is Jewish, and very easily. Orthodox and ultra-Orthodox Jewish men are recognizable by their head covering and, in many cases, distinctive clothing. Jewish homes and shops are often identified by a mezuzah prominently affixed to the outside doorway. Many surnames are also frequently associated with Jewish identity. And Jews can also easily be found congregating at or near synagogues, Jewish community centers, and Jewish day schools. In other words, those antisemites looking for Jews or Jewish targets have a much easier time of it than Goldberg's remarks might have suggested.

Has racial antisemitism evolved over time?

"Scientific" notions of Jews constituting an inferior race led to the Nazi annihilation of 6 million Jews in the Holocaust. Indeed, to this day, the extreme right does not consider Jews "pure" or "White."

However, with the eruption in the 21st century of extreme-left antisemitism, Jews, as explained below, have become the epitome of "Whiteness" for some.

The fixation of the extreme left on overthrowing "unequal power structures," including colonialism and capitalism, would not be applicable to Jews if they were considered non-White. Thus the antisemitism on the extreme left and extreme right splinters, even if in both cases it leads to singling out the Jews for special attention, if not obsession.

Is racial antisemitism consistent in different societies?

No. The contrasting views toward Jews as a "socially inferior" race may be exemplified in the case study of Denmark during the Holocaust.[5] It is estimated that 90% of Danish Jews were

5. "Rescue of the Danish Jews," *Imperial War Museums*, https://www.iwm.org.uk/history/rescue-of-the-danish-jews.

rescued by fellow Danes during World War II. Following the war, when questioned on their rescue efforts, the Danes' most common answer was simply that the Jews were fellow Danes. Needless to say, this approach was the polar opposite to that of Denmark's neighbor Germany, which categorically refused to see Jews as fellow Germans.

What is the difference between racial antisemitism on the far right and on the far left?

The use of racial antisemitism by both the extreme right and the extreme left is testament to the irrationality of antisemitism. Indeed, two seemingly opposite viewpoints unite in their "logic" to single out and demonize Jews. Jews are depicted at once as both poisoning the purity of the White race and exemplifying Whiteness.

The far right views Jews as an ominous threat to the White race. This can most demonstrably be seen in Nazi and neo-Nazi narratives, in addition to those of the Ku Klux Klan, White Aryan Resistance, Christian Identity Movement, and others. On the other hand, racial antisemitism is used by the far left to designate Jews as the embodiment of all sins of White privilege (e.g., colonialism). Racialized antisemitism on the far left can perhaps best be exemplified in extreme anti-Israel narratives, whereby Jews are presented as White, European, settler colonialists, even as the majority of Jewish citizens of Israel today are of direct Middle Eastern origin themselves. Still more important, Jews are indigenous to the land, dating back approximately four millennia.

Are Jews a race, ethnicity, religion, or nation?

It depends on who is answering the question. To the Nazis and to the far left, Jews are a race, though, again, seen through very different lenses. Ask Jews, however, and they would likely define themselves as an ethnicity, religion, nation, tribe, or people, or some combination thereof.

Who gets to define Jewish identity?

Historically, those with the social or political power to determine the status of a minority population often seek to do so in furtherance of an agenda. Consequently, the definition of Jews has often been dictated from outside.

Yet, like other groups, Jews have the right to determine their own identity. While the definition may vary, it is not for outsiders to attempt to impose their own views. Two recent illustrations underscore the point. In the first, Joe Biden, in the heat of the 2020 election, said to a largely Black audience, "If you have a problem figuring out whether you're for me or Trump, then you ain't Black."[6] In a similar vein, in March 2024, Donald Trump asserted, "Any Jewish person that votes for Democrats hates their religion, they hate everything about Israel and they should be ashamed of themselves."[7] Biden and Trump, each in his own way, exemplified the inappropriateness of telling other groups who they are or how they should behave in a free society.

6. BBC News, "Biden Regrets Saying Black Voters Considering Trump 'Ain't Black,'" May 23, 2020, https://www.bbc.co.uk/news/world-us-canada-52773555.
7. Susan Heavey, "Trump Draws Ire for Saying Jews Who Vote for Democrats Hate Their Religion, Israel," Reuters, March 19, 2024, https://www.reuters.com/world/us/trump-draws-ire-saying-jews-who-vote-democrats-hate-their-religion-israel-2024-03-19/.

5

ANTISEMITISM AND THE HOLOCAUST

The Holocaust represents the ultimate evil perpetrated against the Jewish people. During Nazi rule in Germany, 1933–45, 6 million Jews, constituting nearly two-thirds of European Jewry, were murdered, including 1.5 million Jewish children. The killing machinery was systematized in a unique way, employing a new alphabet of genocide—itself a new word coined as a result of the Holocaust or, as the Nazi regime called it, the Final Solution (*Endlösung*). That alphabet ranged from "A" for Auschwitz, the infamous death and slave labor camp, to "Z" for Zyklon-B, the killing agent used in the gas chambers. How did Germany, viewed by so many as a leader in culture and education, descend into such antisemitic barbarism? What were the steps that led from the dehumanization to the destruction of the Jewish people? And what about the hurdles encountered by Holocaust survivors after the war, whether in returning to their homes, trying to reach British-administered Palestine, or seeking to resettle elsewhere?

What explains Adolf Hitler's virulent antisemitism?

There is an extensive body of literature exploring the roots of Hitler's virulent antisemitism, and there are various theories about the contributing factors.

What is clear is that he was greatly influenced by the mayor of Vienna, Karl Lueger, whom Hitler called "the greatest German mayor of all time" in his manifesto, *Mein Kampf*. A rabid Jew-hater himself, Lueger once proclaimed, "I decide who is a Jew."[1] He invoked various forms of antisemitism, from racial to religious to economic, at a time when it could well serve his political ambitions. He was mayor from 1897 until his death in 1910.

In addition, Hitler, who fought in World War I and was severely injured, could not accept the defeat of Germany and Austro-Hungary in 1918. He searched for scapegoats to blame and was drawn to the "stab-in-the-back" theory (*Dolchstoßlegende*). Someone had deliberately caused this humiliation, the theory proclaimed, and that someone was a combination of Jews, Communists (or "Bolsheviks"), and Social Democrats (Figure 5.1).

Incidentally, an estimated 100,000 Jews fought on the German side in World War I, a number of whom received the Iron Cross for valor. But to the antisemite searching for a scapegoat, such contrary facts were immaterial.

Hitler became obsessed with the Jews as an enemy, and they served as the archvillains in his emerging worldview. And since Jews could be found among both Communists and Social Democrats, the "treachery" of the Jews, according to Hitler, knew no limits.

Here are excerpts from what is believed to be his first written statement, dated September 16, 1919, highlighting his views, at age 30, on Jews. Note his emphasis on Jews as a race, which is critical to an understanding of Hitler's annihilationist policy once he gained power. In this letter, he also speaks about other allegedly nefarious Jewish traits, such as the unquenchable quest for wealth and the pursuit of global domination:

1. "Karl Lueger (1844–1910)," *Jewish Virtual Library*, https://www.jewishvirtuallibrary.org/lueger-karl-x00b0.

Figure 5.1 A hook-nosed, grinning Jew stabbing a German soldier in the back.

"Illustration of the 'Stab-in-the-Back' Legend (de:Dolchstoßlegende) from an Austrian Postcard, 1919. 26 March 1919 76 Stab-in-the-back postcard," *Alamy*, https://www.alamy.com/illustration-of-the-stab-in-the-back-legend-dedolchstolegende-from-an-austrian-postcard-1919-26-march-1919-76-stab-in-the-back-postcard-image211073558.html?imageid=8A7CDFDF-15E8-4C05-9AE2-D421AA7A2E8C&p=706922&pn=1&searchId=31830000abeeaf2b50988d8b8ef36d9b&searchtype=0.

Antisemitism as a political movement may not and cannot be defined by emotional impulses, but by recognition of the facts. The facts are these: First, Jewry is absolutely a race and not a religious association.

Their dance around the golden calf is becoming a merciless struggle for all those possessions we prize most highly on earth.

His power is the power of money, which multiplies in his hands effortlessly and endlessly through interest, and which forces peoples under the most dangerous of yokes.

Everything men strive after as a higher goal, be it religion, socialism, democracy, is to the Jew only means to an end, the way to satisfy his lust for gold and domination.

In his effects and consequences, he is like a racial tuberculosis of the nations.[2]

More insight into Hitler's views on Jews, notably on racial purity and impurity, was offered in the work he is most associated with, *Mein Kampf* (*My Struggle*). This book was written in 1924 while he was in prison in Landsberg on charges of treason, after his attempted putsch the previous year:

> With satanic joy in his face, the black-haired Jewish youth lurks in wait for the unsuspecting girl whom he defiles with his blood, thus stealing her from her people. With every means he tries to destroy the racial foundations of the people he has set out to subjugate. Just as he himself systematically ruins women and girls, he does not shrink back from pulling down the blood barriers for others, even on a large scale. It was and it is Jews who bring the Negroes into the Rhineland, always with the same secret thought and clear aim of ruining the hated white race by the necessarily resulting bastardization, throwing it down from its cultural and political height, and himself rising to be its master.
>
> For a racially pure people which is conscious of its blood can never be enslaved by the Jew. In this world, he will forever be master over bastards and bastards alone.
>
> And so he tries systematically to lower the racial level by a continuous poisoning of individuals.
>
> And in politics he begins to replace the idea of democracy by the dictatorship of the proletariat.
>
> In the organized mass of Marxism, he has found the weapon which lets him dispense with democracy and in

2. Jewish Virtual Library, "Adolf Hitler: First Anti-Semitic Writing," September 16, 1919, https://www.jewishvirtuallibrary.org/adolf-hitler-s-first-anti-semitic-writing.

> its stead allows him to subjugate and govern the peoples with a dictatorial and brutal fist.
>
> He works systematically for revolutionization in a twofold sense: economic and political.[3]

When Hitler was released from prison after serving only nine months of a five-year term, the *New York Times* published a report, dated December 20, 1924, with the headline "Hitler Tamed by Prison" and including the following sentence: "It is believed he will retire to private life, and return to Austria, the country of his birth."[4]

Instead of being tamed and retiring, however, just over eight years later, on January 30, 1933, Hitler became chancellor of Germany. And on March 23, after the German Parliament overwhelmingly approved the Enabling Act, he became the all-powerful leader. He could now simply bypass Parliament. This gave him the unchallenged authority to put his views on Jews into action as a matter of state policy.

How were Jews depicted in Nazi propaganda?

Propaganda was a key weapon in the Nazi arsenal.

From 1933 until 1945, it was largely in the hands of Joseph Goebbels, an early Nazi Party stalwart who often expressed his adoration for Hitler. In his diary, apart from voicing his "love" for Hitler, he wrote, "Such a sparkling mind can be my leader. I bow to the greater one, the political genius."[5]

Goebbels had received his doctorate in philology from one of the world's finest centers of higher education at the

3. Yad Vashem, "Extracts from Mein Kampf by Adolf Hitler," accessed April 21, 2025, https://www.yadvashem.org/docs/extracts-from-mein-kampf.html.
4. *New York Times*, "Hitler Tamed by Prison," December 21, 1924.
5. Joseph Bottum, "Satan's Spokesman," *Washington Free Beacon*, June 6, 2015, https://freebeacon.com/culture/satans-spokesman/.

time, Heidelberg University. He was named head of the Nazi Ministry for Public Enlightenment and Propaganda just six weeks after Hitler became chancellor in 1933.

Both Hitler and Goebbels understood the power of communications—of indoctrinating and mobilizing the masses—to serve the Nazi agenda. They took full advantage of all the platforms at their disposal, including radio, films, cartoons, rallies, pageantry, and newspapers. Just imagine for a moment how much greater their global reach and impact would have been had they had the tools of 21st-century media available to them.

They were assisted by many, including Julius Streicher, who, from 1923 to 1945, published *Der Sturmer*, a popular weekly paper that was viciously antisemitic and which depicted Jews in the most grotesque manner possible.

Central to all the messaging was the unquestioned superiority of the Aryan, or "master," race, in stark contrast to the lowest form of humanity, the Jew, described as subhuman (*Untermensch*), a germ or virus.

The Jew was simultaneously seeking to become rich at the expense of non-Jews, while, conversely, trying to impose Marxism-Bolshevism on the people. He was part of a cabal scheming to take power and exert control for its own nefarious interests, just as the infamous *Protocols of the Elders of Zion* had reported. He was looking for Christian blood to fulfill alleged Jewish religious needs, even as the Nazi leaders had their own tenuous relationship with the churches.

In short, the Jew was the implacable enemy of everything the Third Reich stood for and therefore had to be removed entirely, one way or another, from German society. To allow the Jew to remain was to "contaminate" the German people and "poison" the Aryan race.

For Hitler, this was precisely the point: Jews were not White. To the contrary, the Nazis alleged in their nonstop propaganda that Jews were out to destroy the White race, nothing less. When neo-Nazis marched in Charlottesville, Virginia, in 2017, one of their oft-repeated chants was "Jews will not replace us," referring to the White supremacy belief that Jews are not White and indeed pose an existential threat to the White race.

Hitler took the notion of racial antisemitism to the ultimate degree not by stigmatizing, isolating, or discriminating against Jews, as had been done before him, but rather by plotting to remove them entirely as a physical presence. And the more the Jews could be vilified and dehumanized by Nazi propaganda, the easier it would become to enlist the non-Jewish population in achieving the goal.

For Goebbels, as Germany's propaganda minister, the messaging was simple, shouted from the rooftops and endlessly repeated: "Never forget it, Comrades, and repeat it a hundred times so you will say it in your dreams—'THE JEWS ARE TO BLAME!' "[6]

Blame for what? For everything deemed wrong with the country. Germany's loss in World War I? Blame the Jews. Germany's onerous reparations to the victorious World War I nations? Blame the Jews. Hyperinflation? Blame the Jews. Unemployment? Blame the Jews. Communist threat? Blame the Jews.

As antisemitic measures were adopted in the 1930s, how did Jews in Germany react?

As discussed, antisemitism in Germany did not begin with the advent of the Nazis in the 20th century. Its roots go deeper and were manifested, over many centuries, in religious, racial, social, and political beliefs, including from individuals like 16th-century theologian Martin Luther, 19th-century journalist and politician Wilhelm Marr, and 19th-century composer Richard Wagner.

6. Jewish Virtual Library, "Time Magazine Reveals Nazi Attitude toward Jews," July 10, 1933, https://www.jewishvirtuallibrary.org/time-magazine-reveals-nazi-attitude-toward-jews.

Yet when Hitler gained power in 1933, the Jewish community in Germany numbered 525,000, and whatever antisemitic experiences they may have encountered or heard about in prior years, they by and large felt an integral part of German society and were big devotees of German culture.

Their degree of assimilation was quite high, as a considerable number were only loosely connected to Jewish life and would describe themselves as Germans of Jewish faith, while some had married non-Jews or even converted to Christianity, the dominant religion in Germany.

They were acutely conscious of the 100,000 Jews who served in the German army in World War I, during which as many as 12,000 gave their lives in defense of their homeland, while 18,000 received the Iron Cross for valor (Figure 5.2). It was one of Hitler's commanding officers, Lieutenant Hugo Gutmann,

Figure 5.2 A weeping mother, a grave of 12,000 Jewish soldiers, and a reference to Christians and Jews having defended the country together, published by German Jewish veterans of World War I.

"12000 Juden fielen im Kampf," Leo Baeck Institute, https://www.lbi.org/griffinger/record/5523254.

a Jew, who nominated Hitler for an Iron Cross, the coveted medal for valor that he displayed all his life.[7]

Jews played an outsized role in many spheres of German life, including law, medicine, science, commerce, culture, and media. For example, Albert Einstein received the Nobel Prize in Physics in 1922, one of several German Jews to win the prestigious award in the sciences.

When Hitler began his anti-Jewish policies almost immediately after taking the reins of power in 1933, it was not long before Jews felt the effects: scapegoating for all of Germany's alleged ills; legislation that increasingly marginalized, segregated, disenfranchised, and dehumanized them; boycotts of Jewish-owned businesses in German ("Deutsche, Kauft nicht bei Juden"; "Germans, don't buy from the Jews"); beatings by Nazi mobs; and restrictions on just about everything, including which benches Jews could sit on in Berlin's parks.

During this five-year period (1933–38) of ever-increasing threats to Jews, Hitler was still willing to let them leave the country and "solve the Jewish problem" by their emigration. Some German Jews who could see the handwriting on the wall from the very beginning tried to emigrate as fast as they could, heading in whatever direction possible: elsewhere in Europe, British-administered Palestine, North or South America, China, and beyond. Perhaps they had family abroad that could assist with entry, or professional connections, or luck with visa applications, or a chance to incentivize foreign consular officials or border guards.

For others who took longer to grasp that the Germany of their nostalgic past was not about to return anytime soon and had been replaced by a Nazi dictatorship hellbent on

7. Anne Frank House, "Hitler as a Soldier in the First World War," July 1, 1916, https://www.annefrank.org/en/timeline/139/hitler-as-a-soldier-in-the-first-world-war/#:~:text=In%20December%201914%2C%20Hitler%20received,soldiers%20in%20the%20German%20army.

eliminating Jews, the chances of finding an exit strategy rapidly decreased.

To frame the two different types of responses in a more individualized way, Billy Wilder, the Academy Award–winning film director and a Jew born in the Austro-Hungarian Empire, came to America in 1934, one year after the rise of the Nazis. At war's end, he summed up the prewar choice in one sentence: "The optimists died in the gas chambers, the pessimists have pools in Beverly Hills."[8]

On the other hand, in German historian Joachim Fest's memoir *Not Me*, he recalled his late father's comments about prewar Jewish friends whom he called " 'the last Prussians': self-disciplined, quietly polite, brilliant without sentimentality, but now without 'the instinct for danger which had preserved them through the ages.' "[9] Those friends of Johannes Fest waited too long, their attachment to all things German too strong, their faith in the land of Beethoven and Goethe having delayed their full understanding of the radical shift to Hitler and Himmler, and they now faced exit doors slammed shut.

Alas, most countries in the 1930s were unwilling to open their doors to large numbers of German Jews. Edith Frank, the mother of the teenage diarist Anne Frank, said in 1937, "I think that all the German Jews are searching the world today and there is no room for them anymore."[10] Eight years later, Edith Frank perished in Auschwitz and her daughters, Anne and

8. Jordan Hoffman, "Director Billy Wilder's Pre-WWII European Journalism Is Revealed—and Revealing," *Times of Israel*, May 15, 2021, https://www.timesofisrael.com/director-billy-wilders-pre-wwii-european-journalism-is-revealed-and-revealing/.
9. "Closing Keynote—Bret Stephens at the Z3 Conference 2019," *The Z3 Project*, https://www.z3project.org/blog/closing-keynote-2019-bret-stephens.
10. Gertjan Broek, "The (Im)Possibilities of Escaping: Jewish Emigration 1933–1942," Anne Frank House, accessed April 21, 2025, https://www.annefrank.org/en/anne-frank/go-in-depth/impossibilities-escaping-1933-1942/#:~:text=In%20a%20letter%20to%20an,no%20room%20for%20them%20anymore.%E2%80%9D.

Margot, in Bergen-Belsen, two of the infamous Nazi German concentration camps.

In the lead-up to the war, how did Western nations respond to the growing plight of Jews?

The short answer is they responded with relatively little interest, much less sympathy.

While some nations accepted small numbers of Jews seeking to flee Germany from 1933 onward and, later, German-annexed Austria in 1938, followed by other countries in the crosshairs of the Nazis, the overall record was large-scale indifference.

Throughout the 1930s, American immigration policy was determined by country quotas, very different from today. Jews had to apply, navigate the labyrinthine process, and, among other criteria, prove they would not be a financial burden on the United States. There was no special refugee policy at the time, much less a fast track for those in imminent danger.

Antisemitism, isolationism, economic insecurity resulting from the Great Depression, and xenophobia were all very much alive in the 1930s. Their repercussions could be felt in Washington's political circles.

In the decade of the 1930s, the U.S. country quota for Germany (and, later, Germany and Austria combined) was filled only once, in 1939. Otherwise, there were actually unfilled slots each year. This was not for lack of applicants. Vast numbers of Jews, not to speak of others, sought admission. But the State Department bureaucracy was in no hurry to take them, especially, as studies have shown, when it came to Jews.[11] While Jews still had the chance to leave Nazi-occupied lands, many could not because of closed doors elsewhere.

11. David S Wyman, *The Abandonment of the Jews: America and the Holocaust 1941–1945* (Pantheon, 1984); Arthur Morse, *While Six Million Died: A Chronicle of American Apathy* (Hart, 1968).

In 1938, at the behest of the United States and, some observers argue, to deflect attention from Washington's own restrictive policies, an international conference on European refugees was convened in Evian, France.[12] Thirty-two nations attended. This was at a time when Hitler was still teasing the world, saying essentially *If you care so much about the Jews, take them. Germany will not prevent them from leaving*.

But the response in Evian told Hitler all he needed to know. With the notable exception of the Dominican Republic, no country was prepared to open its doors more than a crack to Jews desperate to leave. Thomas White, the Australian delegate, put it bluntly: "As we have no real racial problem, we are not desirous of importing one by encouraging any scheme of large-scale foreign migration." Note that he spoke not of a religious but a "racial" problem prompted by the prospect of Jewish refugees.[13]

This reaction surely signaled to Hitler that, even if some nations occasionally issued statements condemning German policies such as the Nuremberg Laws, which, again, based on racial criteria, stripped German Jews of their citizenship, they were not prepared to act. Thus they would presumably be unwilling to do anything if Hitler went the next step and began to round up the Jews, put them in concentration camps, and work them to death or simply kill them outright.

Several months after the Evian Conference, in November 1938, the Nazis in Germany and Austria unleashed *Kristallnacht*, the Night of Broken Glass. Jews were murdered in the streets, Jewish-owned shops were vandalized, and synagogues were burned.

12. Gordon Sander, "Inside America's Failed, Forgotten Conference to Save Jews from Hitler," *Washington Post*, July 15, 2023, https://www.washingtonpost.com/history/2023/07/15/holocaust-hitler-fdr-jewish-evian-conference/.
13. The Holocaust, "Australia's Response to the Plight of European Jewry," accessed April 21, 2025, https://holocaust.com.au/the-facts/australias-response-to-the-plight-of-european-jewry/.

Yet even as 94% of Americans condemned the Nazi treatment of Jews, in a poll taken by Gallup two weeks after *Kristallnacht*, 72% of those surveyed said no when asked the question "Should we allow a large number of Jewish exiles from Germany to come to live in the United States?"[14]

More evidence of anti-immigrant sentiment came in May 1939, when an ocean liner, the SS *St. Louis*, departed Hamburg, Germany, with 937 passengers on board. The vast majority were Jewish refugees. The first destination was Havana, but the Cuban authorities would allow only a handful of the passengers to disembark, despite previous assurances to some others on board.[15] Nor, subsequently, would the American government accept even one single passenger while the ship itself was just off the coast of Miami Beach, close enough for those on board to see the skyline. Nor would the Canadian government.[16] The ship had no choice but to return to Europe with its passengers. As many as 254 of them were later murdered in the Holocaust.

In the 1930s, the British governed Palestine under a League of Nations mandate. Some European Jews tried to make their way to what they hoped was the safety of this strip of land on the eastern shore of the Mediterranean Sea, where a Jewish community had re-established itself. But Britain issued a White Paper in 1939 announcing that the quota for Jewish entry would be strictly limited to a total of 75,000 over the next five years.

On the eve of the Second World War, which began when German troops invaded Poland on September 1, 1939, there

14. Daniel Greene and Frank Newport, "American Public Opinion and the Holocaust," Gallup, April 23, 2018, https://news.gallup.com/opinion/polling-matters/232949/american-public-opinion-holocaust.aspx.
15. U.S. Holocaust Memorial Museum, "Voyage of the St Louis," accessed April 21, 2025, https://encyclopedia.ushmm.org/content/en/article/voyage-of-the-st-louis-1.
16. To understand Canada's immigration policy regarding Jews at the time, see Harold Troper and Irving Abella, *None Is Too Many: Canada and the Jews of Europe 1933–1948* (Key Porter Books, 2002).

were approximately 9.5 million Jews in Europe, 3.5 million in Poland alone. And the bulk of the other Jews were in countries that would soon be Nazi targets, including Czechoslovakia, France, Belgium, the Netherlands, Norway, the Baltic states, Romania, Hungary, Yugoslavia, Bulgaria, Greece, and the Soviet Union, not to mention Germany itself, where Jews had been in ever-growing danger since 1933, and Austria since the *Anschluss* (joining Austria to Germany) in 1938.

By and large, those Jews were trapped, even as some managed to escape, perhaps through good luck, with the help of Righteous Gentiles, bribable border guards, or, in a few cases, special professional talents that were in demand.

As Chaim Weizmann, a future president of Israel, put it when testifying before the British Peel Commission as early as 1936, "[For the Jews of Europe], the world is divided into places where they cannot live and where they cannot enter."[17]

What was the Wannsee Conference, and why was it so crucial to Hitler's aims?

The Wannsee Conference was a crucial stepping stone on the path to the Nazi plan for the extermination of the Jewish people in Europe. The meeting, in an elegant, lakeside villa on the outskirts of Berlin, took place on January 20, 1942. Chaired by Reinhard Heydrich, a top Nazi security leader, 15 high-ranking officials met to discuss the implementation of Hitler's aim for the "Final Solution of the Jewish Question" ("Endlösung der Judenfrage").

They were not there to debate it. The genocidal policy was set by the *Führer*. No one at the table voiced any disagreement or qualms. Their mandate was to coordinate the plan across the various ministries and offices that would be involved. And, it

17. Yad Vashem, "The Outbreak of World War II and Anti-Jewish Policy," accessed April 21, 2025, https://www.yadvashem.org/holocaust/about/outbreak-of-ww2-anti-jewish-policy.html.

should be noted, more than half of the meeting's participants had a PhD, underscoring that higher education was not necessarily a guarantor of humanistic values in Germany.

Heydrich cited a figure of 11 million Jews in Europe, including the unoccupied United Kingdom and neutral countries such as Switzerland and Spain, and set forth the agenda: "During the course of the Final Solution, the Jews will be deployed under appropriate supervision at a suitable form of labor deployment in the East. In large labor columns, separated by gender, able-bodied Jews will be brought to those regions to build roads, whereby a large number will doubtlessly be lost through natural reduction. Any final remnant that survives will doubtless consist of the elements most capable of resistance. They must be dealt with appropriately, since, representing the fruit of natural selection, they are to be regarded as the core of a new Jewish revival."[18]

In other words, the concentration of the Jews would be "in the East," principally Nazi camps built in occupied Poland. Some "able-bodied" Jews would be used as slave labor for the Nazi machine, while those deemed not capable of the work would be disposed of quickly. The word "extermination" was never formally used, perhaps as a way of seeking to protect themselves if later accused by Allied forces of complicity in mass murder. And "the final remnant that survives" would "be dealt with appropriately," again deliberately vague, though everyone at the table surely understood the intent.

At this stage, the Nazis were already experimenting with Zyklon B, a killing agent that would be used in the gas chambers to annihilate Jews on an industrial scale. The earlier Nazi method of mass shootings of Jews by the *Einsatzgruppen*, the

18. U.S. Holocaust Memorial Museum, "Wannsee Conference and the 'Final Solution,'" accessed April 21, 2025, https://encyclopedia.ushmm.org/content/en/article/wannsee-conference-and-the-final-solution.

frontline death squads deployed to Eastern Europe, was proving too labor-intensive and cumbersome to achieve the larger aims.

How did Nazi Germany implement the Final Solution?

Nazi Germany utilized a variety of means in its attempted annihilation of the Jewish people. Principally, it was through a series of death, slave labor, and concentration camps built in Germany and Eastern Europe. Their names are etched in the history of the Holocaust: Auschwitz-Birkenau, Belzec, Bergen-Belsen, Buchenwald, Chełmno, Dachau, Majdanek, Mauthausen, Ravensbrück, Sachsenhausen, Sobibor, Stutthof, Treblinka . . .

To take one example, between 450,000 and 500,000 Jews were deported to the Nazi German death camp in Belzec, located in southeastern Poland. The sole purpose of the camp was extermination. In one year, 1942–43, virtually all the Jews were murdered in the gas chambers, their bodies then burned in the crematoria. Fewer than 10 Jews survived.

The toll was even higher in Auschwitz-Birkenau, located in southern Poland and used for both slave labor and extermination, where an estimated 1 million Jews—and 100,000 non-Jews—were killed during the camp's five years of operation, 1940–45.

An estimated 2 million Jews were slaughtered by the Nazi killing squads in Eastern Europe, in such places as Babi Yar (Ukraine), Rumbala (Latvia), and Ponary (Lithuania). In a number of cases, the Nazi forces were aided by local collaborators, whether in the camps or killing fields. And in the case of Romania, as reported in the *Holocaust Encyclopedia*, "[e]ven before Romania fell into the orbit of Nazi Germany, Romanian authorities pursued a policy of harsh, persecutory antisemitism."[19]

One of the tragic consequences was the pogrom in the city of Iasi, in June 1941, where thousands of Jews were murdered on

19. Holocaust Encyclopedia, "Romania," accessed April 21, 2025, https://encyclopedia.ushmm.org/content/en/article/romania.

the instructions of the country's virulently antisemitic prime minister, Ion Antonescu. (Antonescu was tried, convicted, and executed as a war criminal in Romania in 1946.)[20] In all, approximately 380,000 Romanian Jews were exterminated between 1940 and 1945, half of the country's total Jewish population.

Elsewhere, in the Polish town of Jedwabne, as told by Jan Gross in his book *Neighbors: The Story of the Annihilation of a Jewish Town*, dozens of local Poles assisted the occupying Germans to round up the town's Jews, lock them in a barn, and set the barn on fire.[21] In Belzec, Ukrainian guards, outnumbering the Germans running the camp, helped implement the mass slaughter of Jews.

There were many more such instances of deadly collaboration, from France to the Baltic lands, from Slovakia to Croatia, and elsewhere.

In addition to the camps and the killing squads, the Nazis, as a first step, often arrested Jews en masse and forced them into ghettos, including in Warsaw, Łódź, Minsk, and Vilnius. Severe food shortages and disease took their toll on many Jews even before the cattle cars transported them to the camps.

The Nazis were not keen for the world to know about the crimes against humanity taking place. They feared eventual retribution. It led them to try to depict the camps as nothing more than a work assignment rather than a journey to likely death. Of course, this also served to reduce any chance of Jewish resistance or rebellion along the way.

Moreover, the Nazis operated one ghetto or camp, Theresienstadt, in Czechoslovakia, as a "model" to deceive the world. And they were quite successful. When a delegation from the Geneva-based International Committee of the Red Cross came on an inspection tour in June 1944, they saw

20. Holocaust Encyclopedia, "Trial of Ion Antonescu," accessed April 21, 2025, https://encyclopedia.ushmm.org/content/en/film/trial-of-ion-antonescu.

21. Jan Gross, *Neighbors: The Story of the Annihilation of a Jewish Town* (Princeton University Press, 2001).

well-fed inmates gardening, playing soccer, and organizing cultural events. It was an elaborate hoax carefully staged by the Nazis. The ICRC fell for it. Decades later, the global organization apologized for its "moral failure" in not seeing behind the truth of Theresienstadt.[22]

The attempted Final Solution of the Jewish Question involved a massive number of personnel, both German and other nationalities, dealing with, among other key elements of the plan, identification, roundups, deportation, transportation, administration of ghettos and camps, industrial production of killing agents and equipment, guards, torturers, medical experimenters, and executioners. As one window into this massive mobilization, historian Christopher Browning authored in 1992 *Ordinary Men: Reserve Police Battalion 101 and the Final Solution in Poland.*[23] Ordinary men, indeed.

In August 1941, upon hearing reports of the mass killings by the *Einsatzgruppen*, British prime minister Winston Churchill said in a radio address to his countrymen, "We are in the presence of a crime without a name."[24] It was not until 1944 that Raphael Lemkin, a Polish-born Jew and lawyer who found refuge in the United States a few years earlier, coined the word "genocide." He wrote, "By 'genocide' we mean the destruction of a nation or ethnic group. This new word . . . is made from the ancient Greek word *genos* (race, tribe) and the Latin *cide* (killing)."[25]

22. Sébastien Farré, "The ICRC and the Detainees in Nazi Concentration Camps (1942–1945)," *International Review of the Red Cross* 94, no. 888 (2012), doi:10.1017/S1816383113000489.
23. Christopher Browning, *Ordinary Men: Reserve Police Battalion 101 and the Final Solution in Poland* (Aaron Asher Books, 1992).
24. Prime Minister Winston Churchill's Broadcast to the World about the Meeting with President Roosevelt, August 24, 1941, https://www.ibiblio.org/pha/timeline/410824awp.html.
25. Facing History & Ourselves, "Excerpt from Axis Rule in Occupied Europe by Raphael Lemkin," March 16, 2008, https://www.facinghistory.org/resource-library/excerpt-axis-rule-occupied-europe-raphael-lemkin.

Figure 5.3 The meeting between Hitler and al-Husayni took place in Berlin on November 28, 1941.

Now the crime at least had a name.

Who was Muhammad Amin al-Husayni?

Muhammad Amin al-Husayni was the mufti, or senior Muslim cleric, in Jerusalem for many years, an Arab nationalist, and an avowed antisemite. In his relentless determination to remove Britain (and the Jews) from the Middle East, he sided with the Third Reich, spending time in Berlin, meeting with Hitler, spreading Nazi propaganda in Arabic, and supporting the annihilation of the Jewish people (Figure 5.3). How influential he actually was in Berlin has long been a matter of debate, but his record of Nazi collaboration is beyond dispute.[26]

26. U.S. Holocaust Memorial Museum, "Hajj Amin al-Husayni: The Mufti of Jerusalem," *Holocaust Encyclopedia*, accessed April 21, 2025, https://encyclopedia.ushmm.org/content/en/article/hajj-amin-al-husayni-the-mufti-of-jerusalem.

Were there countries and individuals who actively opposed Hitler's Final Solution?

There were. Not nearly enough, but those who acted, often at great risk, offer timeless examples of moral clarity and courage.

Among countries, Denmark is a particularly compelling case study. The occupying Germans were planning a roundup of the nation's Jewish community, numbering about 7,800, in 1943. The Danish underground got wind of the plan and hastily organized the evacuation of just over 7,200 Jews—and several hundred non-Jewish spouses—to neighboring Sweden, which was neutral in World War II but opened its doors to the fleeing Jews, keeping them safe until the war's end in 1945.

When the Jews were able to return to their homes in Denmark, they found them largely intact and cared for, unlike the experiences of many surviving Jews in Eastern Europe, whose homes were often occupied and furnishings stolen, with a clear message that the Jews were not welcome back. When Danes were asked why so many of them participated in the rescue effort, the most common answer was quite simply that the Jews were fellow Danes. That reply was often accompanied by regret that some 600 Danish Jews could not be rescued and were seized by the Nazis. In the context of the Holocaust, what happened in Denmark is a towering example of how a nation can react when fellow citizens are collectively endangered.

There were other stirring examples of national rescue, including in Albania, Bulgaria, and Morocco.

Indeed, Albania, occupied by the Italian fascists and then the German Nazis, managed to not only protect but grow its Jewish community considerably by the war's end due to an inflow from other nations. The Albanian code of honor, known as *Besa*, played a big role.

Bulgaria was a different story. It was an ally of Germany, yet when the Nazis demanded that Sofia round up and deport its large Jewish community, resistance emerged from the church, parliament, royal family, and some political parties. Thus the

Bulgarian Jewish community survived the war. At the same time, Bulgarian troops, collaborating with Germany in occupied Macedonia and Thrace, helped deport thousands of Jews to the death camps.

And in Morocco, King Mohammed V protected the Jewish community, numbering 250,000, from deportation. When the collaborationist French Vichy regime demanded the turnover of the Jews, the king's reported reply was "There are no Jews in Morocco. There are only Moroccan subjects."[27]

Yad Vashem, the Israeli center for Holocaust education, research, and remembrance, seeks to identify individuals who saved Jewish lives during the Holocaust. As of 2023, it had honored 28,486 Righteous Among the Nations, as they are called. The countries most represented are, in descending order, Poland, the Netherlands, France, Ukraine, and Belgium.

One of the most powerful stories of rescue occurred on the Greek island of Zakynthos. When the occupying Germans called in the mayor and bishop to demand a list of the island's 275 Jews, they came back the next day with a list of just two names, their own. Meanwhile, the 275 Jews were hidden and survived the war.

Another inspiring illustration was the French town of Le Chambon-sur-Lignon. Led by Pastor André Trocmé and his wife, Magda, the town offered refuge to thousands of Jews and others fleeing the Nazis. One young Jew, Elizabeth Koenig-Kaufman, who found safety there later said, "Nobody asked who was Jewish and who was not. Nobody asked where you were from. Nobody asked who your father was or if you could pay. They just accepted each of us, taking us in with warmth,

27. Sadik Rddad, "The Conflicting Moroccan Responses to Normalization with Israel," Washington Institute, April 12, 2021, https://www.washingtoninstitute.org/policy-analysis/conflicting-moroccan-responses-normalization-israel.

sheltering children, often without their parents—children who cried in the night from nightmares."[28]

Numerically, the rescuers were few considering the size of country populations across occupied Europe. But each story is a powerful testament to humanity, whether motivated by faith, friendship, family, or simple decency. There is much to be learned from the examples—however many, however few—of the saviors and their life-risking responses to genocidal antisemitism.

When did the United States learn about the Holocaust, and how did it respond?

The news of Hitler's anti-Jewish campaign, which began when he became chancellor in January 1933, was not a secret to anyone. It was very public. And until December 1941, when Germany declared war against the United States, there was an American embassy in Berlin, Germany's capital, and American journalists on the ground. Thus there was no shortage of first-hand reports being sent back to the United States, whether in diplomatic pouches or via the news wires.

As discussed earlier, these troubling reports did not change American immigration policy. There were no increased quotas, no exceptions for the cumbersome application process, and no accelerated entry for people whose lives were at stake. To repeat, only once in the entire decade of the 1930s was the country quota for Germany even filled, despite the long lines desperate for admission.

After America joined the war effort, reports continued to arrive in Washington. If this no longer occurred via American

28. U.S. Holocaust Memorial Museum, "Le Chambon-sur-Lignon," accessed April 21, 2025, https://encyclopedia.ushmm.org/content/en/article/le-chambon-sur-lignon#:~:text=%22Nobody%20asked%20who%20was%20Jewish,in%20the%20night%20from%20nightmares.%22.

diplomats and journalists in Germany, then it happened through underground and resistance movements in German-occupied Europe; some diplomats of neutral countries, often in contravention of their official orders; and a few Jews who managed to escape from the clutches of the Nazis.

As one illustration, Gerhart Riegner, a German-born Jew working for the World Jewish Congress (WJC) in neutral Switzerland, got horrifying information that he composed in a telegram in August 1942: "Received alarming report about plan being discussed and considered in Führer headquarters to exterminate at one fell swoop all Jews in German-controlled countries comprising three and a half to four million after deportation and concentration in the east, thus solving Jewish question once and for all stop campaign planned for autumn methods being discussed including hydrocyanic acid."[29] He asked the American consulate in Geneva to forward the telegram to his WJC colleagues in the United States, since he feared the Swiss telegraph agency was compromised by the Germans. His request was refused, with the explanation that it was due to the "fantastic nature of the allegation and the impossibility of our being of any assistance if such action were taken."[30]

In July 1943, President Franklin Roosevelt met in the White House for one hour with Jan Karski, a Polish underground courier. Karski had risked his life time and again to bear witness to the German annihilation policy against the Jews, and then, in another extraordinary act of courage, made his way across German-occupied Europe to London and, later, Washington to

29. World Jewish Congress, "70 Years Ago: Riegner Telegram Alerts World of Nazi Holocaust," August 8, 2012, https://www.worldjewishcongress.org/en/news/70-years-ago-riegner-telegram-alerts-world-of-nazi-holocaust.

30. Gregory J. Wallance, "WJC 1936–2021: The World Jewish Congress during World War II," World Jewish Congress, accessed April 21, 2025, https://www.worldjewishcongress.org/en/85th-anniversary/the-world-jewish-congress-during-world-war-ii.

report his findings. Karski said that the American president "did not ask one question about the Jews."[31]

During the same visit, he met with Supreme Court justice Felix Frankfurter, a Jew born in Austria. Frankfurter explained his reaction to Karski's harrowing account of the systematic slaughter of millions of Jews this way: "I did not say he was lying. I said I could not believe him. There is a difference."[32]

What was going on? Was it a failure of imagination, as in the case of Frankfurter, to believe the flow of information about mass annihilation? Was it widespread antisemitism in Washington officialdom, starting with the State Department, that prevented any empathy for those at risk or any special action on their behalf? Or was it, as President Roosevelt contended, a belief that the best way to end the nightmare was to finish the war as quickly as possible, and without any diversion of resources or rethinking of priorities even to save Jewish lives?

A question that remains hotly debated to this day is whether the United States should have bombed the rail lines taking deported Jews to Auschwitz-Birkenau, as well as at least some of the facilities in the sprawling camp itself, which included dozens of factories using slave labor. The opponents, including U.S. government officials at the time, argued that innocent lives would have been lost, vital military targets might have been skipped, and, like a steady drumbeat, that nothing should be done to divert resources from defeating the Germans as quickly as possible. Proponents assert that innocent lives could have been saved, and U.S. Air Force planes were flying sorties in the area, including bombing synthetic oil and rubber works literally a few miles from the Auschwitz rail lines, gas

31. Andrew Glass, "Holocaust Eyewitness Briefs FDR, July 28, 1943," *Politico*, July 28, 2018, https://www.politico.com/story/2018/07/28/holocaust-eyewitness-briefs-fdr-july-28-1943-735759.

32. Facing History & Ourselves, "The Difference between Knowing and Believing," August 2, 2016, https://www.facinghistory.org/resource-library/difference-between-knowing-believing.

chambers, and crematoria. Moreover, a clear message would have been sent to Berlin about American revulsion regarding the machinery of the Holocaust. However, the proponents did not succeed in changing policy.

But one American position did shift, largely at the behest of Secretary of the Treasury Henry Morgenthau Jr., a close friend of the president and a Jew. As a result of his persistence, President Roosevelt established the War Refugee Board in 1944. It was led by John Pehle, a Department of Treasury official and one of the authors of a damning 1944 report titled "Report to the Secretary on the Acquiescence of This Government in the Murder of the Jews."[33]

In its relatively brief lifespan, the War Refugee Board demonstrated its worth—and disproved those who claimed the United States could do nothing to save endangered Jewish lives other than vanquishing the Third Reich as quickly as possible. Perhaps its most dramatic move was to hire Raoul Wallenberg, a citizen of neutral Sweden and graduate of the University of Michigan. In July 1944, Wallenberg traveled to Budapest on a Swedish diplomatic passport. With extraordinary courage, ingenuity, and determination, and aided by a fellow Swedish diplomat, Per Anger, he helped thousands of Hungarian Jews escape deportation and death. By issuing protective Swedish passports and creating safe Swedish "territories" in the Hungarian capital, he gave the Jews a special status, which kept them in Hungary—and not in sealed box cars to Auschwitz.

When the Soviet Red Army was at the doorstep of Budapest in January 1945, agents of SMERSH, the Soviet counterintelligence agency, seized Wallenberg, allegedly on suspicion of espionage. He was never seen again. Reports varied about what

33. Jewish Virtual Library, "The Acquiescence of the U.S. Government in the Murder of the Jews," accessed April 21, 2025, https://www.jewishvirtuallibrary.org/the-acquiescence-of-the-u-s-government-in-the-murder-of-the-jews.

exactly happened after his arrest, but he indisputably died in Soviet detention.

In 1981, Congressmen Tom Lantos, a Jew from Hungary whose life was saved by Wallenberg and who migrated to the United States after the war, led a successful effort in the U.S. Congress to confer honorary citizenship on the Swedish hero. It was only the second time in American history that honorary citizenship had been granted, the first recipient being Winston Churchill. Other countries—Australia, Canada, Hungary, Israel, and the United Kingdom—also made him an honorary citizen.

Wallenberg and his extraordinary work on behalf of the U.S. War Refugee Board are a reminder of lives saved under the most harrowing circumstances. And they raise an uncomfortable question: Could more lives have been saved had Washington acted earlier than 1944?

Why did survivors of the Holocaust experience such difficulty in resettling after the war?

The war in Europe ended on May 8, 1945, nearly six years after it began with Nazi Germany's invasion of Poland. For the surviving Jews, it was a cause for celebration, of course, but it was far more complicated than that.

Their world had been turned upside down. Their previous lives had been destroyed. Almost two-thirds of Europe's Jews had been murdered. Their great centers of Jewish prayer and study had gone up in flames. Their families were torn apart. They had been subjected to indescribable cruelty. They had witnessed barbarism on a daily basis. They suffered from disease, despair, and dehumanization. They were emaciated. Survival was a 24-hour struggle. Their faith had been challenged as never before. And they knew they had been largely abandoned by an indifferent world.

And why? Simply because they were Jews. That was their "crime." There was no other. The Jewish "race" needed to be annihilated, the Nazis asserted. How else to explain the 1.5 million Jewish children murdered systematically by the Nazis and their collaborators? What had these children done that warranted arrest, deportation, imprisonment, and death in the gas chambers by Zyklon B or in the forest by bullets, other than being born to Jewish parents and representing a Jewish future?

The months and years that followed May 8, 1945, therefore, presented their own multifaceted challenges for the survivors. Where would they go? Could they return to their homes? In the case of Belgium, France, the Netherlands, and some other countries, the answer was possibly, even if it was not always problem-free. Annemiek Gringold, principal curator of the National Holocaust Museum in Amsterdam, explained, "Jewish survivors were ostracized out of fear that they would reclaim property . . . that many Dutch Christians had appropriated. The Jews were a searing reminder that the post-war national self-image—of a plucky, upright folk that had resisted the Nazis to the best of their abilities—was, in many cases, bogus."[34]

But in other cases, such as Hungary and Poland, it was even less clear. In Poland, for example, returning Jews were often met with hostility, if not outright violence. Local populations were not eager to see Jews reclaim their homes, belongings, and jobs.

In Krakow, a rumor circulated that Jews had abducted Christian children, yet another blood libel accusation, just two months after the war's end. Mob violence against Jews was unleashed. A 56-year-old survivor of Auschwitz was murdered. A synagogue was torched, worshipers were beaten. And in Kielce, in another paroxysm of Jew-hatred based on a false rumor of Jews kidnapping an eight-year-old Polish

34. Tunku Varadarajan, "The Netherlands' Unrighteous Gentiles," *Wall Street Journal*, July 18, 2024, https://www.wsj.com/articles/the-netherlands-unrighteous-gentiles-world-war-ii-holocaust-collaboration-ddf13d7d.

Catholic boy, Poles killed 42 Jews and wounded another 40 on July 4, 1946.

Meanwhile, the United States, Canada, and other countries, reluctant to accept Jewish immigrants before and during the war, did not suddenly change their attitude afterward, notwithstanding the suffering Jews had endured. And the British were still unwilling to open the gates of Palestine, the territory they administered under the League of Nations mandate, to larger numbers of Jews. Thus there were heartbreaking scenes of Holocaust survivors on battered ships trying to reach the shores of Palestine, only to be turned away by British authorities unless they could somehow sneak by—the desperate passengers sent back to the haunting memories of continental Europe or placed behind barbed wire in British camps on the island of Cyprus. In fact, more than 2,000 Jewish children were born to Holocaust survivors in those camps in Cyprus, until Israel's rebirth in 1948, when Jews, including survivors, could enter freely.

It is striking that hundreds of thousands of Holocaust survivors ended up in Displaced Persons camps in Germany, Austria, and Italy, the former Axis countries. They simply had nowhere else to go. Eastern Europe was largely unsafe. The antisemites had not suddenly disappeared, and the conquering Soviets were unlikely to treat Jews any better, as the Communist record showed. Palestine was largely closed. And the "new world" showed little interest in addressing their fate.

A German army barracks site near Bergen-Belsen, the infamous Nazi concentration camp where Anne Frank and her sister were imprisoned and died, became a Displaced Persons camp after the war for thousands of survivors. To be sure, the conditions were different, but the painful reminders and ghostlike apparitions were never far away. To make matters worse, initially the surviving Jews were placed in the camps with non-Jews who had nowhere to go, but who, in some instances, mocked or menaced the Jews until administrators finally separated and protected them. The last camps did not actually close until the early 1950s. By then, the remaining Jewish survivors had found their way to Israel or to the United States, Canada, or Australia after their immigration policies changed.

Of course, the psychological damage could not be undone even by a new start in life. Trauma lived on long past resettlement. Given what they had endured and witnessed, how could it not? Survivor and Nobel laureate Elie Wiesel summed it up in his best-selling book *Night*:

> Never shall I forget that night, the first night in camp, that turned my life into one long night seven times sealed.
> Never shall I forget that smoke.
> Never shall I forget the small faces of the children whose bodies I saw transformed into smoke under a silent sky.
> Never shall I forget those flames that consumed my faith forever.
> Never shall I forget the nocturnal silence that deprived me for all eternity of the desire to live.
> Never shall I forget those moments that butchered my God and my soul and turned my dreams to ashes.
> Never shall I forget those things, even were I condemned to live as long as God Himself.
> Never.[35]

Eleanor Roosevelt, the widow of President Franklin Roosevelt, who died on April 12, 1945, just weeks before the war's end in Europe, visited a Displaced Persons camp in Germany in 1946. She described the scene: "There is a feeling of desperation and sorrow in this camp which seems beyond expression. An old woman knelt on the ground, grasping my

35. Elie Wiesel, *Night* (Penguin, 2008), 34.

knees. I lifted her up, but could not speak. What could one say at the end of a life which had brought her such complete despair?"[36]

And what could the life of Otto Frank ever become after surviving Auschwitz but seared by the knowledge that his wife and two daughters were among the 6 million victims of the Nazi Final Solution?

Why is the Holocaust still such a current, often politically charged issue in some countries?

The subject of how countries have dealt with the legacy of their own connection to the Holocaust is varied and complex.

West Germany acknowledged its catalytic role shortly after its establishment in 1949. It offered public apologies, reparations, and indemnification and established a special link with Israel. Communist East Germany took a radically different approach, insisting it was an antifascist state and bore no responsibility for the crimes of the Third Reich.

For decades, Austria hid behind the 1943 Moscow Declaration of the Allies, which claimed it was the first victim nation of the Nazi juggernaut. The Allied step was actually an effort to try to separate Austria from Germany during wartime. But, in fact, Austria was fully engaged in the war. Not only was Hitler himself an Austrian, but a disproportionate number of the elite SS corps and concentration camp heads were also Austrians.

It was not until 1990 that Austrian chancellor Franz Vranitzky began the public reckoning with the past, which by then also included the controversial election of Kurt Waldheim as the country's president, 1986–92, despite having sought to bury his wartime role as a Nazi officer in the Balkans.

36. Eleanor Roosevelt, "My Day," George Washington University, February 16, 1946, https://www2.gwu.edu/~erpapers/myday/displaydoc.cfm?_y=1946&_f=md000264.

In France, it was not until 1995, five decades after the war's end, that a French president, Jacques Chirac, admitted the complicity of France, through the Vichy government, in the Nazi crimes, including the roundup and deportation of thousands of Jews to German concentration camps. He said, "There are moments in the life of a nation that hurt the memory and the view one has of one's country. . . . These dark hours soil forever our history and are an injury to our past and our traditions. Yes, the criminal folly of the [German] occupier was assisted by the French, by the French state."[37]

And Switzerland, neutral in the Second World War, was dragged, kicking and screaming, in the mid-1990s into an investigation of its banking system's role during the war and after, when, for example, it demanded official death certificates of Auschwitz victims before releasing funds in their bank accounts. Of course, the Nazis never issued death certificates for Jews, much less made them available to surviving family members. The banks were simply reluctant to part with the funds they held. Eventually, due to U.S. government pressure, advocacy by the WJC, and relentless media coverage that exposed the banks' resistance and greed, they had no choice.

Today Holocaust-related issues and controversies tend to come up most frequently with respect to Poland and the Vatican. In 2018, a law was enacted making it a crime to claim that Poland was in any way complicit in the crimes of the Holocaust. Poland was a target of the Nazis and endured a brutal German invasion and occupation. Nonetheless, there were frequent allegations, whether from Polish scholars like Jan Gross and Barbara Engelking or Jewish sources, that Poles, driven by their own antisemitism, helped kill Jews during the war and despite the fact that both Poles and Jews were targets of the Nazis. The 2018 law created a firestorm, including public tensions between the governments of Poland and Israel.

37. Michel Zlotowski, "July 16, 1995: Chirac Admits France's Role in Nazi Crimes," *Jewish Chronicle*, September 26, 2019, https://www.thejc.com/news/world/july-16-1995-chirac-admits-frances-role-in-nazi-crimes-onm0x7bx.

No sooner did that die down, after some amendments to the law, when, in 2021, the Polish Parliament enacted a new measure that set a statute of limitations for wartime restitution claims. While not specifically aimed at Jews, mutual accusations swiftly resurfaced and Israel recalled its ambassador from Warsaw. Poland reciprocated, sending its ambassador in Israel to serve in Washington instead. And while Israel sent an ambassador back to Warsaw the next year, no Polish ambassador was named for the post in Israel until 2024.

In addition to the two Polish laws, other Holocaust-related matters have kept coming up, including unpaid private property restitution for the families of Polish Holocaust survivors. Some Poles have claimed that they are depicted unfairly as perpetrators instead of as victims of Holocaust crimes, given they lost 3 million non-Jewish citizens during the war. As well, they have complained that commemorative trips by Jewish youth groups to Poland tend to focus only on the past, ignoring the rebirth of Jewish life in the post-Communist era.

Meanwhile, some Jewish and Israeli voices counter that Poland is unwilling to admit its own history of prewar, wartime, and postwar antisemitism, and instead tries to present a much rosier picture than its record warrants.

Finally, as discussed earlier, there is the debate about the Vatican's wartime role and whether Pope Pius XII could have done more to call attention to the plight of the Jews. That long-standing debate is neatly summed up in this 2020 report from National Public Radio: "Vatican officials have always insisted Pope Pius XII did everything possible to save Jewish lives during World War II. But many scholars accuse him of complicit silence while some 6 million Jews were killed in the Holocaust."[38]

38. Sylvia Poggioli, "Records from Once-Secret Archive Offer New Clues into Vatican Response to Holocaust," NPR, August 29, 2020, https://www.npr.org/2020/08/29/907076135/records-from-once-secret-archive-offer-new-clues-into-vatican-response-to-holoca.

Why did the Hamas-triggered invasion of Israel on October 7, 2023, evoke analogies to the Holocaust?

First, it was the sheer magnitude of the Hamas-triggered attack, making it by far the deadliest single day for the Jewish people since the Holocaust. The death toll on October 7 was 1,200, while 250 people were kidnapped and taken to Gaza.

To put these numbers in proportional U.S. terms, it would be the equivalent of 42,000 people murdered in a single day, dwarfing by far the deadly attacks by Imperial Japan on Pearl Harbor in 1941 and al-Qaeda on 9/11, and more than 8,000 kidnapped. As a reminder, those two attacks on American targets triggered prolonged wars, whereas when 52 Americans were held hostage in Iran for 444 days in 1979–81, the United States was totally focused on seeking their freedom.

Second, it was the indescribable brutality of what happened on October 7 that served as a painful reminder of Nazi crimes. It was seen by many in Israel as a genocidal invasion, with the intention of inflicting as much harm as possible on anyone Hamas could find and consistent with the annihilationist language of the Hamas Charter. Entire families were murdered. Children were killed, kidnapped, separated from their families. Women were sexually assaulted, kidnapped, or murdered. The elderly, including Holocaust survivors, were shot to death or seized and taken to Gaza. The stories were endlessly frightening, traumatizing, and reminiscent of another era in Jewish history.

And third, unlike even the Nazis, who created a special unit, *Sonderaktion* 1005, to try to hide evidence of their crimes against humanity, the invaders on October 7 trumpeted their attacks on Israel, as caught on their own videos and phone calls gleefully telling family and friends in Gaza how many Jews they had stabbed or shot to death.

What is Holocaust denial, and why does it matter?

The International Holocaust Remembrance Alliance is an intergovernmental organization of 35 countries, including the United States and Israel, and 10 observer nations. It was launched in 1998 at the initiative of Swedish prime minister Göran Persson. IHRA has issued a comprehensive definition of Holocaust denial:

> Holocaust denial is discourse and propaganda that deny the historical reality and the extent of the extermination of the Jews by the Nazis and their accomplices during World War II, known as the Holocaust or the Shoah. Holocaust denial refers specifically to any attempt to claim that the Holocaust/Shoah did not take place.
>
> Holocaust denial may include publicly denying or calling into doubt the use of principal mechanisms of destruction (such as gas chambers, mass shooting, starvation and torture) or the intentionality of the genocide of the Jewish people.
>
> Holocaust denial in its various forms is an expression of antisemitism. The attempt to deny the genocide of the Jews is an effort to exonerate National Socialism and antisemitism from guilt or responsibility in the genocide of the Jewish people. Forms of Holocaust denial also include blaming the Jews for either exaggerating or creating the Shoah for political or financial gain as if the Shoah itself was the result of a conspiracy plotted by the Jews. In this, the goal is to make the Jews culpable and antisemitism once again legitimate.
>
> The goals of Holocaust denial often are the rehabilitation of an explicit antisemitism and the promotion of political ideologies and conditions suitable for the advent of the very type of event it denies.[39]

39. International Holocaust Remembrance Alliance, "Working Definition of Holocaust Denial and Distortion," accessed April 21, 2025, https://holocaustremembrance.com/resources/working-definition-holocaust-denial-distortion.

Perhaps the most famous trial involving Holocaust denial occurred in London, when "historian" David Irving sued Professor Deborah Lipstadt of Emory University for her assertion in a 1993 book, *Denying the Holocaust*, that he was a denier. She decisively won the case in 2000 and later wrote a book about it, *Denial: Holocaust History on Trial.*[40]

There is at least one aspect of Holocaust denial, however, that IHRA members cannot agree on: whether it should be criminalized. A number of European countries, including Austria, France, Germany, and Switzerland, have laws that permit prosecution. The United States does not, believing that it would curtail the First Amendment's protection of freedom of speech. Notably, Lipstadt herself opposes prosecution, including when Austrian officials pressed charges against the very same David Irving in 2006 for, among other denials, referring to the "gas chambers fairy tale." Here's how she explained her view in a National Public Radio interview:

> Well, let me say this, first and foremost, generally, I'm against laws that censor. I don't believe in censorship. I don't. I'm a free speech traditionalist, as most Americans are, and I don't, but also, I don't think censorship is efficacious. I think that, certainly, in the case of Holocaust denial, we won my case, in which David Irving was trying to curtail my freedom of speech and force me to pulp my books and, you know, apologize to him, but we won not by relying on the law, we won by relying on history, on facts, on material evidence, on interviews.[41]

40. Deborah Lipstadt, *Denying the Holocaust* (The Free Press, 1993); Deborah Lipstadt, *Denial: Holocaust History on Trial* (Ecco, 2017).
41. National Public Radio, "Austrian Court Jails Historian Who Denied Holocaust," February 21, 2006, https://www.npr.org/transcripts/5226811.

Is there survey data measuring awareness of the Holocaust in the 21st century?

Yes, there is some, notably in the United States and Europe. Of greatest concern are the findings from young people.

In the United States, the Conference on Jewish Material Claims Against Germany sponsored an unprecedented 50-state survey of Americans, ages 18 to 39, in 2020. Among the key findings:

- More than 10% of respondents never heard of the word "Holocaust" in relation to Jews.
- Sixty-three percent could not correctly identify that 6 million Jews were annihilated in the Holocaust; 36% thought the number was "two million or fewer Jews."
- Nearly half could not name a single Nazi concentration camp or ghetto, not even Auschwitz or the Warsaw Ghetto.
- Eleven percent of Millennials and Gen-Z respondents "believe Jews caused the Holocaust." Strikingly, in New York, the state with the largest Jewish population in America and greatest number of Holocaust survivors, the figure was 19%, the highest in the nation.
- Approximately 49% reported seeing "Holocaust denial or distortion posts on social media or elsewhere on line."[42]

That same year, the Pew Research Center, polling a representative sample of the adult American population, reported that 84% understood correctly the meaning of "Holocaust," yet only a minority, 45%, knew that 6 million Jews were murdered.[43]

42. Claims Conference, "First-Ever 50-State Survey on Holocaust Knowledge of American Millennials and Gen Z Reveals Shocking Results," September 16, 2020, https://www.claimscon.org/millennial-study/.
43. Pew Research Center, "What Americans Know about the Holocaust," January 22, 2020, https://www.pewresearch.org/religion/2020/01/22/what-americans-know-about-the-holocaust/.

The Conference on Jewish Material Claims Against Germany also conducted a survey in the Netherlands, a country under Nazi occupation from 1940 to 1945 and where more than 100,000 of the prewar Jewish population of 140,000 were annihilated.[44] The principal finding was that "23 percent of adults under 40 and 12 percent of all respondents believe the Holocaust is a myth or the number of Jews killed has been greatly exaggerated." Moreover, 54% of all respondents, and 59% of those under 40, were unaware that 6 million were killed in the Holocaust.

A survey by the same organization in the United Kingdom in 2021 found:

- Eighty-nine percent of respondents said they had heard about the Holocaust, and some 75% knew that it involved the mass murder of Jewish people, but there are significant gaps in knowledge and understanding.
- Fifty-two percent of respondents did not know 6 million Jews were killed during the Holocaust. Nearly one-quarter (22%) believe 2 million or fewer were killed.
- Nearly one-third of respondents (32%) were unable to name a single one of the more than 40,000 camps or ghettos established during World War II.
- A majority of respondents (56%) believe something like the Holocaust could happen again.
- Fifty-seven percent agree that fewer people seem to care about the Holocaust today than they used to.[45]

44. Claims Conference, "New Study Reveals Nearly One Quarter of Dutch Millennials and Gen Z Believe the Holocaust Was a Myth or Exaggerated," January 25, 2023, https://www.claimscon.org/netherlands-study/.
45. Claims Conference, "New Study Reveals U.K. Respondents Believe Two Million or Fewer Jews Were Killed in the Holocaust," November 10, 2021, https://www.claimscon.org/uk-study/.

With the passage of time and ever-growing dependence on the internet, including social media, where misinformation and disinformation thrive, future surveys are likely to reveal even higher levels of Holocaust ignorance and greater openness to Holocaust denial or distortion—unless new strategies can somehow be found to convey relevant and accurate information to future generations.

6

ANTI-ZIONISM AS ANTISEMITISM

In November 1947, the UN General Assembly voted to recommend that separate Jewish and Arab states replace the British mandate. The Arab world categorically rejected the plan. Notwithstanding, the Jews announced the establishment of Israel on May 14, 1948. Since then, many believe that a new form of antisemitism has emerged: anti-Zionism. Rather than focus on the individual Jew or Judaism or the Jewish "race," the target is the Jewish state. Its exponents often claim their rejection of Israel is not antisemitic but rather state-driven. Others insist the two cannot be separated. Is calling for Israel's destruction inherently antisemitic? Does any attempt to compare Israel's actions to those of Nazi Germany or apartheid South Africa cross a line into antisemitism? Does treating Israel differently at the UN compared to other member states constitute antisemitism? If Israel's overseas supporters are accused of "dual loyalty," meaning their loyalty to Israel is seen as in conflict with loyalty to their country of citizenship, is this antisemitism?

When does criticism of Israel become antisemitism?

Natan Sharansky was a leader of the Jewish and human rights movements in his native USSR. He was arrested for his activities and sent for nine brutal years, 1977–86, to the Soviet Gulag, where he became one of the world's best-known political prisoners. He was finally allowed to leave the USSR in 1986 and resettled in Israel. Fifteen years later, he was the Israeli minister of diaspora affairs. As he said at the time, while witnessing a surge in antisemitism starting in Europe, he "was grappling with the question of how to distinguish between legitimate criticism of Israel and antisemitism." He came up with a formula, known as the 3D test, that has been widely used by mainstream Jewish organizations and various Israeli governments. Here is his explanation:

> These 3Ds—demonization, delegitimization and double standards—are the three main tools that anti-Semites employed against Jews throughout history.
>
> For thousands of years, Jews were demonized, they were charged with blood libels, with poisoning wells, and, later, with controlling the global banking system.
>
> The Jewish faith and the Jewish claim to nationhood was delegitimized.
>
> And double standards were applied to Jews, either through the imposition of special laws—from the Middle Ages in Europe, to the Russian Empire and Nazi Germany—or through de facto government policy discriminating against Jews, as I experienced in the Soviet Union.
>
> Throughout history, demonization of Jewish people, delegitimization of their faith or nationhood, and double standards applied to Jews created fertile soil for pogroms, expulsions and genocide.
>
> My 3D test shows that if we see these same tools of delegitimization, demonization and double standards that were used against Jews in the past being used against the collective Jew, the Jewish State, today—we know we are witnessing a new face of the old anti-Semitism.[1]

1. Natan Sharansky, "Why BDS Fails My 3D Test on Anti-Semitism: Opinion," *Newsweek*, September 25, 2019, https://www.newsweek.com/antisemitism-bds-natan-sharansky-3d-test-1461305.

What is the Boycott, Divestment and Sanctions movement?

According to Boycott, Divestment and Sanctions (BDS) proponents:

> In 2005, Palestinian civil society organisations called for boycotts, divestment and sanctions (BDS) as a form of non-violent pressure on Israel.
>
> The BDS movement was launched by 170 Palestinian unions, refugee networks, women's organisations, professional associations, popular resistance committees and other Palestinian civil society bodies.

They claim:

> Israel is occupying and colonising Palestinian land, discriminating against Palestinian citizens of Israel and denying Palestinian refugees the right to return to their homes. . . . Israel maintains a regime of settler colonialism, apartheid and occupation over the Palestinian people. This is only possible because of international support. Governments fail to hold Israel to account, while corporations and institutions across the world help Israel to oppress Palestinians.

The movement targets "Israeli sporting, cultural and academic institutions," in addition to "international companies" engaged with Israel.[2] In other words, it seeks to isolate and delegitimize Israel on the global stage, as steps toward its eventual demise as a Jewish-majority, sovereign nation.

2. BDS Movement, "What Is BDS?," accessed April 21, 2025, https://bdsmovement.net/what-is-bds.

Is the BDS movement against Israel antisemitic by definition?

This is a controversial issue that has been the focus of attention in legislative chambers and courtrooms in the United States and Europe.

Supporters of the BDS movement have argued they have every right to pursue these strategies, which they claim are peaceful in nature, because of opposition to a variety of Israeli policies, if not to Israel's very existence. They assert that these actions are protected by freedom of speech guarantees and that their campaign against a nation is not the same as targeted, and outlawed, discrimination against a group based on race, religion, or ethnicity.

When the issue came before the Federal Administrative Court in Leipzig, Germany, in 2020, the court ruled against banning BDS events, noting that German law "guarantees everyone the right to freely express and disseminate their opinion."[3]

Opponents of the BDS movement have a radically different perspective. First, they argue that the movement is inherently discriminatory. Of the 193 United Nations member states, only one, Israel, faces a three-pronged policy of boycott, divestment, and sanction. And while Israel is a democracy and peace-seeking nation grappling with constant threats to its existence, there is no BDS focus on nondemocratic and aggressor nations, such as China, Iran, Russia, or Syria. Why, they ask? Could it be because Israel is the only Jewish-majority country in the world?

Further, BDS opponents take issue with the attempt to distinguish between anti-Zionism and antisemitism. Zionism, they insist, is the self-determination of the Jewish people. The vast majority of Jews, surveys affirm, fully support this belief,

3. *Middle East Monitor*, "Germany: Federal Court Rules Anti-BDS Policy to Be 'Unconstitutional,'" January 26, 2022, https://www.middleeastmonitor.com/20220126-germany-federal-court-rules-anti-bds-policy-to-be-unconstitutional/.

which does not necessarily mean, similar to other democratic countries, the same level of support for each and every administration.[4] Nonetheless, to try to deny the Jewish people their own homeland, while claiming this is not antisemitism, rings hollow.

At least two European parliaments formally agree with the opponents of BDS. The German Bundestag, in opposing the movement, made specific reference to the belief that BDS has all-too-familiar echoes of Nazi-era boycotts of Jewish-owned businesses. The resolution, adopted in 2019, states, "The argumentation patterns and methods used by the BDS movement are anti-Semitic."[5]

The following year, the Austrian Parliament's National Council unanimously approved a measure to "strongly condemn the BDS movement and its goals, especially the call for a boycott of Israeli products, businesses, artists, scientists or athletes." In the same spirit, it "emphatically condemns all kinds of anti-Semitism, including Israel-related anti-Semitism, and calls on the federal government to confront these tendencies resolutely and consequently."[6]

In several other countries, leaders spoke out clearly against the BDS campaign, in some cases explicitly calling it antisemitic.

In 2022, Australian prime minister Scott Morrison stated, "We stand totally against the BDS campaign. As I said on

4. American Jewish Committee, "The State of Antisemitism in America 2023," accessed April 21, 2025, https://www.ajc.org/AntisemitismReport2023#prioritybox.
5. Joseph Nasr and Riham Alkousaa, "Germany Designates BDS Israel Boycott Movement as Anti-Semitic," Reuters, May 18, 2019, https://www.reuters.com/article/world/germany-designates-bds-israel-boycott-movement-as-anti-semitic-idUSKCN1SN1Z2/.
6. World Jewish Congress, "Austrian Parliament Unanimously Condemns BDS Movement," February 28, 2020, https://www.worldjewishcongress.org/en/news/austrian-parliament-unanimously-condemns-bds-movement-3-2-2020?print=true.

Holocaust Remembrance Day, "The virus of antisemitism still lives in our world. We know its symptoms. The de-platforming, the cancelling and silencing of Jewish people. The boycotting of Jewish businesses and Jewish artists—hidden under the guise of geo-political lobbying. The threats to Jewish leaders, the attacks on Jewish places of worship. The blaming of Jewish people for every ill in the world."[7] Canadian prime minister Justin Trudeau commented at a town hall meeting in 2019, "In Canada, we have to recognize that there are things that aren't acceptable, not because of foreign policy concerns, but because of Canadian values. It's not right to discriminate or to make someone feel unsafe on campus because of their religion, and, unfortunately, the BDS movement is often linked to those kinds of frames. So yes, I will continue to condemn the BDS movement."[8] And in his first year in office in 2017, French president Emmanuel Macron declared, "France has already condemned boycotting Israel, and I have no intention of changing this position."[9] In the United States, as of mid-2024, 38 states have adopted anti-BDS positions, via legislation or executive orders.

Why does Israel get disproportionate attention at the UN? Why is it the target of a majority of the country-specific resolutions?

Israel is the target of vastly disproportionate attention by the United Nations and a majority of the country-specific resolutions each year, which undoubtedly serves to demonize

7. *Australian Jewish News*, "A Message from Scott Morrison," May 19, 2022, https://www.australianjewishnews.com/a-message-from-scott-morrison/.
8. *Times of Israel*, "Trudeau Blasts BDS Movement as Anti-Semitic," January 17, 2019, https://www.timesofisrael.com/trudeau-blasts-bds-movement-as-anti-semitic/.
9. NGO Monitor, "BDS (Boycotts, Divestment, and Sanctions)," accessed April 21, 2025, https://www.ngo-monitor.org/key-issues/bds/bds-condemnation-by-world-leaders/.

Israel as a nation and, many would argue, fans the flames of anti-Jewish prejudice.

For example, the Geneva-based UN Human Rights Council has a standing agenda, with one of its permanent items, #7, focused exclusively on alleged mistreatment of the Palestinians by Israel, while literally all other nations in the world, including serial human rights violators such as Iran, North Korea, and Russia, are bundled together under agenda item #4, which addresses "General debate on human rights situations that require the Council's attention."[10]

According to the nongovernmental organization UN Watch, in 2022 the UN General Assembly adopted 15 resolutions on Israel and 13 resolutions cumulatively addressing all other nations.[11] For context, 2022 was the year that Russia launched a barbaric, illegal, and unprovoked war against Ukraine.

Within the UN megastructure there are special rapporteurs and standing committees whose sole mandate is to scrutinize Israeli actions. There is nothing remotely comparable for any other UN member state. The explanation boils down to a numbers game, as explained below. Consider that the UN, while dealing with tens of millions of refugees across the globe under the auspices of the high commissioner for refugees, has a separate agency, UN Relief and Works Agency for Palestine Refugees in the Near East (UNRWA), to deal exclusively with Palestinians. This agency defines Palestinians as refugees from generation to generation, explaining why their numbers have ballooned from 700,000 in 1948 to 5.9 million in 2023, yet UNRWA makes *no* effort to resettle them. Or that the UN

10. EEAS, "HRC57—Item 4: General Debate on Human Rights Situations That Require the Council's Attention," September 24, 2019, https://www.eeas.europa.eu/delegations/un-geneva/hrc57-item-4-general-debate-human-rights-situations-require-council%E2%80%99s-attention_en?s=62.
11. UN Watch, "2022 UNGA Resolutions on Israel vs. Rest of the World," November 14, 2022, https://unwatch.org/2022-2023-unga-resolutions-on-israel-vs-rest-of-the-world/.

General Assembly has established the Special Committee to Investigate Israeli Practices Affecting the Human Rights of the Palestinian People and Other Arabs of the Occupied Territories (1968), the Committee on the Exercise of the Inalienable Rights of the Palestinian People (1975), and the Division for Palestinian Rights (1977), all standing bureaucracies in the world body that have no equivalent for any other conflict or territory in the world.

It goes deeper. UNRWA schools have been repeatedly accused by Israel of teaching Palestinian children to hate Israel and view it as the enemy, while, particularly since October 7, 2023, evidence has surfaced about UNRWA complicity with Hamas, including overlapping members and the shielding of Hamas terrorist infrastructure.[12] These revelations led the Israeli Knesset in October 2024 to ban UNRWA from operating in Israel.

Francesca Albanese, the special rapporteur "on the situation of human rights in the Palestinian territories since 1967," has been accused more than once of blatant antisemitism, including, according to UN Watch, comparing Israel to Nazi Germany. The American ambassador to the UN in Geneva, Michèle Taylor, posted on X in 2024, "Francesca Albanese has a history of using antisemitic tropes. Her most recent statements justifying, dismissing, & denying the antisemitic undertones of Hamas' October 7 attack are unacceptable & antisemitic. We expect more of independent UN experts and condemn all forms of antisemitism." This was echoed by her colleague, Linda Thomas Greenfield, the U.S. permanent representative to the UN, who declared, "It is clear she is not fit for this or any other position at the UN," as well as by Deborah Lipstadt, the

12. UN Watch, "Updated: Evidence of UNRWA Aid to Hamas on and after October 7th," July 12, 2024, https://unwatch.org/evidence-of-unrwa-aid-to-hamas-on-and-after-october-7th/.

U.S. special envoy to monitor and combat antisemitism, who condemned Albanese's "blatant antisemitic rhetoric."[13]

Albanese is not an outlier. Other examples abound. For instance, in 2023, the director of the New York office of the UN High Commissioner for Human Rights, Craig Mokhiber, called for an end to Israel, which he described as a "European ethno-nationalist, settler colonial project in Palestine." He also rejected accusations of antisemitism directed against Albanese as "a tired old trick" and a "ridiculous campaign of slander."[14]In 2005, the same year Gaza took control of its own destiny, the UN's special rapporteur on food, Jean Ziegler, compared Gaza to an "immense concentration camp," prompting an unusual repudiation by a spokesman for UN Secretary-General Kofi Annan: "The United Nations believes any comparison between conditions in Gaza and those of Nazi concentration camps is irresponsible."[15]

Whereas all this attention zeroes in on Israel, neither the UN General Assembly nor UN Human Rights Council has ever, not once, condemned Hamas by name for its cross-border raids against Israel, such as on October 7, 2023, when 1,200 were murdered and 250 were kidnapped, or the thousands of missile strikes, over many years, against Israeli civilian targets.

13. UN Watch, "Wolf in Sheep's Clothing: Why Democracies Should Sanction UN Rapporteur Francesca Albanese for Propagating Antisemitism and Supporting Terrorism," October 23, 2024, https://unwatch.org/wp-content/uploads/2024/10/Wolf-in-Sheeps-Clothing-Report-on-Francesca-Albanese.pdf; *Jerusalem Post*, "UN Watch Calls for Sanctions against Francesca Albanese over Antisemitism and Terrorism Support," October 24, 2024, https://www.jpost.com/international/article-825935.
14. *Times of Israel*, Luke Tress, "UN Palestinian Rights Investigator Denies 'Jewish Lobby' Comments Are Antisemitic," December 16, 2022, https://www.timesofisrael.com/un-palestinian-rights-investigator-denies-jewish-lobby-comments-are-antisemitic/.
15. Mitchell Bard, "The UN Relationship with Israel," Jewish Virtual Library, 2024, https://www.jewishvirtuallibrary.org/the-u-n-israel-relationship.

To understand these realities is actually quite simple. It is, above all, a numbers game. With the exception of the UN Security Council, where each of the five permanent members has veto power, in every other body the majority rules. And the majority not only adopts resolutions, sets up committees, and calls for investigations, but also appoints leaders of UN bodies. Being a staunch friend of Israel is unlikely to advance anyone's career or any country's ambitions in the UN system.

For the first 50 years of its UN membership, Israel could not join one of the five regional blocs that nominate countries for key leadership posts and committee assignments. Its natural home was Asia, but countries from Iran to Syria, Iraq to Yemen, Malaysia to Pakistan blocked its admission. Finally it was accepted, in 2000, as a temporary member (until it could assume its rightful place in the Asia Group) of the West European and Others Group, which was a step forward but required it to wait in a long line to vie for positions.

Since 1949, when Israel became a UN member, it has *never* sat as a rotating member of the Security Council, a privilege Algeria has enjoyed four times, Egypt five times, Syria three times, Tunisia four times, and Turkey four times. It has not had a seat on the Human Rights Council for decades, while in 2003, for instance, Libya, then led by Muammar Gaddafi, served for one year as the chair of this body, and an Iranian ambassador was chosen to head the 2023 UN Human Rights Council Social Forum.

If the Palestinians wish to see a resolution critical of Israel adopted, they can count on the votes of the other 21 members of the Arab League, as well as the vast majority of the 57 members of the Organization of Islamic Cooperation, plus almost all the 120 members of the Non-Aligned Movement. In these three concentric circles alone there is a guaranteed majority of the 193 member states. That explains the quip of the late Abba Eban, who served as Israel's ambassador to the UN and, later, foreign minister. It is as appropriate today as it was when he said it 50 years ago: "If Algeria introduced a resolution declaring that the earth was flat and that Israel had flattened it, it would pass by a vote of 164 to 13 with 26 abstentions."[16]

Are the movements on university campuses that seek to depict Israel as an "apartheid" or genocidal state antisemitic, or simply critical of Israel?

It depends on who one asks.

Israeli-born Hadas Thier, who is active with a number of left-wing movements in the United States, including the anti-Israel Democratic Socialists of America, wrote an article on the campuses she visited for *The Nation* in May 2024, in which she said, "I have never experienced the level of solidarity and the depth of understanding about antisemitism that I am seeing across college campuses right now. . . . I had never before witnessed such a deliberate commitment to learning about and confronting antisemitism head-on."[17] She also noted that she met self-identified Jews who participated in the encampments and organized a Passover seder.

In contrast, Shabbos Kestenbaum, who was one of six students from Harvard to file a lawsuit against the university alleging failure to protect Jewish students, stated:

> The encampments were blatantly antisemitic, regardless of how many Jews were involved or not. Every single time I walked through the encampment, of course wearing my kippah (skullcap), for three weeks, I was followed. . . . And when you call for the globalization of the intifada—the worst period of violence against the

16. Jewish Virtual Library, "Abba Eban on the UN," accessed April 21, 2025, https://www.jewishvirtuallibrary.org/abba-eban-on-the-un.
17. Hadas Thier, "The Student Encampments Aren't a Danger to Jews. But the Crackdown Is," *The Nation*, May 3, 2024, https://www.thenation.com/article/activism/campus-encampment-police-crackdown-antisemitism-brutality/.

> Jewish people in the 21st century, and when you paint our [university] president with horns and a tail, that is unquestionably antisemitism. . . . Every leader of the encampment has taken it upon themselves to tell Jews what is and isn't antisemitism. There's no other minority group in the world [except the Jews] that is not allowed to define what is dangerous, harmful or offensive to them.[18]

Why did the 1975 UN General Assembly resolution that declared Zionism to be a form of racism outrage both Israel and Jews around the world?

On November 10, 1975, the United Nations General Assembly adopted Resolution 3379, which "[d]etermines that Zionism is a form of racism and racial discrimination." The vote was 72 in favor, 35 against, with 32 abstentions.

Those voting in favor were primarily the Muslim-majority nations and the Soviet bloc. Indeed, it was widely believed that the resolution itself was a product of Soviet-Arab collaboration, designed to isolate Israel as a "pariah" nation.[19] Those opposed were overwhelmingly the democratic states of the Western world.

This moment was viewed by Israel and its friends as perhaps the darkest day in the history of the world body since its founding in 1945—on the ashes of the Holocaust, it should be noted. Specifically, to label Zionism, the quest for Jewish

18. Jewish Broadcasting Service, "Defending Israel," August 21, 2024.
19. For example, Alex Ryvchin, "Red Terror: How the Soviet Union Shaped the Modern Anti-Zionist Discourse," *Australian Institute of International Affairs*, September 10, 2019, https://www.internationalaffairs.org.au/australianoutlook/red-terror-how-the-soviet-union-shaped-the-modern-anti-zionist-discourse/; see also Yohanan Manor, "The 1975 'Zionism Is Racism' Resolution: The Rise, Fall, and Resurgence of a Libel," Jerusalem Center for Security and Foreign Affairs, May 2, 2010, https://jcpa.org/article/the-1975-zionism-is-racism-resolution-the-rise-fall-and-resurgence-of-a-libel/.

sovereignty in the Jewish ancestral home, as "racism" meant nothing less than to delegitimize the country and effectively call for its dismantlement. Not only did it grotesquely distort the concept of Zionism, but it ignored the reality that Israel sought to enshrine in its founding laws equal rights and equal opportunities for all citizens.

In addition, Jews worldwide who viewed themselves as Zionists—not to mention the founder of modern Zionism, Theodor Herzl—were in the forefront of the broader anti-racism struggle. Indeed, Herzl had written, "Once I witness the redemption of the Jews, I wish also to assist in the redemption of the Africans."[20] He did not live to see either day. He died in 1904.

At the same time, a number of UN member states were actual practitioners of racism and racial discrimination, including in the Arab world, where minorities, from Christians to Kurds, Baha'i to Jews, were systematically mistreated. These countries, however, were untouched by any UN resolutions for the numerical reasons mentioned above, another example of what some referred to as the UN's double standards.

And finally, the date of the resolution's adoption, November 10, was the 37th anniversary of *Kristallnacht*, the 1938 Nazi massacres of Jews in Germany and Austria, further adding insult to injury.

Chaim Herzog, Israel's UN ambassador and, later, the country's president, tore up the resolution from the speaker's podium and said: "For us, the Jewish people, this is but a passing episode in a rich and an event-filled history. We put our trust in our Providence, in our faith and beliefs, in our time-hallowed tradition, in our striving for social advance and human values, and in our people wherever they may be. For us, the Jewish people, this resolution, based on hatred, falsehood

20. Jewish Virtual Library, "Theodor Herzl on Africa," accessed April 21, 2025, https://www.jewishvirtuallibrary.org/theodor-herzl-on-africa.

and arrogance, is devoid of any moral or legal value. For us, the Jewish people, this is no more than a piece of paper, and we shall treat it as such."[21] Sixteen years later, and led by an American diplomatic offensive, Resolution 3379 was repealed by the UN General Assembly, one of only a handful of times the body has ever reversed itself. With the collapse of the Soviet bloc and the prospects for Arab-Israeli peace growing in the wake of the 1991 Gulf War, the timing was right, the first Bush administration concluded.

The canard of "Zionism is racism" has not disappeared, but the original UN resolution that validated it has.

In a similar vein, many Jews viewed the 2001 UN-sponsored World Conference Against Racism, held in Durban, South Africa, as another devastating development in modern-day antisemitism. Why?

The United Nations held the World Conference Against Racism, Racial Discrimination, Xenophobia and Related Intolerance, in Durban, South Africa, in 2001. It was the third such gathering. The first and second were both in Geneva—in 1978 and 1983.

There were two major elements of the Durban gathering (plus a youth track): a governmental forum for UN member states and a nongovernmental forum, the latter attracting well over 1,000 groups and tens of thousands of participants. Initially, Jewish organizations were keen to participate, as many had long been involved in the struggle for civil rights, antiapartheid campaigns, and the social justice movement. But in the lead-up to Durban, and culminating at one of the four regional conferences, in Tehran, the handwriting was on the wall.

21. American Archive of Public Broadcasting, "11/10/1975: Transcript," accessed April 21, 2025, https://americanarchive.org/catalog/cpb-aacip-80-311nsnn5.

Iran, the Arab League, the Organization of Islamic Cooperation, and their allies sought to turn the governmental forum into a targeted assault on Israel and Zionism. They met some resistance from Western nations and ended up with less than they had hoped for, and the United States and Israel withdrew from the conference after concluding it had gone off the rails. Explaining the reasons for the American decision, U.S. secretary of state Colin Powell stated:

> I have taken this decision with regret, because of the importance of the international fight against racism and the contribution that the Conference could have made to it. But, following discussions today by our team in Durban and others who are working for a successful conference, I am convinced that will not be possible. I know that you do not combat racism by conferences that produce declarations containing hateful language, some of which is a throwback to the days of "Zionism equals racism"; or supports the idea that we have made too much of the Holocaust; or suggests that apartheid exists in Israel; or that singles out only one country in the world—Israel—for censure and abuse.[22]

When the nongovernmental organizations assembled, it was equally clear that their focus was not only going to be on Israel and Zionism, but on Jews. As reported by accredited participants at the NGO forum, "The stand of the Arab Lawyers Union is selling *The Protocols of the Elders of Zion*. Caricatures are hung up. One of them depicts a rabbi with *The Protocols of the Elders of Zion* under his arm and an Israeli army cap on

22. U.S. Department of State, "World Conference Against Racism," accessed April 21, 2025, https://2001-2009.state.gov/secretary/former/powell/remarks/2001/4789.htm.

his head."[23] Laudatory references to Hitler could be heard and seen. And Jews in attendance not only felt beleaguered and threatened but also vilified and scorned. Their presumed allies in the antiracism trenches disappeared or, worse, turned against them.

Irwin Cotler, one of the world's most prominent human rights lawyers and a Canadian minister of justice and attorney general from 2003 to 2006, commented, "Those of us who personally witnessed the Durban festival of hate—with its hateful declarations, incantations, pamphlets and marches—have forever been transformed. For us, 'Durban' is part of our everyday lexicon as a byword for racism and anti-Semitism, just as 9/11 is a byword for terrorist mass murder."[24] Tom Lantos, the only Holocaust survivor ever to serve as a member of the U.S. Congress, lamented:

> Although the NGO proceedings were intended to provide a platform for the wide range of civil society groups interested in the conference's conciliatory mission, the forum quickly became stacked with Palestinian and fundamentalist Arab groups. Each day, these groups organized anti-Israel and anti-Semitic rallies around the meetings, attracting thousands. One flyer which was widely distributed showed a photograph of Hitler and the question "What if I had won?" The answer: "There would be NO Israel . . ." At a press conference held by Jewish NGOs to discuss their concerns with the direction the conference was taking, an accredited NGO, the Arab Lawyers Union, distributed a booklet filled with

23. Joëlle Fiss, *The Durban Diaries* (American Jewish Committee, 2008) https://www.ajc.org/sites/default/files/pdf/2021-07/THE_DURBAN_DIARIES-AJC.pdf.
24. Irwin Cotler, "Durban & 9/11—Ten Years Later," Conseil Représentatif des Institutions Juives de France, September 15, 2011, https://www.crif.org/fr/actualites/durban-911-ten-years-later-irwin-cotler.

> anti-Semitic caricatures frighteningly like those seen in the Nazi hate literature printed in the 1930s. Jewish leaders and I who were in Durban were shocked at this blatant display of anti-Semitism. For me, having experienced the horrors of the Holocaust first hand, this was the most sickening and unabashed display of hate for Jews I had seen since the Nazi period.[25]

And Joelle Fiss, a young Swiss-British human rights activist, wrote *Durban Diaries*, an anguished reflection on her experience at the UN gathering: "This is the story of a group of young Jews who return from Durban, puzzled and disoriented. For the first time in their lives, they have been subjected to racism—by people who staged anti-racism speeches. Thousands of people united to isolate, offend, and intimidate them—all in the name of antiracism. Their perceptions shift. Nothing seems to be the same. A new phenomenon, Judeophobia, an abstract notion until then, brutally imposes itself."[26]

Hence, for many participants and observers, the Durban events became an inflection point in the mainstreaming of antisemitism and abandonment of Jews—with the imprimatur, alas, of the sponsoring United Nations and UN high commissioner for human rights.

How has Israel chosen to respond to the surge in antisemitism in the Middle East and worldwide?

In 2022, Israel named actress, activist, and author Noa Tishby as its first special envoy for combating antisemitism and the delegitimization of Israel. Until then, these issues were largely handled within Israel's Ministry of Foreign Affairs, Ministry of

25. UN Watch, "Leading International Voices on the 2001 Durban NGO Forum," October 27, 2008, https://unwatch.org/leading-international-voices-on-the-2001-durban-ngo-forum/.
26. Fiss, *The Durban Diaries*, 1 .

Strategic Affairs, and Ministry of Diaspora Affairs, but without a center of gravity.

In making the appointment, Foreign Minister Yair Lapid announced:

> The creation of this post and the appointment of Noa Tishby is another step that will strengthen Israel and our fight against antisemitism internationally at a moment when Jews around the world once again face an alarming and dramatic resurgence in antisemitism. She is a gifted author and thinker who has long been a powerful voice on issues of antisemitism and the delegitimization of the State of Israel. In this fight, it's critically important to tell the Israeli story well, influence decision makers and world opinion, and to be quick and powerful in our response to acts of hate and violence directed against Jews. As one of the world's most influential Jews, few are better prepared to do that on the world stage than Special Envoy Tishby.[27]

Tishby was succeeded a year later by Michal Cotler-Wunsh, a prominent attorney and former member of the Israeli Knesset. She has collaborated closely with special envoys from other countries to highlight and combat surging antisemitism, particularly since October 7, 2023.

In doing so, she has focused on several themes, including, in particular, anti-Zionism as antisemitism. "Jew-hatred

27. Israeli Ministry of Foreign Affairs, "FM Lapid Names Artist, Author and Thought Leader Noa Tishby as First-Ever Special Envoy for Combating Antisemitism and Delegitimization," April 11, 2022, https://www.gov.il/en/pages/fm-lapid-names-noa-tishby-as-special-envoy-for-combating-antisemitism-and-delegitimization-11-apr-2022.

never died," she said. "It just mutated."[28] She noted on another occasion, "There is no chance of combating antisemitism if we do not combat this strain that disguises Jew-hatred as anti-Zionism."[29]

A related topic for Cotler-Wunsh has been reliance on the IHRA's working definition of antisemitism. As she noted, "The IHRA definition is critical to identifying and combating all strains of a pernicious hate that predicts collapse of spaces and places it infects."[30] And she has repeatedly decried what she calls the "normalization of antisemitism" and "international silence, indifference and impunity" too often in response.

More broadly, the Israeli government has not been hesitant to call out criticism of Israel as antisemitic when it believes the label is warranted. Thus, in January 2024, after an International Court of Justice ruling, a headline in *The Guardian* stated, "Israeli officials accuse international court of justice of antisemitic bias."[31] Three months earlier, in October 2023, Lior Haiat, Ministry of Foreign Affairs spokesperson, blasted Amnesty International as "an antisemitic organization that is biased against Israel," after alleging "war crimes, by all parties"[32] in the Hamas-triggered war with Israel.

28. Pamela Paresky, "Michal Cotler-Wunsh: 'Jew Hatred Never Died, It Just Mutated,'" *Quillette*, April 5, 2024, https://quillette.com/blog/2024/04/05/michal-cotler-wunsh-pamela-paresky/.
29. Twitter, @i24NEWS_EN, July 11, 2024, https://x.com/i24NEWS_EN/status/1811324545065754746?lang=en-GB.
30. Twitter, @CotlerWunsh, July 3, 2024, https://x.com/cotlerwunsh/status/1808373002293170313?s=48&t=l723VUxLjCht-d_Od2oIbA.
31. Bethan McKernan, "Israeli Officials Accuse International Court of Justice of Antisemitic Bias," *The Guardian*, January 26, 2024, https://www.theguardian.com/world/2024/jan/26/israeli-officials-accuse-international-court-of-justice-of-antisemitic-bias.
32. Paul Dallison and Peter Wilke, "Israel Blasts 'Antisemitic' Amnesty Over Finding of 'War Crimes, by All Parties'," *Politico*, October 26, 2023, https://www.politico.eu/article/israel-calls-amnesty-international-antisemitic-and-biased-after-it-criticized-war-crimes-by-all-parties/.

Similar accusations against Amnesty International have been leveled in the past, both by the Israeli government and such nongovernmental groups as Israel-based NGO Monitor. Amnesty representatives have rejected the charges, insisting they strongly condemn antisemitism but have the right and obligation to criticize Israel, even in the harshest terms, when they believe it is warranted.

7

ANTISEMITISM IN THE COMMUNIST WORLD

There was a long history of antisemitism during centuries of czarist rule, including pogroms, discriminatory laws, residential restrictions in the Pale of Settlement, and Russian Orthodox Church–inspired hatred and blood libels. As a result, millions of Jews fled to the West at the end of the 19th and beginning of the 20th century, when it became possible to do so. Meanwhile, some Jews regarded the 1917 Bolshevik Revolution as a potentially promising new chapter in Russia. After all, the Communist Party's political slogans included "equality" and "brotherhood." But it would not be long before antisemitism resurfaced with a vengeance. Nonetheless, in 1948 Moscow welcomed Israel's rebirth. Why? And why, 19 years later, did Moscow break diplomatic ties with Israel? What changed for the Kremlin? By the mid-1970s, Moscow was leading a global campaign to brand Zionism as racism, which, in turn, increased antisemitism worldwide. What impact did this Soviet policy have on millions of Jews inside the country until the USSR imploded in 1991?

Was Communism inherently antisemitic?

Communism was an all-enveloping ideology, doctrine, and worldview. It was in stark opposition to organized religion, including Judaism. "Religion is the opium of the masses," Karl

Marx wrote in 1843. It would be replaced by a new doctrine, historical materialism, or Marxism. Not only was Marxism or, as it evolved, Communism staunchly atheist, but it viewed faith groups as dangerous competitors for human allegiance and value systems. In a similar vein, it opposed the Zionist quest in the early 20th century for a Jewish state, seeing its nationalism as a challenge to the clarion call of Communist "universalism."

When Communism surfaced as a political and social force in the 19th century, it appealed to some Jews in Eastern Europe and elsewhere. Indeed, a few Jews became notable in Communist movements. They were drawn by the purported Communist vision of equality and brotherhood, which stood in stark contrast to their harsh life experiences as Jews under czarist and other antidemocratic rule. And they were attracted by what sounded to some like quintessentially Jewish values of justice and fairness.

Between 1791 and World War I, millions of Jews under Russian control were confined to what was called the Pale of Settlement. This severely restricted their mobility, educational opportunities, and economic possibilities. From 1882, under the rule of Czar Alexander III, Jews were additionally saddled with the highly restrictive May Laws, described by future Israeli president Chaim Weizmann, who lived within the Pale's borders as a child, as follows: "This particular set of enactments . . . was prolonged and broadened and extended until it came to cover every aspect of Jewish life."[1] Then, triggered by yet another blood libel accusation of Jews killing Christians, came the devastating pogrom in Kishinev in 1903, one of many to target Jews in Russia at the time, and one that drew worldwide attention, including a powerful poem, "In the

1. Chaim Weizmann, *Trial and Error: The Autobiography of Chaim Weizmann*, book 1 (Greenwood Press, 1972), 159.

City of Slaughter" by Hayim Nachman Bialik, because of its unprecedented scale and ferocity.[2]

In other words, many Jews were desperate to leave czarist rule behind. They fled to the West, others joined the Zionist movement to create a Jewish homeland, and still others hoped that social democracy or even Communism could bring about relief.

Yet once Communism gained power in the Soviet Union in 1917, it revealed its own authoritarian—and biased—traits. Although Vladimir Lenin claimed to oppose antisemitism in the name of "internationalism," Jews did not fare well. Over time, just about all examples of Jewish distinctiveness were targeted and eliminated, including synagogues, Jewish schools, and cultural centers. After all, they were seen as being at odds with the new religion of the land and, therefore, as a threat to the Kremlin's iron-fisted rule.

Also eliminated was any form of what was viewed as Jewish self-expression, be it a sense of group identity, collective memory, or affiliation with Zionism. And for Jews who had been shopkeepers, artisans, traders, merchants, or, in a few cases, entrepreneurs prior to 1917, the anticapitalist thrust of Communism ensured they would soon be attacked as "enemies of the state."

Finally, those Jews who had seen Communism as a hope for humankind, including early leaders of the movement in the Soviet Union and Eastern Europe, often ended up as victims of targeted campaigns, arbitrary arrests, kangaroo courts, and show trials, whether those campaigns were labeled "anticapitalist," "anticosmopolitan," "antibourgeois," or "anti-Zionist." As one rabbi quipped, mindful that the arch-Communist Leon Trotsky was born Lev Bronstein, "It's

2. H. N. Bialik, "The City of Slaughter," in *Complete Poetic Works of Hayyim Nahman Bialik*, vol. 1, ed. Israel Efros (Histadruth Ivrith of America, 1948), 129–43.

the Trotskys who make revolutions, and it's the Bronsteins who pay the price."[3]

Wasn't Karl Marx, one of the founders of Communism, himself a Jew?

Karl Marx, who with Friedrich Engels authored the history-changing *Communist Manifesto* in 1848, had Jewish ancestors but was not himself a Jew. His parents had both converted to Christianity before Marx was born, and he was baptized at the age of six. Thus he never considered himself a Jew and never had any formal or informal Jewish education.

In 1844, Marx wrote an essay titled "On the Jewish Question." To this day there are debates about the degree to which it reflected overt antisemitism on his part. In any case, it is fair to say that Marx never showed any sympathy for Jews or any curiosity about the Jewish roots of his family lineage. To the contrary, some considered him to be a virulent antisemite. That said, it has not prevented antisemites from claiming that Marx was a Jew and that the evils of Communism, by extension, were a "Jewish plot."

Of course, they conveniently sidestep the fact that Marx was born into a Christian home and never had any connection to the Jewish community. Nor do they note that Marx's colleague Engels was raised in a devoutly Christian home, which would further undermine the "Jewish angle" of their claims.

Wasn't the Soviet Union a staunch supporter of Israel's rebirth in 1948? What changed?

Yes, it is true. Speaking on behalf of the Soviet Union in the UN General Assembly in 1947, Ambassador Andrei Gromyko

3. *Jewish Journal*, "A Message from Socialism's Survivors to Local Liberal Jews," October 29, 2020, https://jewishjournal.org/2020/10/29/a-message-from-socialisms-survivors-to-local-liberal-jews/.

dwelled at length, and with surprising compassion, on Jewish suffering during the war and homelessness for the survivors after the war. While Moscow preferred a one-state solution for Arabs and Jews alike in Mandatory Palestine, he said, if that proved unworkable, his country would support an independent Jewish state.[4] Indeed, the one-state idea was a non-starter, and the Soviet Union recognized Israel within 24 hours of its establishment on May 14, 1948.

Despite his earlier opposition to Zionism as an expression of "bourgeois nationalism," Soviet leader Josef Stalin believed the new state could become a socialist outpost in the Middle East. Indeed, many early Zionist leaders embraced socialism as the path forward for the embryonic state. But Stalin turned out to be wrong. In the 1950s, Israel looked west, not east, unwilling to become a Soviet ally. Moreover, Stalin was horrified by the extraordinary reception Israel's first ambassador to Moscow, Golda Meir, received when she visited the main synagogue in the fall of 1948. Thousands of Soviet Jews were there to welcome her. For the Kremlin, this was a rude awakening that 30 years of Soviet rule had not managed to extinguish Jewish collective identity.

It was not long, then, before the Soviets cracked down on the Jewish population, fully embraced Israel's Arab foes, and, in 1967, severed diplomatic ties with Israel.

Why was the Soviet Union behind the "Zionism is racism" campaign that began at the UN in the mid-1970s and spread antisemitism worldwide?

As an outcome of the 1967 Six-Day War, in which Israel achieved a decisive victory against the armed forces of Egypt, Syria, and Jordan, the Arab world suffered the humiliation of defeat and

4. Jewish Virtual Library, "The Partition Plan: United Nations Debate on Partition," accessed April 22, 2025, https://www.jewishvirtuallibrary.org/united-nations-debate-on-partition-november-1947.

the Soviet Union the embarrassment of backing and arming the losing side. To confront the changed realities on the ground and seek additional international support, Moscow and its allies, all of whom, with the exception of Romania, broke diplomatic ties with Israel, came up with a new strategy: depicting Zionism as racism, associating Zionism with the evil of apartheid in South Africa, and even comparing Zionism to Nazism. But, as Soviet-born historian Izabella Tabarovsky noted, while the language may have been new, it drew on familiar antisemitic tropes, transferring them from Jews as a people to Jews as a sovereign state. For her and many other Soviet Jews, there was little question that Moscow's anti-Zionist campaign was, in reality, nothing more than newly packaged antisemitism.[5]

Until then, the conflict in the Middle East was primarily seen as a national and territorial struggle between two peoples. By seeking to inject a racial dimension, the aim was to associate Israel with a demonic force that undermined its reputation, indeed its very legitimacy. After all, if a state's very foundation is deemed racist, it does not deserve to exist. The Soviet-Arab bloc believed they could thereby mobilize greater support in Africa, the larger nonaligned movement, and left-wing political circles in Western countries.

In 1975, the notion of Zionism as racism made its debut at the UN-sponsored international women's summit in Mexico City, followed by the United Nations General Assembly, where it was adopted by majority vote.

In vehemently condemning the resolution, Daniel Patrick Moynihan, American ambassador to the UN at the time, declared:

5. Izabella Tabarovsky, "Soviet Anti-Zionism and Contemporary Left Antisemitism," *Fathom Journal*, May 7, 2019. See also Lenny Fukshansky, "Soviet Antisemitism at California's Claremont Colleges," *Wall Street Journal*, October 2, 2024, https://www.wsj.com/opinion/soviet-antisemitism-at-californias-claremont-colleges-97bd4929.

Indeed, the idea that Jews are a "race" was invented not by Jews but by those who hated Jews. The idea of Jews as a race was invented by nineteenth century anti-semites such as Houston Steward Chamberlain and Edouard Drumont, who saw that in an increasingly secular age, which is to say an age made for fewer distinctions between people, the old religious grounds for anti-semitism were losing force. New justifications were needed for excluding and persecuting Jews, and so the new idea of Jews as a race—rather than as a religion—was born. It was a contemptible idea at the beginning, and no civilized person would be associated with it. To think that it is an idea now endorsed by the United Nations is to reflect on what civilization has come to.[6]

Why did Jews in the Soviet Union begin to campaign for emigration in the late 1960s/early 1970s?

In the late 1960s, a few Jews in the Soviet Union bravely clamored for the right to leave the country and emigrate to Israel. They asserted that Israel was their ancestral homeland and they wished to be repatriated. Moreover, some had relatives in Israel with whom they wanted to be reunited. This movement, which grew rapidly in the 1970s and 1980s, was motivated not only by a desire for repatriation and family reunification but by four powerful forces at work within the Soviet Union.

First, there was totalitarian rule, which touched every aspect of life for Jews and non-Jews alike and every corner of the country. Repression, surveillance, and chronic shortages were the norm for Soviet citizens.

6. UN Watch, "Fighting the 'Zionism Is Racism' Lie: Moynihan's Historic U.N. Speech," November 10, 2015, https://unwatch.org/moynihans-moment-the-historic-1975-u-n-speech-in-response-to-zionism-is-racism/.

Second, Jews were denied the right to learn about their religion, history, and culture, study Hebrew, memorialize the Soviet Jewish victims of the Holocaust, or maintain contact with Jews abroad. While an underground movement developed for Jews seeking to explore and affirm their identity, it entailed the risk of harassment, arrest, job loss, internal exile, or imprisonment.

Third, the impact of the 1967 Six-Day War was galvanizing for many Soviet Jews. There was an incredible surge of pride among Jews, who had been fed a steady diet of Soviet anti-Israel propaganda, and a newfound interest in learning more about Israel, despite Kremlin efforts to depict Israel in the most diabolical manner possible.

Fourth, the Soviet system was antisemitic to its core. In the Soviet Union, everyone at the age of 16 had to obtain an internal passport. This had nothing to do with travel abroad but rather activity within the country's borders, such as applying for a university, job, residence, or transfer to another city.

As Soviet leader from 1923 to 1953, Stalin decreed that a Jew was anyone with two Jewish parents. It did not matter if they "felt" Jewish or not. For Stalin, it was a matter of bloodline. Thus, in the internal passport, which was obligatory till the collapse of the Soviet system, the fifth item was nationality. A 16-year-old with two Jewish parents was listed as a Jew. (If the child came from a mixed marriage, the applicant could choose between the nationalities of the mother and father.) That meant, at every step of their lives, they were known to be Jews and discrimination was inescapable.

This combination of factors—totalitarianism, denial of opportunities to explore Jewish identity, uptick in curiosity about Israel, and discrimination—led to Jewish underground activities and increased interest in emigration. As emigration had essentially been banned for decades—after all, why would anyone seek to leave the "workers' paradise" and "brotherhood of nationalities"?—getting permission to emigrate from the Soviet Union was not a simple or cost-free process. The fact that so many Soviet Jews were willing to take the risk highlighted their desperation to exit the country and start life anew in Israel or elsewhere.

Was there anywhere in the Communist world where Jews felt safe and able to practice their religion freely?

In the Communist bloc outside the Soviet Union, the only countries that had significant Jewish populations after the Second World War and as Moscow extended its reach were in Romania, Hungary, Poland, and Bulgaria. The other countries—East Germany, Czechoslovakia, and Albania—had much smaller Jewish communities.

It needs to be repeated that, with the notable exceptions of Bulgaria and Albania, Jews suffered massive wartime losses in what later became the Soviet orbit. For example, Poland's prewar Jewish population numbered approximately 3.5 million, comprising 10% of the country and 30% of Poland's capital city, Warsaw. Ninety percent of Poland's Jews perished at the hands of the Nazis and their collaborators. Of the survivors, some who sought to return to their homes were met with fierce, at times deadly, resistance from their Polish non-Jewish neighbors. Hence many Polish Jewish survivors quickly left Poland.

On the other hand, although Bulgaria joined the Axis bloc and Hitler urged the Bulgarians to round up and deport Jews to the death camps, Sofia refused. As a result, the number of Jews in the country remained quite constant. It is striking that, after the Communists seized power in Bulgaria, they permitted those Jews wishing to leave for the newly reborn state of Israel to do so. More than 40,000 did, just a few thousand staying behind.

In wartime Albania, the tiny Jewish community of perhaps 200 people was protected by the local population from the occupying Nazis. As a result, this community expanded nearly 10-fold as Jews from nearby countries sought refuge.

Unfortunately, after the war, as Albania experienced harsh Communist rule and almost total isolation, little was heard about the fate of Jews until the regime fell in 1991.

In each nation, as Communist leaders exerted control, Jews experienced more or less the same treatment as in the Soviet Union. Their lives as Jews were restricted, and antisemitism was often used as a tool of government policy. Many chose to distance themselves from any vestiges of Jewish life, either as devoted Communists or as pragmatic careerists who felt they had no other option. Only a few sought to keep afloat Jewish life in any form, be it religious, cultural, or national, and often with attendant risks.

Two events were particularly stark reminders of Jewish vulnerability, even for those who had joined the Communist Party and renounced their Jewish heritage: the 1952 Slansky show trials in Czechoslovakia, in which 14 high-ranking officials, 11 of whom were identified by the prosecutor as being "of Jewish origin," were convicted of "espionage," "conspiracy," "Zionism," "Trotskyism," "imperialism," "collusion with Western intelligence agencies," and more, and the 1968 antisemitic campaign in Poland, led by party leader Władysław Gomułka, which drove thousands of Polish Jews abroad.

Romania and Hungary offer somewhat different stories. Romania allowed a measure of Jewish religious life. Its chief rabbi for many years, Moses Rosen, had a certain national and even international stature. And unlike the other Soviet bloc countries, Romania did not sever diplomatic ties with Israel after the 1967 Six-Day War. Rather, government rulers saw the large Jewish community as a commodity to be sold to Israel or showcased to garner American support. As a result, hundreds of thousands of Romanian Jews were able to move to the Jewish state during the Communist era, while those who stayed behind had at least some trappings of Jewish life. Nevertheless, like other Romanian citizens, they faced a despotic regime.

Hungary, the other sizable community, practiced what was sometimes referred to as "goulash Communism," meaning it was a bit more reform-minded than in the harsher countries like East Germany. Hungary was home to the only rabbinic seminary in Eastern Europe, and there was a modicum of Jewish life available to those who sought it. Again, there were invisible boundaries around what Jews could do but certainly some wiggle room unavailable to Jews in, say, the Soviet Union.

It is noteworthy that as Soviet Communism began to relax a bit in the Gorbachev era, starting after 1985, Hungary and Poland, with others to follow, began to quietly re-establish links with Israel.

How many Jews left the Soviet Union, and where did these refugees go?

Jewish emigration from the Soviet Union began as a trickle in the late 1960s, after decades in which it was essentially banned. The numbers varied from year to year as a result of a deliberately uneven approval process by Soviet authorities—at times slightly more lenient, at other times more restrictive. Consequently, applicants could not know in advance if they would receive an exit visa or a rejection. In the latter case, a category of Jews emerged called "refuseniks," some experiencing repeated denials for a decade or longer because of alleged security reasons or no stated reasons at all. During that period, they most often suffered from harassment and persecution, including job loss. From the early days of the emigration movement until the end of the Soviet Union in December 1991, as many as 2 million Jews and non-Jewish family members of Jews were able to leave.

The largest number, well over a million, resettled in Israel, making a game-changing contribution to every phase of Israeli life. The second largest group went to the United States, principally settling in major cities, starting with New York. As many as 200,000 found a new home in Germany, making it the fastest-growing Jewish community in the world. Smaller groups went to Canada and Australia.

Today there are vibrant Jewish communities in each of the 15 successor republics of the Soviet Union, with synagogues, rabbis, community centers, and schools. Yet even as opportunities for Jewish education and involvement have changed dramatically since the Soviet era, the numbers involved are much smaller due to the mass outflow from the late 1960s to the 1990s. Antisemitism has not entirely disappeared, yet it is noteworthy that Ukraine, for example, has a democratically elected Jewish president, Volodymyr Zelensky, something previously unimaginable.

How did the Soviet Union view the Holocaust and its memory?

At least 2 million Jews in the Soviet Union were murdered by Nazi Germany and its allies in the Holocaust. These Jews principally came from Ukraine, Belarus, Russia, Moldova, Estonia, Latvia, and Lithuania—in other words the western territories occupied by Hitler's forces. Meanwhile, an estimated 500,000 Jews fought in the Soviet armed forces, many paying with their lives in battle or as German prisoners of war.

In January 1945, the Soviet Red Army liberated Auschwitz-Birkenau, the infamous German slave labor and death camp. That day, January 27, has been designated by the United Nations as the annual Holocaust commemoration day. Against this backdrop, the Soviet Union might have been expected to demonstrate a particular sensitivity to the Holocaust and its memory. But this was not to be the case. Instead, Moscow sought to remove any focus on Jews as targets of the Nazis, instead referring to them generically as "antifascist" victims. Once again, the Kremlin's fear of stoking Jewish particularism or nationalism through the power of memory outweighed any willingness to acknowledge the painful truth about the high price paid by Jews in the Second World War or, as the Soviets called it, the Great Patriotic War.

Moreover, insofar as approximately 20 million to 25 million Soviet citizens perished during the war, again there was no desire to single out Jews as a separate group of victims, even if they were part and parcel of the Nazi Final Solution. Most famous, perhaps, was the battle for memory at the site of Babi Yar (in Ukrainian, Babyn Yar), the ravine on the outskirts of Kiev, where more than 33,000 Ukrainian Jews, including several great-uncles of President Zelensky, were murdered on September 29–30, 1941, by Nazi Germans and their Ukrainian collaborators.

In 1961, a young Russian poet, Yevgeny Yevtushenko, visited the massacre site and wrote a poem. Here are the opening words:

> No monument stands over Babi Yar.
> A steep cliff only, like the rudest headstone.
> I am afraid.
> Today, I am as old
> As the entire Jewish race itself.[7]

Yevtushenko, who was not Jewish, took a risk. He sought to expose and condemn the silence surrounding the site. He broke a taboo. For doing so, he could have jeopardized his career, perhaps run the risk of imprisonment. But he succeeded in raising consciousness about Babi Yar, reaching a global audience, and helping trigger efforts to organize annual commemorations at the site, which were regularly disrupted by the authorities. It was only after the implosion of the Soviet Union in 1991 that Jews could begin to create monuments, museums, and memorials to Holocaust victims and raise awareness about Soviet Jewish victims who died in Nazi-administered ghettos

7. Museum of Jewish Heritage, "The Long and Uncertain Journey of the Babyn Yar Memorial," March 24, 2022, https://mjhnyc.org/blog/the-long-and-uncertain-journey-of-the-babyn-yar-memorial/.

or were deported to death camps in Eastern Europe or were killed in assembly-line fashion in forests and ravines: *The Holocaust by Bullets*, in the words of Father Patrick Desbois and the title of a book he wrote in 2008.[8]

Did Communist East Germany follow the West German example of accepting responsibility for the Holocaust and seeking to make amends to Israel and the Jewish people?

After the Second World War, Germany was divided into four occupation zones, each governed by one of the victorious Allied forces. In practice, the zones ruled by the Americans, British, and French cohered into one space, which, in 1949, became the Federal Republic of Germany, or West Germany. The other zone of occupation, under Soviet administration, became the German Democratic Republic, or East Germany.

Led by Chancellor Konrad Adenauer, West Germany took responsibility for the crimes of the Holocaust and negotiated reparations accords in 1952, known as the Luxembourg Agreements. They focused on Jewish survivors and the state of Israel, which bore the heavy responsibility of caring for so many of those who escaped death at the hands of the Nazis. The opening lines of the Agreements are unambiguous:

> Whereas unspeakable criminal acts were perpetrated against the Jewish people during the Nazi-Socialist reign of terror, And whereas by a declaration in the Bundestag (West German parliament) on 27th September 1951, the Government of the Federal Republic of Germany made known their determination, within the limits of their

8. Patrick Desbois, *The Holocaust by Bullets: A Priest's Journey to Uncover the Truth behind the Murder of 1.5 Million Jews* (Palgrave Macmillan, 2008).

> capacity, to make good the material damage caused by these acts.[9]

By contrast, East Germany took no responsibility for the crimes of the Holocaust, offered no indemnification to survivors, and showed no interest in engaging Israel. The East Germans, firmly anchored in the Soviet sphere, asserted that West Germany, not East Germany, was the "successor" state of the Third Reich, whereas they were the antifascists who opposed Nazism and Hitler's 12-year reign. Hence they bore no link to any crimes committed then. To the contrary, they claimed, it was the Communists, whether in the Soviet Union or East Germany, who had ultimately defeated the Nazi regime.

As in the Soviet Union, East Germany deliberately ignored the specificity of the Nazi goal to annihilate the Jewish people in favor of describing all victims as antifascists. Moreover, East Germany evolved into an implacable foe of Israel, providing funding, training, weapons, and refuge to Israel's enemies and offering diplomatic support for the libelous "Zionism is racism" campaign. The few Jews living in East Germany were denied access to Jewish communal life for nearly four decades. Once again, Communism, not Judaism (or any other traditional faith), was viewed as the all-encompassing religion of the land.

After the Berlin Wall, built by the Communist regime in 1961 to keep its own people penned in, dramatically fell in 1989, things in East Germany began to change rapidly. Indeed, when the first freely elected, post-Communist parliament in East Berlin convened in April 1990, one of its earliest decisions, approved with near unanimity, was the adoption of a historic statement. Here are excerpts:

9. United Nations Treaty Collection, "No. 2137 Israel and Federal Republic of Germany," accessed April 22, 2025, https://treaties.un.org/doc/Publication/UNTS/Volume%20162/volume-162-I-2137-English.pdf.

> We, the first freely elected parliamentarians of the GDR (German Democratic Republic), on behalf of the citizens of this land, admit responsibility for the humiliation, expulsion and murder of Jewish men, women and children. We feel sorrow and shame, and acknowledge this burden of German history.
>
> Immeasurable suffering was inflicted on the peoples of the world during the era of National Socialism. We ask all the Jews of the world to forgive us. We ask the people of Israel to forgive us for the hypocrisy and hostility of official East German policies toward Israel and for the persecution and humiliation of Jewish citizens in our country after 1945 as well.[10]

These words came 40 years after the West German acknowledgment, and with much lost time to act, atone, and educate, but they did, at long last, begin to close an open wound.

10. Tamara Jones and Tyler Marshall, "E. Germany Takes Holocaust Blame: Atrocities," *Los Angeles Times*, April 13, 1990, https://www.latimes.com/archives/la-xpm-1990-04-13-mn-1205-story.html.

8

THE RESURGENCE OF ANTISEMITISM IN EUROPE

In 2000–2001, antisemitism in Europe resurfaced in a dramatic way. There were three main sources. First, and deadliest, was jihadist, including fatal attacks in France, Belgium, Bulgaria, Denmark, and elsewhere. The second was the far left, which organized to isolate, demonize, and, ultimately, bring Israel to its knees. The third was the aggressive re-emergence of the far right, including Nazi sympathizers who viewed Jews through a racialized lens. How did European societies react as antisemitism once again surged? Were they alert or asleep? How did the rapidly changing demography in Europe affect the safety of Jewish communities? Is there a future for Jews in Europe? Expressing concern about the fate of Europe's largest Jewish community, former French prime minister Manuel Valls said, "If 100,000 Jews leave, France will no longer be France."[1]

What did Jewish life in Europe look like immediately after World War II?

Before World War II, there were approximately 9.5 million Jews living in Europe, the majority in Central and Eastern Europe.

1. Jeffrey Goldberg, "French Prime Minister: If Jews Flee, the Republic Will Be a Failure," *The Atlantic*, January 10, 2015, https://www.theatlantic.com/international/archive/2015/01/french-prime-minister-warns-if-jews-flee-the-republic-will-be-judged-a-failure/384410/.

During the Holocaust, nearly two-thirds of European Jewry were murdered. In the immediate aftermath of the war, many things were happening more or less simultaneously.

The Jews in Britain, one of the biggest communities, were largely intact, apart from the valiant soldiers who made the ultimate sacrifice and the Jews living in Britain's Channel Islands who were seized by the occupying Nazi armed forces. The Jews in the neutral countries, including Ireland, Portugal, Spain, Sweden, Switzerland, and Turkey, survived, their communal institutions essentially untouched.

It was the Jews in the countries occupied by the Nazis that were most profoundly affected and suffered unimaginable losses, with four notable exceptions: Albania, Bulgaria, Denmark, and Finland.

Elsewhere, the devastation was catastrophic. In such countries as Greece, Poland, and Lithuania, virtually entire Jewish communities disappeared in the death camps, ghettos, and killing fields. The communities in Thessaloniki, Greece, Lublin, Poland, and Vilnius, Lithuania, all renowned centers of Jewish learning, were almost totally wiped out.

Surviving Jews from Poland and Hungary, in particular, who tried to go back home after their ordeal, too often discovered their lodgings taken by neighbors, their belongings stolen, and antisemitic hatred still alive and well. They often ended up in Displaced Persons camps in Austria, Germany, and Italy.

Keeping the survivors alive while they grappled with their horrific experiences was a massive task, for which most victorious armies and well-intentioned welfare organizations were unprepared. So, too, trying to locate surviving family members and reuniting them if possible, all on a continent where survivors most often ended up far from home, multiple languages were spoken, and communications capabilities were limited.

Coping with borders still closed to the vast majority of Jews even after the Holocaust, including the United States, Canada, and the United Kingdom, helps explain the Displaced Persons camps. Some of them continued to operate for years until relief agencies were finally able to find new homes for the refugees.

Then there was the special case of British-administered Palestine. Many Jews in Europe, and especially the survivors, wanted nothing more to do with the European continent, nor with being minority communities in a part of the world where antisemitism had deep roots, wide reach, and deadly consequences. They wanted to start over in a land where Jews could govern themselves and not be subject any longer to the whims of the majority population. But the British authorities, sensitive to Arab concerns, were not keen to permit large-scale Jewish migration to Palestine, even for Holocaust survivors, notwithstanding everything they had been through.

And finally there was the postwar division of Europe into east and west, as the Soviet Union gained control of neighboring countries on its western flank. That prevented many Jews from leaving, and it certainly hindered any chance to reconstitute the structure of Jewish communities, including religious, cultural, political, and social life.

Whereas battered Jewish communities in such countries as Belgium, France, Greece, Italy, the Netherlands, and Norway were able, step by tenuous step, to re-establish themselves, albeit with greatly diminished numbers, the Jews of the Baltic states, Czechoslovakia, Hungary, Moldova, Poland, and elsewhere in the Soviet Empire were almost entirely cut off from their brethren—and from their Jewish roots.

When, where, and why did a resurgence of antisemitism take place in Europe?

It accelerated in 2000–2001, when the second Palestinian intifada (uprising) erupted after Palestinian leaders turned down a two-state deal being urged by Israeli and American leaders. But this happened only in some European countries, not all. The vast majority of incidents, especially acts of violence, occurred in Western European nations. Consequently, it was these governments that needed to develop responses, in some cases, alas, with lengthy delays. At the same time, Jewish communities had to face the challenges of new layers of security—at times with official help, at other times without—and of resilience. In France, for example, the chief rabbi told religious Jews that, if they felt unsafe in public, they did not have to wear a kippah (skullcap) but could wear a baseball cap instead. And a number of French Jews, in particular, began to explore options for moving to Israel. Meanwhile, security expenses skyrocketed to more than one-fifth of the entire community budget in a country like Sweden.

Why was ground zero in Western European countries, including Belgium, France, Germany, the Netherlands, and Sweden? Conventional wisdom based on history suggests that Eastern European nations, such as Croatia, Hungary, Lithuania, Poland, Slovakia, and Ukraine, would be likely candidates.

There is no one-size-fits-all answer; however, there are several possible explanations.

First, the trigger for the new outbreak of antisemitism was Israel's response to the Palestinian intifada. As civilian targets in Israel, including pizzerias, discotheques, buses, and cafes, were being hit by suicide bombings, Israel reacted with force to try to end the string of attacks that left more than 1,000 murdered.

By and large, the countries of Eastern Europe developed close ties with Israel during the post-Communist era, in stark contrast to the Soviet bloc period. They mostly refrained from any criticism of Israel, which was not necessarily the case in Western Europe. This set the tone for the public at large. A Polish official told a visiting American Jewish delegation that anyone could walk across Warsaw, day or night, carrying an Israeli flag and wearing a kippah without incident, while it could be life-threatening in Paris, Brussels, or Berlin.

Second, precisely because the Soviet bloc had routinely used inflammatory anti-Israel and anti-Zionist language as thinly veiled antisemitism, these post-1989 countries clearly understood the slippery slope and blurring of distinctions in a way that was not always grasped in Western Europe.

Third, the antisemitism that emerged in Western Europe was driven by three main sources: the far left, jihadists, and the far right. But in Eastern Europe, the far left constituted a distinct minority because of its association in the public mind with the detested Communist era. And jihadists were few in number, since Muslim populations, where they existed, were long established and linked largely to non-Arab backgrounds, such as Crimean Tatars and converts in the Ottoman Turkish era.

Finally, the media played a catalyzing role in fanning the flames of antisemitism in some Western European nations, Spain being a notable example. Three popular themes emerged in cartoons and elsewhere in the region. These were (1) historical inversion: Israelis as the new Nazis and Palestinians as the victims of a new Holocaust; (2) Israelis as Christ killers, this time the crucified figure on the cross being a Palestinian; and (3) a modern-day version of the blood libel charge: Jews deliberately killing non-Jewish children. All three were superimposed on the lone Jewish-majority nation.

What were some of the deadliest examples of this new chapter in European antisemitism?

Since the new wave of antisemitism began in Europe in 2000–2001, there have been a number of horrifying incidents.

In 2006, Ilan Halimi, 23, was kidnapped, tortured, and, after three weeks in captivity, killed in Paris by a gang with roots in Africa and Iran. Halimi's murderers believed that, as a Jew, he must be rich and could deliver a big ransom.

In the southeastern French city of Toulouse in March 2012, Mohammed Merah, who was described by his brother as being raised in a home that hated Jews, killed three Jewish children, ages eight, six, and three, and a rabbi at Ozar HaTorah school. In a separate incident, he also murdered three French police officers. Merah himself was then killed in a shoot-out with officers.

In July 2012, an explosive went off in a bus carrying Israeli tourists at the airport in Burgas, Bulgaria. Six people were killed, five Israelis and the Bulgarian bus driver. The Bulgarian government launched an investigation and named Hezbollah as the group responsible for the attack, the same month that a Hezbollah-linked plot in Cyprus to track Israelis visiting the island nation was foiled by the authorities.

These incidents led the European Union, in 2013, to designate Hezbollah's "military wing" as a terror organization. The EU took no action against the "political wing." In turn, the decision led to criticism by those arguing that Hezbollah is a single entity that cannot be divided into separate parts. These critics had a boost from Hezbollah leaders themselves, who insisted the organization cannot be artificially divided.

In May 2014, Mehdi Nemmouche, originally from Algeria and a French citizen, killed four people at the Jewish Museum in Brussels. Nemmouche had been a foreign fighter in Syria.

In July 2014, three Palestinian-German men threw Molotov cocktails at a synagogue in Wuppertal, Germany. Arrested afterward, they claimed they were drunk and high on drugs and wanted to express their anger at Israel. They presumably saw the synagogue, a place of Jewish worship, as a "legitimate" target to channel their rage. In a court decision that triggered widespread controversy, the three men were found guilty of arson and given suspended sentences; they were not found guilty, however, of doing so with an antisemitic motive. In reaction, the head of the local Jewish community, Leonid Goldberg, declared the attack "pure antisemitism."[2]

2. Sven Pöhle, "'Pure Anti-Semitism' behind Wuppertal Synagogue Attack," *Deutsche Welle*, January 27, 2015, https://www.dw.com/en/pure-anti-semitism-behind-synagogue-attack-says-wuppertal-jewish-leader/a-18216819.

In January 2015, a young man, Amedy Couliby, with links both to Mali and France and armed with a submachine gun, entered a kosher food shop in Paris and killed four people, while holding others hostage until a policeman shot him and freed those held at gunpoint.

In May 2015, a volunteer guard, Dan Uzan, was shot at a synagogue in Copenhagen, later dying from his wounds. The killer had sworn loyalty to the Islamic State.

In April 2017, a Jewish doctor, Sarah Halimi, was killed in her Paris apartment by a neighbor, described by the BBC as a "Muslim of Malian origin," shouting "Allahu Akbar" ("God is great").[3] The perpetrator, Kobili Traoré, was caught and tried, but the verdict, which set off a firestorm in France, found he was not criminally responsible because he was under the influence of cannabis at the time of the fatal attack.

In 2018, Mireille Knoll, a Holocaust survivor, was murdered in her Paris home in what the authorities labeled an antisemitic hate crime. The perpetrator, Yacine Mihoub, a neighbor whom she had known since his childhood, thought that, as a Jew, she must be rich, and he wanted her money.

The same year, a Norwegian rapper, Kaveh Kholardi, performing at an Oslo concert, wished Muslims in the audience a "blessed feast" to mark the end of Ramadan, then asked if Christians were present and smiled when some responded, and then asked if any Jews were present. He was met with silence, then added, "Fucking Jews . . . just kidding." A few days earlier, he had written on social media that "fucking Jews are so corrupt."[4] He was investigated by the authorities but

3. Hugh Schofield, "Sarah Halimi: How Killer on Drugs Escaped French Trial for Anti-Semitic Murder," BBC, May 3, 2021, https://www.bbc.co.uk/news/world-europe-56929040.
4. European Jewish Congress, "Norwegian Prosecutors Say Rapper Who Used Antisemitic Insult Was 'Criticising Israel,'" March 13, 2019, https://eurojewcong.org/news/communities-news/norway/norwegian-prosecutors-say-rapper-who-used-antisemitic-insult-was-criticising-israel/.

not charged with a hate crime for his comments because, the prosecutors concluded, they could be viewed as criticism of Israel.

In 2019, a far-right assailant, Stephan Balliet, tried to attack a synagogue on Yom Kippur, the holiest day of the Jewish calendar, in Halle, Germany. He was unable to gain entry, so he turned his gun on a passerby and killed her. In court, Balliet apologized for killing her only because he "didn't want to kill whites."[5] In Nazi-like fashion, he saw the Jews in the synagogue, whom he could not reach, as non-White people.

In May 2024, police killed a man from Algeria who was suspected of starting a fire at a synagogue in Rouen, France. The French minister of interior, Gerald Darmanin, described the incident as "clearly" antisemitic. And in August 2024, French police arrested a man reportedly carrying a Palestinian flag, who attacked a synagogue in Nimes. President Emmanuel Macron called it "a terrorist act."[6]

In November 2024, indeed on the eve of the 86th anniversary of *Kristallnacht*, there was an explosion of antisemitism on the streets of Amsterdam. Several thousand soccer fans from Israel had traveled to the Netherlands to attend a soccer match. According to multiple reports, a "Jew hunt" (*jodenjacht*, in Dutch) was planned locally beforehand, largely by Arabic-speaking individuals, and it resulted in widespread assaults, injuries, and damage.[7] It was followed by more violence a few

5. Kirsten Grieshaber and Volkmar Kienoel, "Yom Kippur Synagogue Attacker Goes on Trial in Germany," *Washington Post*, July 21, 2020, https://www.washingtonpost.com/world/europe/yom-kippur-synagogue-attacker-goes-on-trial-in-germany/2020/07/21/1e81ac70-cb27-11ea-99b0-8426e26d203b_story.html.
6. Malu Cursino and Jaroslav Lukiv, "French Police Arrest Synagogue Blast Suspect," BBC, August 24, 2024, https://www.bbc.co.uk/news/articles/c5y3d4v43gjo.
7. Stacy Meichtry, Kim Mackrael, and Anat Peled, "Calls for 'Jew Hunt' Preceded Attacks in Amsterdam," *Wall Street Journal*, November 10, 2024, https://www.wsj.com/world/europe/calls-for-jew-hunt-preceded-attacks-in-amsterdam-e3311e21.

days later and slogans of "Cancer Jew" (*Kanker joden*).[8] Jews were compelled to flee, hide, and await rescue. The Dutch king, Willem-Alexander, referring to the first day of Jews fleeing from the frenzied mobs, said, "We failed the Jewish community of the Netherlands during World War II, and last night we failed again."[9] U.S. president Joe Biden noted that the assaults "echo dark moments in history when Jews were persecuted."[10]

Several weeks after the pogrom in Amsterdam, the Dutch chief rabbi, Binyomin Jacobs, declared: "It's not like in Nazi Germany. The authorities are not antisemitic. But for every word spoken about violence against Jews, immediately a whole conversation on Islamophobia is started to deflect from the problem. There is a powerful Islamic and left-wing political lobby at work. I don't want to over-generalize, but the other day I took out my calculator and added up all the support I received from the left and from Muslims. The final number was zero."[11]

When Russian president Vladimir Putin claimed he invaded Ukraine in 2022 to "denazify" it, what did he mean?

In February 2022, Russia's armed forces invaded neighboring Ukraine. It was an unprovoked and illegal attack under international law. Yet the Kremlin sought to justify the

8. Yuval Barnea and Danielle Greyman-Kennard, "'Cancer Jews: Trams Set Alight, Violence Erupts in Amsterdam in Second Wave of Violence," *Jerusalem Post*, November 12, 2024, https://www.jpost.com/breaking-news/article-828672.
9. Teri Schultz and Scott Simon, "Violence Broke Out After a Soccer Match in Amsterdam," *NPR*, November 9, 2024, https://www.npr.org/2024/11/09/nx-s1-5184414/violence-broke-out-after-a-soccer-match-in-amsterdam.
10. Paul Kirby, "We Must Not Turn Blind Eye to Antisemitism, Says Dutch King After Attacks On Israeli Football Fans," *BBC News*, November 8, 2024, https://www.bbc.co.uk/news/articles/cx2y33ee1klo.
11. Bart Schut, "Last Straw: Amsterdam 'Jew Hunt' Triggers Push for Dutch Jewish Migration to Israel," *Times of Israel*, November 28, 2024, https://www.timesofisrael.com/last-straw-amsterdam-jew-hunt-triggers-push-for-dutch-jewish-migration-to-israel/.

aggression in a rather unusual way. Russian Federation president Vladimir Putin asserted that the war's aim was to "denazify" Ukraine. Immediately after the invasion, the Russian strongman stated: "The purpose of this operation is to protect people who for eight years now have been facing humiliation and genocide. To this end, we will seek to demilitarize and denazify Ukraine."[12] The claim was indefensible on its face. Putin, however, continued to press the theme, attempting to demonize Ukraine in the eyes of the world, as well as rallying the Russian people by stirring patriotic memories of World War II, when 20 million to 25 million Soviets were killed.

Why was the claim of denazification ludicrous? For starters, Ukraine had a democratically elected president, Volodymyr Zelensky, who was a Jew and made no secret of it. Zelensky often referred to his grandfather's brothers, all of whom were murdered as Jews by the Nazis in Babi Yar. Also Ukraine's defense minister at the time, Oleksii Reznikov, was a Jew. How, then, could Zelensky and his government be seen in Moscow as the embodiment of nazification?

While Russian disinformation sought to focus on Ukraine as a hotbed of unrepentant fascists, more than 73% of Ukrainian voters supported Zelensky in his 2019 landslide victory.

Longtime Russian foreign minister Sergei Lavrov added another element to the Kremlin disinformation campaign against Ukraine in May 2023, asserting that Hitler, the author of the genocide against the Jewish people, himself "had Jewish blood." He went on to say, "For a long time now, we have been hearing the wise Jewish people say that the biggest antisemites are the Jews themselves."[13]

12. Rachel Treisman, "Putin's Claim of Fighting Against Ukraine 'neo-Nazis' Distorts History, Scholars Say," *NPR*, March 1, 2022, https://www.npr.org/2022/03/01/1083677765/putin-denazify-ukraine-russia-history.
13. BBC News, "Israel Outrage at Sergei Lavrov's Claim That Hitler Was Part Jewish," May 2, 2022, https://www.bbc.co.uk/news/world-middle-east-61296682.

The world of antisemitism is infinitely versatile. Yet again defying all logic and reason, Jews were accused of being responsible for monstrous crimes against their own people, thus seeking to lift and divert responsibility from the actual perpetrators.

Or, as Yair Lapid, Israel's foreign minister at the time, put it, "The lowest level of racism against Jews is to accuse Jews themselves of antisemitism."[14]

Why did Poland and Israel have a rupture in diplomatic relations over Holocaust-related issues?

Perhaps more than in any other country in Europe today besides Germany, the history of World War II, the Holocaust, and their aftermath is very much alive in Poland, where debate and controversy continue to surface.

On September 1, 1939, Poland became the first country attacked by Nazi Germany. While Polish forces fought valiantly, they were overwhelmed by the German blitzkrieg. What followed was a brutal occupation. Approximately 6 million people in Poland were killed during the nearly six-year war—3 million Jews, from a prewar Jewish population of 3.5 million, and 3 million non-Jews, including tens of thousands murdered in Auschwitz.

Unlike France, Norway, and several other occupied countries, Poland never had the equivalent of a collaborationist regime like Vichy or Quisling. It did, however, have a well-developed resistance movement, not to mention as many as 150,000 Poles fighting from abroad against the Nazis, including in the British

14. Andrew Roth, and Bethan McKernan, "Russia Accuses Israel of Backing 'neo-Nazis' in Kyiv as Diplomatic Row Grows," *The Guardian*, May 3, 2022, https://www.theguardian.com/world/2022/may/03/russia-accuses-israel-backing-neo-nazis-kyiv-diplomatic-row-grows.

Royal Air Force and British intelligence nerve center at Bletchley Park and in the epic battle at Monte Cassino, Italy.

This background is important to an understanding of Poland today. For many Poles, the story of the war is, above all, an unalloyed story of Polish valor, courage, and sacrifice. And there are reminders everywhere throughout the country: monuments, memorials, plaques, ceremonies, and school curricula.

But for many Jews, the Polish story is more complex. Yes, Poland was on the Allied side. Yes, Poles fought tenaciously against Nazi Germany. And yes, more Poles than citizens of any other country have been honored by Israel's Yad Vashem for their efforts to save Jewish lives (even as far more Jews lived in Poland than any other European country). All true.

Yet they also view Poland as a country with a long history of virulent antisemitism that predated the war. It continued during the war even as Jews and other Poles were on the same side against the Nazis, and it resurfaced in the postwar Communist era.

In 1998, the Polish Parliament enacted a law creating the Institute of National Remembrance and its Commission for the Prosecution of Crimes against the Polish Nation. Twenty years later, the law was amended to criminalize public speech, including research and writing, that linked "Poland or the Polish nation" to any responsibility for the Holocaust. The measure triggered an international outcry, most notably in Israel.

Defending the law, and in another glaring example of victim-blaming, Polish prime minister Mateusz Morawiecki declared that "there were Jewish perpetrators" of the Holocaust[15] in addition to Germans. Israeli Knesset member Yair Lapid, the son of a Holocaust survivor and future foreign minister and prime

15. Tamara Zieve, "Polish PM: There Were Jewish Perpetrators of the Holocaust," *The Jerusalem Post*, February 17, 2018, https://www.jpost.com/international/polish-pm-there-were-jeiwsh-perpetrators-of-the-holocaust-542857.

minister, responded forcefully, "The Jewish state will not allow the murdered to be blamed for their own murder."[16]

While the criminal penalties in the 2018 amendment were later revoked, the exchange of angry words between Polish and Israeli leaders continued.

Three years later, Poland's Parliament approved a law setting a 30-year statute of limitations on all property restitution cases, effectively ending any further legal claims from the wartime era, 1939–45. Another firestorm erupted, with Lapid, now foreign minister, describing the law as "antisemitic and immoral."[17] Diplomatic ties suffered. The Israeli ambassador in Poland and the Polish ambassador in Israel were recalled by their respective governments. Bilateral relations have not fully recovered, and the historical issues sparking such crises still elude resolution between the two nations.

Does the growing popularity of extreme right-wing political parties pose a threat to Jews and Jewish life in Europe?

The short answer is yes. The genocidal legacy of the Nazis and their collaborators across much of Europe serves as a stark reminder of the profound dangers of the far right, all the more so when its political fortunes were rising in 2024. But it gets more complicated. Far-right parties are not all monolithic in today's Europe.

There are hardcore, ultra-nationalist, antisemitic parties nostalgic for the Nazi era. The Golden Dawn in Greece, which rose to prominence earlier this century, becoming the third

16. Tamara Zieve, "Polish PM: There Were Jewish Perpetrators of the Holocaust," *The Jerusalem Post*, February 17, 2018, https://www.jpost.com/international/polish-pm-there-were-jeiwsh-perpetrators-of-the-holocaust-542857.
17. "Poland's President Signs Bill to Curb Claims On Property Seized by Nazis," *The Guardian*, August 14, 2021, https://www.theguardian.com/world/2021/aug/14/polands-president-signs-bill-to-curb-claims-on-property-seized-by-nazis.

largest bloc in the Greek Parliament in 2015, is one example. Today, with some of its leaders found guilty of criminal activity, it is no longer in the Parliament, but its unabashed neo-Nazism—in a country that was utterly devastated by the Nazis decades earlier—was no impediment to its decade-long electoral success.

In Europe's most populous nation, the far-right, xenophobic Alternative for Germany (AfD) has shown political strength, particularly in the former East German territory, where it led all parties in the June 2024 voting for European Parliament seats. Overall, it won 15.9% of the national vote, topping the governing Social Democratic Party, led by Chancellor Olaf Scholz. Felix Klein, Germany's federal antisemitism commissioner, minced no words in the media: "Klein accused the AfD of condoning antisemitism and backing forces that have sought to downplay the Holocaust—the Nazi genocide of 6 million Jews or two-thirds of Europe's Jewish population—during World War II."[18]

Then there are the parties that were once in more or less the same category but have sought to reinvent themselves by redirecting their focus on such "mainstream" issues as Euroskepticism, the belief that the European Union project was gaining too much power at the expense of national sovereignty, and immigration. It is more often than not a code word for hostility to Muslims or believing Islam is incompatible with prevailing European values. These groups, therefore, make a special effort to reach out to Jews, voice support for Israel, and reject any nostalgia for the Nazi past.

Three examples are the National Rally in France, led by Marine Le Pen; Brothers of Italy, headed by Giorgia Meloni, Italy's prime minister since 2022; and the Dutch Party for Freedom, founded by Geert Wilders in 2006.

18. *Deutsche Welle*, "German AfD: Revival of Far-Right a 'Threat to Jewish Life,'" May 8, 2023, https://www.dw.com/en/german-afd-revival-of-far-right-a-threat-to-jewish-life/a-66447819.

In the French case, the founding party, National Front, was created by Jean-Marie Le Pen, Marine's father. He harbored deeply antisemitic views, once described the Holocaust and its gas chambers as nothing more than a "detail" of history, for which he was found guilty of denying crimes against humanity in a French court, and acted as an apologist for Vichy France, the regime that collaborated with Nazi Germany from 1940 to 1944.

Marine took over the party, ousted her father and his kindred spirits, and renamed it. In the June 2024 European Parliament elections in France, National Rally came in first. The party platform rejects antisemitism and Holocaust denial and supports Israel, yet, periodically, reports surface of a party member caught on camera with Nazi paraphernalia, such as Ludivine Daoudi. She was forced to withdraw her 2024 candidacy after a photo emerged of her wearing a Nazi cap.

This attempted restart has triggered a major debate among French Jews. Can the National Rally be trusted? Is it the "same old" in shiny new packaging, or has it genuinely put its antisemitic past behind it?

These debates took place as the French center collapsed in the first round of voting for the French National Assembly in 2024. In many districts, that left a choice between National Rally and a left-wing coalition, New Popular Front, which included Jean-Luc Mélenchon, whom *Politico* described as "the former-socialist-turned-radical-leftist,"[19] and which aroused its own concerns about deep-seated hostility to Israel and accusations of antisemitism.

Le Pen asserted, "The best shield for our fellow French citizens of Jewish faith today is the National Rally. It's the only movement with the will, the conviction and the means to fight Islamist fundamentalism, which is the major danger facing

19. Nicholas Vinocur, "Macron's Gamble Ends in Leadership Crisis," *Politico*, July 8, 2024, https://www.politico.eu/newsletter/brussels-playbook/macrons-gamble-ends-in-leadership-crisis/.

them."[20] Serge Klarsfeld, a renowned Nazi hunter, said he would vote "without hesitation" for the National Rally if the choice came down to left versus right, because "Marine Le Pen is the head of a party which supports Israel and which supports the Jews."[21] On the other hand, Shannon Seban, a French Jew and candidate for the centrist party, denounced both far right and far left: "Far left, far right—for me, it's a choice between the plague and cholera."[22]

In the face of the country's prospect of one political extreme or another, a prominent Paris rabbi, Moshe Sebbag, declared, "It is clear today that there is no future for Jews in France. I tell everyone who is young to go to Israel or a more secure country."[23]

In Italy, the Brothers of Italy party has its roots in the postwar neofascist movement, anchored in longing for the era of Benito Mussolini. But under the leadership of Giorgia Meloni, it has sought to recast itself as a classic conservative party, and since 2022 Meloni has served as Italy's prime minister. Disputes continue in the media and elsewhere about how to describe her party most accurately: far right? neofascist? right-wing?

20. Victor Goury-Laffont, "In France, (Some) Jews Are Voting Far Right," *Politico*, July 5, 2024, https://www.politico.eu/article/france-election-2024-some-jews-are-voting-far-right/#:~:text=%E2%80%9CThe%20best%20shield%20for%20our,the%20major%20danger%20facing%20them.%E2%80%9D.
21. Sylvie Corbet and Jeffrey Schaeffer, "Renowned Nazi Hunter in France Advises Jews to Choose Far Right over Far Left in Elections," AP News, July 3, 2024, https://apnews.com/article/france-election-far-right-nazi-hunter-antisemitism-dbe220c915894f6aded6f3547c05aae0.
22. John Leicester and Alex Turnbull, "In France's High-Stakes Election, a Jewish Candidate Faces Hate and Division," *Times of Israel*, June 28, 2024, https://www.timesofisrael.com/in-frances-high-stakes-election-a-jewish-candidate-faces-hate-and-division/.
23. Michael Starr, "Paris Grand Synagogue Rabbi: 'There Is No Future for Jews in France,'" *Jerusalem Post*, July 1, 2024, https://www.jpost.com/diaspora/article-808521.

center-right? And questions persist about whether the party has truly purged itself of its fascist links.

Prime Minister Meloni has tried to reassure the 30,000-member Italian Jewish community. On October 16, 2023, she declared:

> On 16 October 1943, one of the most heinous crimes in Italian history was committed. In the early hours of the morning, Nazi troops, with the complicity of the Italian fascist regime, began a ruthless manhunt in the capital. 1,259 innocent people were taken away from their homes and deported to the death camps. Among them were also more than two hundred children, torn from their innocence and sentenced to death. Only 16 returned from the abyss of Auschwitz. An atrocity that has marred the history of the Italian people forever, and that must serve as a warning against anything similar ever happening again, also in other forms. Today, we renew our commitment to keep the memory of those terrible events alive and to fight the virus of anti-Semitism in all its forms, new and old. The Government expresses its closeness to the Jewish Community of Rome, to the relatives and descendants of the deported. Today more than ever, following the terrible attack by Hamas, we reiterate our solidarity with the entire population of Israel, hurt once again by anti-Semitic hatred.[24]

In the Netherlands, Geert Wilders has been both a prominent and highly controversial politician, whose party in the most recent Dutch elections in 2023 came out on top and is the

24. Governo Italiano, "President Meloni Receives President of the Jewish Community of Rome on 80th Anniversary of the Rounding Up of Jews in the City during WWII," October 16, 2023, https://www.governo.it/it/node/23950.

largest in the governing coalition. Wilders offers another case study in European right-wing complexity.

He is a populist, a belittler of Islam, which he calls an "ideology," not a religion, a fierce critic of migration from Muslim countries, and a Euroskeptic. At the same time, he has gone to considerable lengths to defend Israel, saying, "If Israel falls, the West falls."[25] He was a volunteer on a kibbutz in his youth and is married to a Jewish woman.

For some Dutch Jews primarily concerned about growing antisemitism from within Muslim communities in Europe, rising hostility toward Israel, and abandonment by the left, Wilders offers a political pathway. But other Dutch Jews distrust him and fear that, behind the face mask, he represents a combustible cocktail of racism, populism, and xenophobia.

As in France and Italy, so, too, in the Netherlands, deeply divided Jewish communities are having fierce debates about unabashedly right-wing parties making overtures to Jewish voters.

Meanwhile, it must also be noted, though it is not the focus of this book, that Muslims have faced violence, the threat of violence, and social discrimination at times in Europe, primarily from nationalist, populist, right-wing forces. Most devastating was the systematic, cold-blooded murder of more than 8,000 people, primarily Muslim and male, in Srebrenica, Bosnia-Herzegovina, in 1995 at the hands of Bosnian Serbs and notwithstanding the presence of Dutch peacekeeping forces.

Does the growing population of Muslims in Europe, many of whom arrived from countries with strong antisemitic traditions, pose a threat to Jews and Jewish life in Europe?

The short answer, as to the previous question, is yes.

25. Memy Peer, "'If Israel Falls, the West Falls': Geert Wilders is Europe's Last Stand Against Islam—Opinion," *The Jerusalem Post*, July 3, 2024, https://www.jpost.com/opinion/article-808875.

Not all Muslims who live in Europe pose a threat to Jews and Jewish life. Not at all. Muslims are not a monolithic community, but rather embody different traditions and outlooks. Some have made interfaith understanding and cooperation, including outreach specifically to the Jewish community, a priority, including in defense of circumcision and kosher/halal food requirements, when they have been challenged in Germany, Sweden, Switzerland, and elsewhere. That said, there are dangers for Jews from those Muslims who harbor hardcore antisemitic beliefs, be they from mosques, madrasas, media, or family. And their numbers are not insignificant.

A poll commissioned by the Henry Jackson Society, a London-based think tank, and released in April 2024 reported:

- Almost half of British Muslims say Jews have too much power over U.K. government policy, with similar numbers thinking the same for U.S. foreign policy.
- British Muslims are more likely to have a positive than a negative view of Hamas, a proscribed terrorist organization in the United Kingdom.
- Thirty-two percent of British Muslims favor the implementation of Shari'a law, and the same number the declaration of Islam as a national religion.
- Extreme views were generally more likely to be found in the youngest age cohort of 18–34, among graduates of all ages (as opposed to nongraduates) and British-born rather than foreign-born Muslims, suggesting British integration policy is failing and needs urgent revision.[26]

26. Henry Jackson Society, "Only One in Four British Muslims Believe Hamas Committed Murder and Rape in Israel on October 7th," April 8, 2024, https://henryjacksonsociety.org/2024/04/08/only-one-in-four-british-muslims-believe-hamas-committed-murder-and-rape-in-israel-on-october-7th/.

A 2022 survey of Muslims in France by Fondapol and the American Jewish Committee revealed:

- Thirty-six percent of Muslims say there is too much talk about antisemitism, compared to 15% in the general population.
- Fifteen percent of Muslims admit to feeling antipathy toward Jews, compared to 5% of the general French population.
- Forty percent agree with the statement "Jews use their status of victims of the Nazi genocide during the Second World War to their own advantage."
- However, young Muslims seem to be less inclined to hold certain antisemitic stereotypes than the older generation.[27]

As the Muslim population in Europe grows rapidly, particularly in such countries as Belgium, France, Germany, the Netherlands, Spain, Sweden, and the United Kingdom, if a significant minority are avowedly antisemitic, the sheer numbers pose threats to Jews and Jewish life.

For Jewish leaders in Europe, discussing this topic is not always easy. As a minority community themselves, Jews wish to be sensitive to the challenges faced by other such groups, especially newer ones still finding their way. All too familiar with attempts to stereotype an entire group or assign it collective blame, many Jews seek to tread carefully. There is also awareness that voicing concern about antisemitism within the Muslim population could be misinterpreted as Jews trying to hold back another group's development.

27. American Jewish Committee, "American Jewish Committee Surveys French Jewish, Muslim, and General Populations' Perspectives on Antisemitism," February 2, 2022, https://www.ajc.org/news/american-jewish-committee-surveys-french-jewish-muslim-and-general-populations-perspectives-on-antisemitism.

Moreover, in some European countries, there is an unwillingness to categorize antisemitic incidents by the ethnic or religious affiliation of the perpetrators, even as the data could be important for tracking antisemitism and understanding societal dynamics. In Germany, for example, antisemitic hate crimes have been broadly attributed either to "right-wing extremists" or "others." And France and Sweden do not identify perpetrators by ethnic or racial identity. So data is uneven, depending on the country and its laws and methodologies.

When Chancellor Angela Merkel chose to welcome more than a million newcomers to Germany in 2015, while encouraging other European countries to open their doors as well, she created a conundrum for many Jews. Her rationale, she said, was to demonstrate that the new Germany was open to people fleeing their countries, and thereby put another nail in the coffin of the Nazi legacy. But those entering were overwhelmingly from nations in North Africa and the Middle East, starting with Syria, which have deeply rooted antisemitic traditions.

For many Jews in Germany, this was tricky. On the one hand, the German population was largely in favor of the influx, and it would have been misunderstood had Jews voiced misgivings. On the other hand, the likelihood that a considerable number of the newcomers might bring antisemitic sentiments to their new homes could not be downplayed.

The larger question of whether millions of Muslim immigrants to Europe will be assimilated and acculturated, including to values of respect for and peaceful coexistence with other religious minorities, sensitivity to Europe's Holocaust history, and recognition of Europe's long-standing ties with Israel, remains to be seen.

In 2024 Germany's minister of interior, Nancy Faeser, announced that the country was adding a series of Israel-related and Jewish-related questions to its citizenship test. This was unprecedented. She explained, "From the German crime against humanity that was the Holocaust come our special responsibilities to protecting Jewish people and the State of Israel."[28]

The pessimists point to places like Malmö, Sweden, where the Jewish community has dwindled in size because of repeated threats from within the large Muslim immigrant population, not to mention the deadly attacks against Jews by jihadists in Brussels, Copenhagen, Paris, Toulouse, and elsewhere. The optimists cite elected officials like Sadiq Khan, mayor of London since 2016, who has maintained cordial ties with the city's large Jewish community, and Hassen Chalghoumi, imam of the mosque in Drancy, France, who has marched against antisemitism and stressed interreligious dialogue.

If the optimists prevail, there can be a future for Jews in Europe. But if the pessimists are proved correct, combined with the extreme right's rise (which is in large part fueled by a reaction to the rising Muslim population in countries like France and Germany), then declining numbers of Jews in Europe can be anticipated, as more move to Israel and elsewhere.

What steps have the European Union and individual European nations taken to combat antisemitism?

Here is the essence of the European Union approach, which is entitled "EU Strategy on Combating Antisemitism and Fostering Jewish Life (2021–2030)":

> Antisemitism is incompatible with Europe's core values. It represents a threat not only to Jewish communities and to Jewish life, but to an open and diverse society, to democracy and the European way of life. The European Union is determined to put an end to it.

28. Germany Visa, "Germany Will Include 12 New Questions Related to Judaism and Israel on Its Citizenship Test," https://www.germany-visa.org/news/germany-will-include-12-new-questions-related-to-judaism-israel-on-its-citizenship-test/.

Contemporary antisemitism occurs in many forms, old and new: from online hate speech to hate crimes and attacks on Jewish people, their properties and institutions, to desecration of synagogues, cemeteries and memorials. It occurs in the daily lives of Jewish people in the form of casual remarks or actions at work, private conversations, in public places, in the media, sports and culture or when Jewish people are practicing their religion. Antisemitism manifests itself as racial, ethnic or religious discrimination, stereotyping and hatred of Jews and people perceived as Jewish. It can lead to violent and lethal attacks such as those on the Ozar Hatorah school in Toulouse in 2012, the Jewish Museum in Brussels in 2014, the Hypercasher in Paris in 2015, or on the Synagogue in Halle in 2019.

In addition, the COVID-19 pandemic has shown how old antisemitic prejudices can resurge and fuel new conspiracy myths and hatred online and offline. Jewish people have been one of the most attacked communities during the pandemic; they have been unjustifiably blamed for creating the virus and for developing vaccines to make a profit.

This is compounded by comparisons of pandemic measures with policies that led to the genocide of the Jewish people that minimise and trivialise the experiences of Holocaust victims and survivors.

Jewish life in the EU in the 21st century

In recent years, the Jewish population in the EU has been declining, due in large part to migration to outside of the EU. This is linked to several factors, in particular to security concerns, as well as to the perceived lack of determination of some governments to address antisemitism and the politicisation of public debates around Jewish customs and traditions.

Stepping up the fight against antisemitism

Crucially, this strategy seeks to go beyond responding to antisemitism alone and step up action to actively prevent and combat it in all its forms and to ensure that Jewish life continues to thrive in an inclusive and diverse EU. The strategy comprises three pillars:

1—Preventing and combating all forms of antisemitism
2—Protecting and fostering Jewish life in the EU
3—Education, research and Holocaust remembrance.[29]

Is there any polling data on attitudes toward Jews in European countries?

In 2019, the Pew Research Center Global Attitudes Survey published findings on views of Jews in several European countries.[30] The results varied quite markedly.

The countries with the most favorable numbers were Sweden and the Netherlands, where 92% of those surveyed had a positive opinion of Jews. Just 3% in Sweden and 5% in the Netherlands had an unfavorable attitude. They were followed by the United Kingdom (90% favorable to 6% unfavorable), France (89% to 6%), and Germany (86% to 6%).

At the other end of the spectrum, Greece had the highest unfavorable view, 38%, while a slim majority, 51%, had a favorable opinion. Slovakia came next (58% favorable to 30% unfavorable), then Poland (59% favorable to 31% unfavorable), Hungary (60% favorable to 18% unfavorable), and the Czech Republic (65% favorable to 17% unfavorable).

29. European Commission, "EU Strategy on Combating Antisemitism and Fostering Jewish Life (2021–2030)," September 30, 2021, https://commission.europa.eu/document/6160ed15-80da-458e-b76b-04eacae46d6c_en.
30. Richard Wike, Richard Wike, Jacob Poushter, Laura Silver, Kat Devlin, Janell Fetterolf, Alexandra Castillo and Christine Huang, "Views on Minority Groups across Europe," Pew Research Center, October 14, 2019, https://www.pewresearch.org/global/2019/10/14/minority-groups/.

The other European countries surveyed, including Italy, Spain, Bulgaria, and Lithuania, plus Ukraine and Russia, came out in the middle of the rankings.

As mentioned earlier, these European numbers overall are markedly better disposed toward Jews than the Pew findings in seven countries in the Muslim world.

The Pew report also offered some insight into the European results: "There are few demographic differences in attitudes toward Jews. However, in many of these countries, those with more education tend to have more positive attitudes than do those with less education, though majorities at both levels have favorable views. The biggest such difference is in the Czech Republic, where 81% of those with more education have a favorable view of Jews, compared with 60% among those with less education."

The same year, 2019, the Anti-Defamation League reported the findings of its surveys linked to the *ADL Global 100: An Index of Anti-Semitism*. On Europe, the organization reported: "About one in four Europeans polled harbor pernicious and pervasive attitudes toward Jews. While anti-Semitic attitudes held mostly steady in Western Europe, the poll found hateful notions about Jews are rising in Eastern and Central European countries polled, where long-held tropes about Jewish control of business and finance and of 'dual loyalty' remain widespread."[31]

Is there data available on how Jews in Europe assess the danger of antisemitism?

In 2019, the European Union Commission and London-based Institute for Jewish Policy Research jointly published a study

31. Anti-Defamation League, "ADL Global Survey of 18 Countries Finds Hardcore Anti-Semitic Attitudes Remain Pervasive," November 21, 2019, https://www.adl.org.il/en/research/adl-global-survey-of-18-countries-finds-hardcore-anti-semitic-attitudes-remain-pervasive/.

titled "Young Jewish Europeans: Perceptions and Experiences of Antisemitism." The findings of the 2,700 respondents, ages 16 to 34, in 12 EU countries with sizable Jewish communities, were striking.[32]

More than 80% said antisemitism is a current problem in their countries and that antisemitism is on the rise. Forty-four percent indicated that they themselves had experienced an antisemitic incident at least once in the previous year, whether online or in person. And 41% of these young Europeans "have considered emigrating from the countries in which they currently live out of fear for their safety as Jews."

In 2022, the American Jewish Committee conducted a survey of Jews in France, the largest Jewish community in Europe and the world's third biggest, after Israel and the United States. The survey's conclusions:

> 85% of French Jews say antisemitism is a widespread phenomenon in France today, and 73% say it has been increasing over the past ten years.
>
> Three-quarters, 74%, of French Jews, have been victims of antisemitic acts during their lives. Assaults have included derogatory remarks (68%), threats on social media (28%), verbal threats (24%), and physical violence (20%).
>
> More than one-third, 37%, say they feel threatened because of their religious affiliation. 35% say they have avoided wearing a style of dress that identifies them Jewishly, and 41% have avoided displaying mezuzas and other religious symbols.[33]

32. Jonathan Boyd, "An In-Depth Study of the Identities of Young Jews in Europe," Institute for Jewish Policy Research, July 5, 2019, https://www.jpr.org.uk/reports/young-jewish-europeans-perceptions-and-experiences-antisemitism.
33. American Jewish Committee, "American Jewish Committee Surveys French Jewish, Muslim, and General Populations' Perspectives on Antisemitism."

Given that antisemitism has spiked since 2023, such surveys now would likely yield even more troubling results.

In France, according to Conseil Représentatif des Institutions Juives de France, the umbrella body of French Jewry, antisemitic incidents quadrupled in 2023 compared to 2022. On November 12, 2024, French interior minister Bruno Retailleau reported, "Our compatriots of Jewish faith represent less than one percent or the French population, yet they are victims of 57 percent of all racist, of all anti-religious attacks."[34] In the United Kingdom, the Community Security Trust reported that recorded incidents of antisemitism in 2023 more than doubled from the previous year.[35] The United Kingdom is home to Europe's second largest Jewish population. And in Germany, Europe's third biggest Jewish community, the Federal Association of Research and Information Centers on Antisemitism revealed that antisemitic incidents in 2023 were 80% higher than in the previous year.[36]

In July 2024, the European Union's Fundamental Rights Agency released the results of its omnibus survey of 8,000 Jews in 13 of the 27 EU member states. The survey was conducted prior to the Hamas-launched invasion of Israel in October 2023. A full 96% of the respondents said they had encountered antisemitism, whether online, on the street, or at work, while 76% reported "they hid their Jewish identity at least occasionally."[37]

34. @DavidSaranga, *X*, November 13, 2024, https://x.com/DavidSaranga/status/1856538833770209518.
35. "Antisemitic Incidents 2023," *Community Security Trust* (2024), https://cst.org.uk/public/data/file/9/f/Antisemitic_Incidents_Report_2023.pdf.
36. "Antisemitic Incidents in Germany 2023," *Federal Association of Departments for Research and Information on Antisemitism e.V.* (2024), https://report-antisemitism.de/documents/2024-06-2024_Antisemitic_incidents_in_Germany_Annual-Report_Federal_Association_RIAS_2023.pdf.
37. BBC, "Europe Facing 'Wave of Antisemitism,' Survey Finds," July 11, 2024, https://www.bbc.co.uk/news/articles/c147w9572dvo.

9

ANTISEMITISM TRAVELS ACROSS THE ATLANTIC

Few in the American Jewish community were prepared for the shock of growing antisemitism at home, even as they observed its resurgence in Europe since 2000–2001. The shock was compounded by the fact that incidents, including violent acts, came from multiple sources. Meanwhile, the explosion of social media triggered fierce debates about the extent to which these platforms, in the name of free speech, were spreading antisemitism. In the spring of 2023, the Biden administration took the unprecedented step of announcing "The U.S. National Strategy to Combat Antisemitism," the first-ever such plan in American history. What could explain the turn of events? The Jewish community has lived proudly on American soil since 1654, even despite having experienced episodic antisemitism from extremist groups ranging from the Ku Klux Klan to the Nation of Islam, discriminatory immigration laws, and restrictive entry during the Holocaust. Was this a reaction to specific events, or did it reflect a fundamental change in the nature of American society?

Historically, was antisemitism in the United States a major concern for Jews?

Jews first arrived in what is today America in 1654. Twenty-three Jews left Brazil, which had become subject to the

Portuguese Inquisition. They got a mixed reception in New Amsterdam, the Dutch outpost that later became New York. The governor, Peter Stuyvesant, no friend of the Jews, wanted to expel them. He was overruled by his bosses at the Dutch West India Company. The Jewish pioneers stayed. Others followed.

In 1751, the speaker of the Pennsylvania Assembly wanted a bell for the legislature. And on the bell, he chose words not from the Christian Bible but from Leviticus in the Hebrew Bible: "Proclaim LIBERTY throughout the Land unto all the inhabitants thereof." Those words remain to this day on one of the iconic symbols of the United States.

George Washington, America's first president, wrote on June 14, 1790, to the Hebrew Congregation in Savannah, Georgia, "May the same wonder-working Deity; who long since delivering the Hebrews from their Egyptian Oppressors planted them in the promised land—whose providential agency has lately been conspicuous in establishing these United States as an independent nation—still continue to water them with the dews of Heaven and to make the inhabitants of every denomination participate in the temporal and spiritual blessings of that people whose God is Jehovah."[1] Two months later, Washington sent a similarly remarkable letter to the Hebrew Congregation of Newport, Rhode Island, that set the crystal-clear tone for the new country's approach to religious freedom and religious pluralism. The letter's most cited paragraphs:

> The Citizens of the United States of America have a right to applaud themselves for having given to mankind examples of an enlarged and liberal policy: a

1. Library of Congress, "George Washington to Savannah, Georgia, Citizens, May 13, 1791," https://www.loc.gov/resource/mgw2.039/?sp=78&st=image.

policy worthy of imitation. All possess alike liberty of conscience and immunities of citizenship. It is now no more that toleration is spoken of, as if it was by the indulgence of one class of people, that another enjoyed the exercise of their inherent natural rights. For happily the Government of the United States, which gives to bigotry no sanction, to persecution no assistance requires only that they who live under its protection should demean themselves as good citizens, in giving it on all occasions their effectual support.

It would be inconsistent with the frankness of my character not to avow that I am pleased with your favorable opinion of my Administration, and fervent wishes for my felicity. May the Children of the Stock of Abraham, who dwell in this land, continue to merit and enjoy the good will of the other Inhabitants; while every one shall sit in safety under his own vine and figtree, and there shall be none to make him afraid. May the father of all mercies scatter light and not darkness in our paths, and make us all in our several vocations useful here, and in his own due time and way everlastingly happy.[2]

When the First Amendment to the U.S. Constitution was added in 1791, two protections in particular signaled the nation's direction: "Congress shall make no law respecting an establishment of religion, or prohibiting the free exercise thereof."

When Reverend Ezra Stiles was president of Yale College in the late 18th century, he adopted the Hebrew words *Urim v'Tumim*, "Light and Truth," as the university's motto and required all students to study Hebrew. That reflected a

2. National Archives, "From George Washington to the Hebrew Congregation in Newport, Rhode Island, 18 August 1790," https://founders.archives.gov/documents/Washington/05-06-02-0135.

widespread interest among early political and social leaders in Judaism, the Hebrew Bible and identification with the Exodus story, the image of Jerusalem as the shining city on the Hill, and the age-old quest for religious liberty.

This is important not merely as historical curiosity but as an explanation for what made America so appealing to Jews elsewhere and led to the mass migrations, when they were possible, to start new lives in what was later referred to, in Yiddish, as *Di Goldene Medina*, "the Golden Country."

In reality, it was not always easy for Jews living in the United States or seeking to resettle there. Far from it. Those lucky enough to arrive usually had to start from scratch, residing in ramshackle tenement buildings, eking out a meager living in often unsafe conditions, seeking to bring family to escape persecution and discrimination elsewhere, overcoming language issues, and grappling with an entirely new culture.

There were barriers aplenty, including widespread antisemitism, but what separated America from Europe for so many was that the bigotry, where it existed, was rarely lethal or baked into the laws and system of justice. There was no equivalent of the pogroms in Eastern Europe, the Inquisitions in Spain and Portugal, the centuries-long expulsion from England and other countries and cities, the blood libels from England to Ukraine, the confining ghettos from Rome to Venice, the kidnaping of Jewish children and their forced conversion to Christianity, or the many cultural, intellectual, and political spaces where only Christians could apply, work, and advance.

In other words, antisemitism in the United States was real, it was shameful, and it was costly, but it never came close to reaching the levels in Europe, where so many Jews had fled from.

Nevertheless, it prevented many Jews, even as they climbed up the economic ladder, from living in certain neighborhoods where restrictive covenants explicitly excluded Jews. It also blocked Jews from joining some social and recreational clubs that barred even Jewish guests, matriculating in a number of prestigious universities that maintained overt or discreet Jewish quotas, working in many banks and law firms, or practicing medicine in some hospitals right up until the mid-20th century.

In 1862 General Ulysses S. Grant issued an unprecedented order expelling all Jews from his military jurisdiction in several states, an order rescinded by President Abraham Lincoln and for which Grant subsequently apologized over and over again. Leo Frank, a Jew, was lynched by an antisemitic mob in Georgia, in 1915, on the unjust accusation of killing a child. In 1924, Congress passed new immigration legislation designed to keep out as many Jews (and Catholics) as possible. In the 1920s and 1930s, antisemitism was strong and quite widespread, fueled by the likes of Henry Ford, Father Charles Coughlin, Charles Lindbergh, and Gerald Smith, not to mention the Ku Klux Klan, America First Committee, German-American Bund (which organized a sold-out, pro-Nazi rally in New York's famed Madison Square Garden in 1939), and others. There were several bombings of synagogues in 1957–58 in the South, in Atlanta, Miami, and Nashville, and one in Peoria, Illinois, all associated with segregationists who opposed Jewish support for racial integration. Fortunately, there were no fatalities. Chicago-based Nation of Islam leader Louis Farrakhan for decades made Jews a centerpiece of his hateful rhetoric, referring to them as "satanic" and "my enemy."

All of this was painfully true, it was in the public arena, and it affected Jews in many ways, but it never dimmed their views of America as a unique country in the sweep of Jewish diaspora history. Indeed, it could fairly be called a love affair. America was free and open compared to their previous lives. Even if there were hurdles, Jews found ways to leap over them or find pathways around them or combat them head-on through their own and allied organizations.

American Jews established new neighborhoods in which to live and new law firms and hospitals in which to practice. And, eventually, Jews' faith in America told them the doors would one day fully open because merit and coexistence would triumph over quotas and bias—and America would eventually fulfill its promise for all, not just a privileged elite.

It was not until 1970 that any of the eight Ivy League universities appointed a Jew as president. That was not for lack of qualified candidates, but there were those nasty social barriers preventing it. But once the gates opened, at the University of Pennsylvania, then Dartmouth, discrimination quickly became a receding memory.

When Irving Shapiro was named chairman and chief executive officer of the chemical giant DuPont in 1973, it made headline news, as he was reportedly the first Jew picked to head a Fortune 500 company. Afterward it became commonplace, and most people stopped paying attention.

Perhaps the most significant coming-of-age moment occurred in 2000, when the Democratic Party nominated Joseph Lieberman as the running mate to Albert Gore on the presidential ballot. Lieberman was a Modern Orthodox Jew. He respected the Sabbath and ate kosher food. Yet this was not seen as an impediment to the ticket. Indeed, Gore-Lieberman won the popular vote, though ultimately lost the election in a 5–4 Supreme Court decision.

Twenty-four years later, in the 2024 presidential race, the possibility of another Jewish vice-presidential candidate arose, as Vice President Kamala Harris considered her running mate. Attention turned to Josh Shapiro, the governor of Pennsylvania, a critical battleground state in what was expected to be a nail-biting election. In the end, however, she opted for Tim Walz, the governor of Minnesota. A debate arose as to whether Shapiro was passed over because he was Jewish (or "too" Jewish or Zionist), or if the choice was driven by entirely different considerations. Shapiro himself emphatically rejected any antisemitic motives, as reported by NBC News: "Antisemitism played absolutely no role in my dialogue with the vice president. Absolutely none."[3] On the other hand, the Republican vice-presidential candidate, JD Vance, asserted in a Fox News interview, "The fact that you're letting antisemites within the Democratic Party drive so much of the conversation, and so much of the decision-making for Kamala Harris, is a really worrying sign."[4]

No, antisemitism never disappeared from the American scene, and in the 21st century it is markedly on the rise—on university campuses, in social media, on the streets, and even in the extreme wings of Congress. However, that Jewish love affair with America, and the recognition that the country, since its founding, has offered Jews a welcome mat unlike anywhere else on earth outside Israel, explains the special attachment American Jews have felt for their country.

There have been a number of deadly attacks in the United States in recent decades. Were the motives of the perpetrators all similar?

The fatal attacks against Jews in America in recent decades, so rare previously, have come from multiple sources.

In 1991, a car in a police-escorted motorcade in Brooklyn for Rabbi Menachem Schneerson, the revered leader of the Chabad movement, unintentionally struck two children, one of whom, seven-year-old Gavin Cato, died. As the driver of the car was Jewish and the children were Black people, the situation quickly escalated. In the ensuing violence directed against

3. Natasha Korecki, "Josh Shapiro Says Antisemitism Played No Role in VP Discussions and Slams Trump's Comments," *NBC News*, August 19, 2024, https://www.nbcnews.com/politics/2024-election/josh-shapiro-says-antisemitism-played-no-role-vp-discussions-slams-tru-rcna167167.
4. Ron Kampeas, "Vance Says Democrats Made Josh Shapiro 'Run from His Jewish Heritage,'" *Times of Israel*, August 7, 2024, https://www.timesofisrael.com/vance-says-democrats-made-josh-shapiro-run-from-his-jewish-heritage/.

Jews in the Crown Heights neighborhood, a visiting Jewish scholar from Australia, Yankel Rosenbaum, was stabbed to death. Other Jews were beaten and several Jewish-owned businesses were vandalized.

While some leaders on both sides were meeting privately in an effort to defuse tensions—which related not only to the tragic car accident and the murder of Rosenbaum but also to long-simmering clashes over access to city services, claims of preferential treatment, disputes over scarce housing and differing lifestyles—others in the Black community, including Reverend Al Sharpton, were invoking antisemitic slogans to keep people in the streets and temperatures high.

This saga was described by some as a "pogrom," referring to organized attacks against Jewish communities in Eastern Europe; others, including the mayor at the time, David Dinkins, rejected the term. It was perhaps the single worst act of mob violence against Jews up to that point in American history.

Three years later, a van carrying 15 Chabad students across New York's Brooklyn Bridge was struck with gunfire by a Lebanese-born driver, Rashid Baz. One boy, Ari Halberstam, 16, died from gunshot wounds. Another, Nachum Sossonkin, 18, suffered permanent brain injury. Earlier that day, Baz had reportedly listened to an antisemitic sermon in a Brooklyn mosque.

Initially, law enforcement categorized the tragedy, to the astonishment of some, as due to "road rage" on Baz's part. It took years, but the verdict eventually changed to terrorism, thanks to the determination of Ari Halberstam's mother, Devorah. As Baz himself admitted 13 years after the shooting, "I only shot them because they were Jewish."[5]

5. Menachem Wecker and David Swicker, "$50,000 Reward Offered for Info on 1994 NYC Antisemitic Murder," *Jewish Chronicle*, July 11, 2023, https://www.thejc.com/news/world/50-000-reward-offered-for-info-on-1994-nyc-antisemitic-murder-vgn96pbk.

The most deadly attack, indeed the worst ever against a Jewish target since Jews arrived on American shores in 1654, took place in Pittsburgh on October 27, 2018. The target was the Tree of Life Synagogue while a Shabbat worship service was underway. Eleven people were killed and six wounded by a gunman, Robert Bowers, an avowed White supremacist.

Bowers had been active on Alt-Right, dark web sites. He frequently displayed hatred for Jews and Black people; believed that White people were being displaced in America by minorities—the so-called "Great Replacement Theory"—and that Jews were among those principally responsible for the new immigrants; peddled multiple other conspiracy theories; denied the Holocaust; embraced neo-Nazis; and detested "globalists" as opposed to "nationalists" like himself.[6]

Exactly six months later, the Chabad of Poway synagogue was the target of another attack, again on Shabbat and again by a White supremacist, John Earnest. One congregant, Lori Kaye, was killed; three others, including the rabbi, were wounded. Later, it was revealed that Earnest had attempted to torch a mosque in Escondido, California, a month earlier. The investigation revealed that he admired Bowers, the perpetrator of the Pittsburgh massacre, and also Brenton Tarrant, another White supremacist who attacked two mosques in Christchurch, New Zealand, in March 2019, killing dozens of Muslim worshipers. And, like Bowers, Earnest was convinced that White people were imperiled and that Jews were a major reason why. In his writing, he claimed to have been inspired not only by Bowers and Tarrant, but also by some Christian religious figures and Adolf Hitler.

In disavowing their son's heinous crime, Earnest's parents stated, "To our great shame, he is now part of the history of

6. "Jew-hatred Keeps Mutating to Survive," *The Economist*, November 3, 2018, https://www.economist.com/international/2018/11/03/jew-hatred-keeps-mutating-to-survive.

evil that has been perpetrated on Jewish people for centuries."[7] The Orthodox Presbyterian Church where Earnest belonged declared, "We deplore and resist all forms of anti-Semitism and racism," adding, "Such hatred has no place in any part of our beliefs or practices."[8]

Four people were killed at a kosher grocery store in Jersey City, New Jersey, on December 29, 2019. But unlike in Pittsburgh and Poway, the two assailants were Black Israelites, who insist they are the authentic Jews and that other Jews are "imposters who inhabited synagogues of Satan." One of the killers, David Anderson, was recorded during the attack as saying, "They [Jews] stole our heritage, they stole our birthright, and they hired these guys to stop us."[9]

A day earlier, a knife-wielding man, Grafton Thomas, entered the Rockland County, New York, home of a Hasidic rabbi during a Hanukkah celebration and stabbed five people before being forced out. One of the wounded, Rabbi Josef Neumann, later died. Thomas was reportedly linked to the Black Israelites and, it was later learned, had searched the internet for "Why did Hitler hate the Jews?"[10]

On January 15, 2022, Malik Faisal Akram, a British citizen whose family originated in Pakistan, entered the United States

7. Doha Madani, "'Our Great Shame': Poway Shooting Suspect's Family Releases Public Apology," *NBC News*, April 29, 2019, https://www.nbcnews.com/news/us-news/our-great-shame-family-poway-shooting-suspect-releases-public-apology-n999731.
8. Zachary R. Keele, "A Public Statement from the OPC on the Shooting at the Chabad Synagogue," *Aquila Report*, May 1, 2019, https://theaquilareport.com/a-public-statement-from-the-opc-on-the-shooting-at-the-chabad-synagogue/.
9. Bruce Golding, "Jersey City Killers' Bomb Could Have Killed People 5 Football Fields Away: Feds," *New York Post*, January 13, 2020, https://nypost.com/2020/01/13/jersey-city-killers-bomb-could-have-killed-people-5-football-fields-away-feds/.
10. "Monsey Stabbing: Journals of Attacker 'REFERENCED Jews'," *BBC News*, December 30, 2019, https://www.bbc.co.uk/news/world-us-canada-50952441.

legally and eventually made his way to Congregation Beth Israel in Colleyville, Texas, during a Shabbat service. Armed with a gun, he took four people hostage. The hostages all survived. Akram was shot by the police, who were alerted to the crisis by a worshiper's 911 call.[11]

In November 2023, Paul Kessler, 69, attended a pro-Israel demonstration in Los Angeles. He was struck by a pro-Palestinian protester, Loay Abdelfattah Alnaji, who was at a nearby rally, and died the next day. Alnaji was charged with involuntary manslaughter.[12]

In October 2024, a Jewish man walking to synagogue in Chicago on Shabbat was shot. The suspect, Sidi Mohammed Abdullahi, is accused of terrorism and a hate crime. "Evidence from the offender's phone indicated he planned the shooting and specifically targeted people of Jewish faith," said Chicago police chief Larry Snelling.[13]

A more complete list would include death threats against Jews; thwarted attempts to target Jewish schools, centers, and synagogues; neo-Nazis marching and chanting in Charlottesville, Virginia, "Jews will not replace us"; numerous street attacks on "identifiable" Jews, most notably in New York; assaults against Jews where the motives were not immediately clear but nonetheless suspicious; and menacing statements by pro-Palestinian individuals or groups for Zionists to get off

11. Jacob Magid, "Hostage: Attacker Chose Synagogue, Thinking Jews Powerful Enough to Free 'Sister'," *The Times of Israel*, January 18, 2022, https://www.timesofisrael.com/hostage-attacker-chose-synagogue-thinking-jews-powerful-enough-to-free-sister/.
12. "Man Accused of Killing Jewish Protester in Thousand Oaks Pleads Not Guilty," *CBS News*, June 11, 2024, https://www.cbsnews.com/losangeles/news/man-accused-of-killing-jewish-protester-in-thousand-oaks-pleads-not-guilty/.
13. Maher Kawash, "Hate Crime, Terrorism Charges Filed in Chicago Shooting of Jewish Man Walking to Synagogue," *ABC 7*, October 31, 2024, https://abc7chicago.com/amp/post/chicago-police-give-update-jewish-man-shot-west-rogers-park-amid-calls-hate-crime-charges-sidi-mohamed-abdallahi/15493546/.

the subway in New York, Jews to identify themselves at a Los Angeles restaurant, or Jewish students to "go back to Germany or Poland" or hearing chants of "Gas the Jews."

In sum, antisemitism in America today is a clear and present danger. It can be lethal, and it comes from multiple sources.

Is there recent data on American Jewish assessments of the threat of antisemitism in the United States?

In its annual survey of American Jews in the fall of 2023, the American Jewish Committee (AJC) reported that 93% of the respondents said antisemitism is "a very serious problem" or "somewhat of a problem."[14] In 2020, the comparable figure was 88%, but those saying it was "a very serious problem" jumped from 37% in 2020 to 53% in 2023.

Eighty-seven percent said antisemitism has increased "a lot" or "somewhat" in the past five years. In 2020, the figure was 82%. Twenty-six percent said that in the previous 12 months they had "avoided publicly wearing, carrying or displaying things that might help identify [them] as a Jew out of fear of antisemitism." In 2020, it was 24%. A similar number acknowledged that they "avoided certain places, events or situations out of concern for [their] safety or comfort as a Jew out of fear of antisemitism."[15]

When asked in the 2023 AJC survey "Do you view the statement, 'Israel has no right to exist' " as antisemitic, 85% said it is antisemitic. In 2020, the result was identical.

More than 60% of respondents said they had seen or heard "antisemitic content (such as comments or posts) online or on

14. American Jewish Committee, "The State of Antisemitism in America 2023: AJC's Survey of American Jews," 2023, https://www.ajc.org/AntisemitismReport2023/AmericanJews.
15. U.S. Department of Justice, "2020 FBI Hate Crimes Statistics," https://www.justice.gov/crs/highlights/2020-hate-crimes-statistics.

social media," the principal platforms mentioned being, in descending order, Facebook, X, YouTube, Instagram, and TikTok.

Separately, the Pew Research Center conducted a comprehensive survey of Jews in the United States and published the findings in 2020. Here is the summary from the Pew report:

> Although in many ways the U.S. Jewish population is flourishing, concerns about anti-Semitism have risen among American Jews. Three-quarters say there is more anti-Semitism in the United States than there was five years ago, and just over half (53%) say that "as a Jewish person in the United States" they feel less safe than they did five years ago. Jews who wear distinctively religious attire, such as a kippa or head covering, are particularly likely to say they feel less safe. But the impact on behavior seems to be limited: Even among those who feel less safe, just one-in-ten—or 5% of all U.S. Jews—report that they have stayed away from a Jewish event or observance as a result.[16]

As background, in 2022 the FBI reported that 55% of all religiously motivated hate crimes which were reported to the law enforcement agency targeted Jews. In other words, a community comprising just over 2% of the American population was the victim of more than half of all such reported crimes. No other faith community—not Catholics, Muslims, Sikhs, Mormons, or others—was even listed in double-digit figures. And these numbers were largely consistent with previous years' data.[17]

16. Pew Research Center, "Jewish Americans in 2020," May 11, 2021, https://www.pewresearch.org/religion/2021/05/11/jewish-americans-in-2020/.
17. "FBI Releases Supplement to the 2021 Hate Crime Statistics," *U.S. Department of Justice*, https://www.justice.gov/archives/crs/highlights/2021-hate-crime-statistics.

Has antisemitism been a factor in contemporary American politics?

To some extent, yes, although, at least until recently, it had been largely taboo in mainstream circles.

Since the Second World War, two presidents, Harry Truman and Richard Nixon, were known to have voiced explicitly antisemitic sentiments, though not in public. And even as they did, their records in office on matters directly affecting the Jewish people were considered positive.

According to David McCullough, author of the Pulitzer Prize–winning biography *Truman*, "In private, Truman was a man who still, out of old habits of the mouth, could use [an antisemitic slur] or, in a letter to his wife, dismiss Miami as nothing but 'hotels, filling stations, Hebrews, and cabins.'"[18] Later, as president, he wrote in his diary, largely as a reaction to Jews pressing for American recognition of Israel, "The Jews have no sense of proportion nor do they have any judgment on world affairs" and "The Jews, I find, are very, very selfish."[19]

Yet the very same Truman, as a senator from Missouri, was outspoken during the war in calling attention to the plight of the Jews in Nazi-occupied Europe and, as president, in ignoring the opposition of his State Department to recognize the newly reborn nation of Israel in May 1948. As a former president, he spoke out against antisemitism. A May 12, 1964, headline from the *New York Times* read, "Truman Cautions on Anti-Semitism: Calls It Challenge as Grave as Equality for Negroes."

Nixon, again in private but recorded on White House tapes, had some harsh things to say about Jews. For example, in conversations with his chief of staff, Bob Haldeman, he said, "The Jews are all over the government" and "But, Bob,

18. David McCullough, *Truman* (Simon Schuster, 1992), 286.
19. Harry S. Truman, "Truman Diary Entry Disparages Jews," Jewish Virtual Library, July 21, 1947, https://www.jewishvirtuallibrary.org/truman-diary-entry-disparages-jews.

generally speaking, you can't trust the bastards [the Jews]. They turn on you. Am I wrong or right?," though he made exceptions, he said, for some of his key staff, including his national security advisor, Henry Kissinger.[20]

Nonetheless, it was Nixon who made the fateful decision in October 1973 to resupply Israel's military during the extended Yom Kippur War, helping Jerusalem turn the tide of battle and defeat the aggressors, Egypt and Syria.

A third president, Donald Trump, prompted some Jews to question whether he harbored antisemitic prejudices. Trump supporters vehemently rejected the accusation, citing his consistent support for Israel as president, as well as his own Jewish family members, including his daughter Ivanka. Critics cited his comments after the 2017 White nationalist march in Charlottesville, Virginia, and his postpresidency dinner in 2022, with Kanye West and Nick Fuentes, both of whom have expressed virulently antisemitic views.

In Congress, extreme voices in both parties have said and done things widely regarded as antisemitic.

In the Democratic Party, perhaps the most egregious cases involved Ilhan Omar, a representative from Minnesota. Prior to being elected, in 2012 she tweeted, "Israel has hypnotized the world, may Allah awaken the people and help them see the evil doings of Israel."[21] And after her election to Congress, in 2019 she tweeted about "the Benjamin's baby," referring to what she implied was a Jewish, pro-Israel effort to buy influence in Washington.

That led to her apology and an effort to censure Omar in the House of Representatives, while President Trump called

20. Miller Center, "Richard Nixon and H. R. 'Bob' Haldeman on 3 July 1971," Presidential Recordings Program, accessed April 22, 2025, https://prde.upress.virginia.edu/conversations/4006745.
21. Reuters, "Fact Check: Trump Quoted Ilhan Omar Tweet Saying 'Israel Hypnotized the World,'" October 12, 2023, https://www.reuters.com/fact-check/trump-quoted-ilhan-omar-tweet-saying-israel-hypnotized-world-2023-10-12/.

her an "anti-Semite." By the time the nonbinding House legislation was finally adopted in March 2019, the text was so broadened to include "Islamophobia, racism and other forms of bigotry," and so nonspecific about culprits, that Omar herself voted in favor. But in 2024, visiting Barnard College, where her daughter was a student, she again raised eyebrows when she said: "I think it is really unfortunate that people don't care about the fact that all Jewish kids should be kept safe and that we should not have to tolerate antisemitism or bigotry for all Jewish students, whether they are pro-genocide or anti-genocide."[22] That led some Jewish leaders, including Jonathan Greenblatt of the Anti-Defamation League, to accuse Omar of spreading a modern-day blood libel by suggesting that any Jews who support Israel are, in her formulation, endorsing genocide.

Another Democrat in Congress who aroused concern was Rashida Tlaib of Michigan. A Jewish group, StopAntisemitism, named her the 2023 "Antisemite of the Year." The group's executive director, Liora Rez, commented: "Rep. Tlaib's well-earned title reflects a long history of antisemitism, but her statements in the wake of Hamas's October 7 attacks were particularly unconscionable. Tlaib not only victim-blamed Israel, but she also accused it of committing genocide against the Palestinians and continues to defend calls to ethnically cleanse Israel of Jews and genocide."[23] And Congresswoman Cori Bush, a Democrat from St. Louis who was defeated in a 2024 primary contest, triggered an angry letter, dated November 1, 2023, from 30 local Jewish organizations that read in part: "To accuse Israel of ethnic cleansing as it seeks to defend itself and

22. Mychael Schnell, "Nebraska Republican Introduces Resolution to Censure Ilhan Omar," *The Hill*, May 7, 2024, https://thehill.com/homenews/4648913-ilhan-omar-censure-resolution/.

23. *Jerusalem Post*, "Rashida Tlaib Crowned 'Antisemite of the Year' 2023 by StopAntisemitism," January 9, 2024, https://www.jpost.com/diaspora/antisemitism/article-781331.

locate hundreds of hostages still held captive in Gaza—taken only because they were assumed to be Jews—is sickening, The 60,000 Jewish members of the St. Louis community deserve an apology for her lack of decency, disregard for history, and for intentionally fueling antisemitism and hatred, especially at a time when law enforcement in America is recording an all-time high in violent attacks against Jews."[24]

On the Republican side of the aisle, there were also positions and statements that sparked concern.

Marjorie Taylor Greene, a congresswoman from Georgia, claimed, in her first term in office, that the 2018 California wildfires were the result of a space laser controlled by a corporate cabal, including the Rothschild family—a name that over the centuries has been repeatedly invoked by antisemitic conspiracy mongers, mostly regarding financial allegations but, more recently, it seems, climate accusations as well.[25]

Apropos, in March 2018, an elected member of the Council of the District of Columbia, Trayon White Sr., declared in a Facebook video, "Man, it just started snowing out of nowhere this morning, man. Y'all better pay attention to this climate control, man, this climate manipulation. And D.C. keep talking about, 'We a resilient city.' And that's a model based off the Rothschilds controlling the climate to create natural disasters they can pay for to own the cities, man. Be careful."[26]

24. Jewish Federation of St. Louis, "Statement from the Jewish Community of St. Louis," November 1, 2023, https://www.jfedstl.org/2023/11/01/statement-from-the-jewish-community-of-st-louis/.
25. Jonathan Chait, "Marjorie Taylor Greene Blamed Wildfires on Secret Jewish Space Laser," *Intelligencer*, January 28, 2021, https://nymag.com/intelligencer/article/marjorie-taylor-greene-qanon-wildfires-space-laser-rothschild-execute.html.
26. BBC News, "Lawmaker Sorry for Spreading Anti-Semitic Weather Conspiracy," March 19, 2018, https://www.bbc.co.uk/news/world-us-canada-43460263.

Greene also shared a video propagating the myth of the "Great Replacement Theory," namely, that Jews are responsible for seeking to import millions of non-White people to replace native White populations to commit "the biggest genocide in history."

Congressman Paul Gosar, a Republican from Arizona, has been accused of associating with Nick Fuentes, the White supremacist who dined with President Trump. Fuentes has complimented Hitler, belittled the Holocaust, and called Jews "evildoers." Gosar also spoke at Fuentes's America First Political Action Conference.[27]

In the same vein, Steve King, a Republican member of Congress from Iowa who served from 2003 to 2021, was identified with White nationalist ideologies that marginalized and denigrated minority groups; sought out kindred spirits in Europe, including leaders of Austria's Freedom Party, a group that evokes memories of the country's Nazi past; and endorsed a mayoral candidate in Toronto who embraced the "Fourteen Words," a neo-Nazi slogan to protect "the future for white children" and "the beauty of the white Aryan woman."[28]

What explains the dramatic surge in antisemitism on U.S. university campuses, particularly since October 7, 2023?

The question itself is in dispute. Some would argue that it is not antisemitism but anti-Zionism that has erupted on a number of American campuses, even noting that a certain number of the demonstrators identify as Jews. And they strenuously distinguish between antisemitism, which they insist they reject,

27. "AFPAC III: Elected Officials Support White Supremacist Event," *Anti-Defamation League*, February 27, 2022, https://www.adl.org/resources/article/afpac-iii-elected-officials-support-white-supremacist-event.
28. "Letter to House Leaders Regarding Rep. Steve King," *Anti-Defamation League*, January 14, 2019, https://www.adl.org/resources/letter/letter-house-leaders-regarding-rep-steve-king.

and anti-Zionism. Illustrative of this view is Benjamin Moser, writing in the *Washington Post* in January 2024, who said that some Jews like himself reject "the idea of ethnic nationalism." It is the concept of Jewish statehood he rejects, while embracing a "commitment to universalism."[29] Others counter that the two cannot be separated. Cary Nelson, professor emeritus of English at the University of Illinois, commented, "Anti-Zionism suffered a huge wound on October 7. We need to understand antisemitism differently. Anti-Zionism and antisemitism have completely fused."[30]

This second group also asserts that chants on campuses calling for the end of Israel and a global intifada—"From the river to the sea, Palestine will be free," "Globalize the intifada," "Khaybar, Khaybar, oh Jews, the army of Mohammed will return"—threaten Jews everywhere. (According to the 2024 AJC survey of American Jews, at least 85% of the respondents identify as Zionists.)

Those who have sounded the alarm on surging antisemitism on American campuses, most notably since October 7, 2023, cite the following factors as possible explanations for what has been happening on campuses for many years—and, they would add, which too often have been neglected or downplayed by university administrators.

First, foreign funding. The Institute for the Study of Global Antisemitism and Policy (ISGAP) launched a "follow the money" project several years ago and has since issued a series of reports about Qatar as the principal overseas donor to American higher education.

Why, ISGAP asks, would Qatar, a tiny nation of barely 350,000 citizens, thousands of miles from America's shores,

29. Benjamin Moser, "Opinion: Anti-Zionism Isn't the Same as Antisemitism. Here's the History," *Washington Post*, January 2, 2024, https://www.washingtonpost.com/opinions/2024/01/02/anti-zionism-antisemitism-israel-jews-came-first/.
30. Jewish Broadcasting Service, "The ISGAP Hour," July 2024.

be donating billions of dollars to these universities? ISGAP's answer? To play the long game and ever so subtly promote hatred of Jews, Israel, and Zionism in American classrooms, while generating sympathy for political Islam and the Muslim Brotherhood, to which Qatar's leaders have given a *baya*, a spiritual oath. Hamas is an offshoot of the Muslim Brotherhood, which calls for a world without Israel and Jews and sees America as evil. Some of the top Hamas leaders live openly in Qatar.

Moreover, the U.S. director of national intelligence, Avril Haines, dropped a bombshell in July 2024: "In recent weeks, Iranian government actors have sought to opportunistically take advantage of ongoing protests regarding the war in Gaza, using a playbook we've seen other actors use over the years. We have observed actors tied to Iran's government posing as activists online, seeking to encourage protests, and even providing financial support to protesters."[31]

Further to the role of outsiders, at a press conference on May 1, 2024, about the protesters at Columbia University, New York mayor Eric Adams commented, "Outside agitators were on their [Columbia's] grounds, training and really co-opting this movement," a charge rejected outright by campus activists.[32]

And the efforts of increasingly well-organized and, it would appear, well-funded organizations like the National Students for Justice in Palestine and its hundreds of campus affiliates

31. Office of the Director of National Intelligence, "Statement from Director of National Intelligence Avril Haines on Recent Iranian Influence Efforts," July 9, 2024, https://www.dni.gov/index.php/newsroom/press-releases/press-releases-2024/3842-statement-from-director-of-national-intelligence-avril-haines-on-recent-iranian-influence-efforts.
32. City of New York, "Transcript: Mayor Eric Adams Briefs Media on Recent Protests at Columbia University with NYPD Commissioner Caban," May 1, 2024, https://www.nyc.gov/office-of-the-mayor/news/337-24/transcript-mayor-eric-adams-briefs-media-recent-protests-columbia-university-nypd.

must be taken into account. According to ISGAP research, these groups "are at the forefront of this ideological warfare on campus, coordinating student organizations, working with radical faculty, and distributing propaganda on campus" which "denies the right of Jewish self-determination (in other words, the right of Israel to exist in any form), diminishes and, at times, denies the Holocaust, and supports global *intifada* (violent resistance) against Jews and Israel."[33]

Second, they argue that expansive Diversity, Equity and Inclusion (DEI) programs on American campuses tend to promote a dichotomous worldview along the lines of race, power, and privilege.[34] Since the advent of the second Trump administration, which has targeted DEI initiatives on campuses and elsewhere, some universities are reportedly reviewing and curtailing their programs or, at a minimum, renaming them. They point out the irony that Jews, who the far right sees as non-White, even as polluters of the White population, are sometimes regarded as quintessential White people—"privileged," "domineering," "all-powerful"—in the DEI construct. As a consequence, Jews have not merited particular attention, much less understanding and sympathy, when they claim bias and fear for their safety.

33. Institute for the Study of Global Antisemitism and Policy, "National Students for Justice in Palestine (NSJP): Antisemitism, Anti-Americanism, Violent Extremism and the Threat to North American Universities," 2024, https://isgap.org/wp-content/uploads/2024/06/SJP_Report.pdf.
34. At the University of Michigan, for example, there were reportedly 241 staff in 2023 focused exclusively on DEI and operating with an annual budget exceeding $30 million. Steven McGuire, "How One College Spends More Than $30M on 241 DEI Staffers . . . and the Damage It Does to Kids," *New York Post*, January 11, 2024, https://nypost.com/2024/01/11/opinion/dei-boondoggle-costs-us-millions-and-harms-students-it-claims-to-help/; see also Nicholas Confessore, "The University of Michigan Doubled Down on D.E.I. What Went Wrong?," *New York Times*, October 16, 2024, https://www.nytimes.com/2024/10/16/magazine/dei-university-michigan.html.

Former Harvard University president Larry Summers, speaking at a Jewish event on campus in November 2023, stated:

> [W]ith few exceptions, those most directly charged with confronting prejudice—Offices of Diversity, Equity, and Inclusion—have failed to stand with Israeli and Jewish students confronting the oldest prejudice of them all.
>
> And there may even have been cases where they did more to support the prejudiced than victims. Ideologies arising out of identity politics have too often had the effect of driving discrimination against groups whose members have been most committed to the values of rigorous study and intellectual inquiry.[35]

Third, with only a few exceptions to date, universities tend to attract faculty, especially in the humanities and social sciences, who position themselves on the liberal/progressive side of the political spectrum. As an illustration, the *Harvard Crimson*'s[36] 2022 survey of Harvard's Faculty of Arts and Sciences revealed that more than 80% described themselves as "liberal" or "very liberal," while 1% described themselves as "conservative." (By contrast, in a 2023 Gallup national survey of Americans generally, 33% described themselves as "liberal" on social issues, while 32% said they were "conservative.")[37]

35. Larry Summers, "Reflections on Antisemitism and the University," November 13, 2023, https://larrysummers.com/2023/11/13/reflections-on-antisemitism-and-the-university/#:~:text=And%20there%20may%20even%20have,rigorous%20study%20and%20intellectual%20inquiry.
36. Meimei Xu, "More than 80 Percent of Surveyed Harvard Faculty Identify as Liberal," *The Harvard Crimson*, July 13, 2022, https://www.thecrimson.com/article/2022/7/13/faculty-survey-political-leaning/.
37. Justin McCarthy, "Increase in Liberal Views Brings Ideological Parity on Social Issues," *Gallup*, June 10, 2024, https://news.gallup.com/

In particular, certain Middle East Studies departments have been dominated by faculty members hostile to Israel and Zionism. Columbia University is often mentioned in this context.[38]

When Hamas invaded Israel on October 7, 2023, the reaction of a few faculty members, whether at Columbia, Cornell, Yale, or other elite institutions, was borderline ecstasy. Illustrative were the comments of Zareena Grewal, an associate professor at Yale: "Israel is a murderous, genocidal settler state, and Palestinians have every right to resist through armed struggle, solidarity. . . . It's been such an extraordinary day."[39] Meanwhile, a Stanford University lecturer, Ameer Loggins, reportedly asked Jewish and Israeli students in his classroom to identify themselves, then separated these students from the others, to lecture on Israel as a "colonizer." And a professor at Columbia University, Joseph Massad, described the Hamas invasion as "astonishing," "astounding," and "awesome," while a Cornell professor, Russell Rickford, declared on October 15, 2023, that he was "exhilarated" by the Hamas invasion of Israel.[40]

poll/645776/increase-liberal-views-brings-ideological-parity-social-issues.aspx.

38. Committee on Education and the Workforce Letter, February 12, 2024, https://edworkforce.house.gov/uploadedfiles/2-12-24_foxx_letter_to_columbia_university.pdf.
39. Nikolas Lanum, "Yale Professor Urged to Resign for 'Vile' Comments about Hamas Attacks on Israel: 'Settlers Are Not Civilians,'" *Fox News*, October 12, 2023, https://www.foxnews.com/media/yale-professor-vile-comments-hamas-attacks-israel-settlers-not-civilians.
40. Stephanie Saul, "Who Are the Columbia Professors Mentioned in the House Hearing?" *The New York Times*, April 17, 2024, https://www.nytimes.com/2024/04/17/nyregion/jospeh-massad-katherine-franke-mohamed-abdou-columbia-university.html; Gabriel Munoz and Julia Senzon, "Rickford's Controversial Remarks Spark Divisions on Campus," *The Cornell Daily Sun*, October 24, 2023, https://www.cornellsun.com/article/2023/10/rickfords-controversial-remarks-spark-divisions-on-campus.

The fraught atmosphere on some campuses led a few Jewish students to file lawsuits, claiming they no longer felt safe and protected as Jews at their schools. In one such lawsuit, two MIT students alleged, "As a result of MIT's blatant and intentional disregard for its legal and contractual obligations to its students, plaintiffs and other students have suffered injury to themselves and their educational experience. Jewish and Israeli students at MIT have felt unsafe attending classes, have in some instances deferred graduation dates or exams, and some professors have left the university."[41] In another lawsuit, claiming that Penn violated Title VI of the 1964 Civil Rights Act, one of the three students filing the case stated, "I have seen and heard first-hand reports of individuals in the encampment, including students, committing acts of violence, intimidating and harassing Jewish students and faculty members, and inciting others to do the same."[42]

On December 7, 2023, the House Committee on Education and the Workforce held a hearing regarding antisemitism on campuses. Presidents Claudine Gay of Harvard and Liz Magill of the University of Pennsylvania were criticized for weak responses when questioned how they would handle calls for genocide against Jews on campus. Magill subsequently resigned, as did Gay, who, separate from the hearing, also faced allegations of plagiarism in her academic work.

Eleven months later, the House committee's chair, Virginia Foxx, a Republican from North Carolina, summed up a yearlong investigation of campus antisemitism: "What we discovered was a massive, systematic failure by university

41. *Times of Israel,* "New Lawsuit against MIT Accuses University of Allowing Antisemitism on Campus," March 7, 2024, https://www.timesofisrael.com/liveblog_entry/new-lawsuit-against-mit-accuses-university-of-allowing-antisemitism-on-campus/.
42. Emily Scolnick, "Students Suing Penn over Antisemitism Response Allege 'Hostility' from Encampment in New Filing," *Daily Pennsylvanian,* May 7, 2024, https://www.thedp.com/article/2024/05/penn-lawsuit-antisemitism-new-declarations-encampment.

administrators to respond to the antisemitic displays roiling their campuses."[43]

In all, according to ISGAP, the U.S. Department of Education has launched approximately 100 investigations of violations of Jewish student rights as of July 2024 under Title VI of the Civil Rights Act.

And, finally, some concerned about the campus situation have pointed to declining numbers of Jews on "elite" campuses, suggesting that Jews have less of a voice and are of less interest because they purportedly no longer represent the kind of diversity universities seek. They contrast this with the golden era of Jewish representation on campuses between 1970 and 2010. With the exception of Brown and Dartmouth, for instance, Jewish student enrollment in the other six Ivy League schools has dropped quite precipitously. At Penn, according to one dean, Jewish enrollment plummeted from an estimated 30% of the student body two decades ago to approximately 12–14% in 2024.

Why have some Jewish organizations felt disappointed that partners in other minority communities failed to speak up in the face of growing antisemitism?

For decades, one of the programmatic pillars of national and local Jewish organizations has been promoting intergroup dialogue and cooperation.

The rationales were twofold. First, in the Jewish tradition it is incumbent to reach out to other minority communities that are disadvantaged or victims of discrimination.

Many Jewish ethical teachings—"We are all created in God's image," "Justice, justice, shalt thou pursue," "We were

43. Virginia Foxx, "These So-Called Elite Universities Have a Glaring Antisemitism Problem," *New York Post*, October 31, 2024, https://nypost.com/2024/10/31/opinion/these-so-called-elite-universities-have-a-glaring-antisemitism-problem/.

once strangers in the land of Egypt," "For the sake of the betterment of society," "If I am not for myself, who will be for me? If I am only for myself, what am I? And if not know, when?," "Love your neighbor as yourself," and "And what does the Lord require of you? To act justly and to love mercy and to walk humbly with your God"—are grounded in a universalist outlook.

These were interpreted as mandating Jewish outreach to others in the spirit of *tikkun olam*, the repair of the world. In practical terms, this meant that, for well over a century, Jewish organizations have been on the front lines of human rights, civil rights, and social justice campaigns to help fulfill the promise of America for all its inhabitants. They have done this while, for many overlapping decades, still struggling to ensure equality of opportunity for, and full integration of, Jews in American society.

Whether in the quest for racial equality, a welcoming and nondiscriminatory immigration policy, generous quotas for refugees, the women's liberation movement, full inclusion of the LGBTQ community, opposition to xenophobia and social hierarchies, or the campaign to open up executive suites, higher education, and elected office to all, the Jewish role in civil rights and social justice movements has been of long standing, prominent, significant, and, at times, fraught with risk. As a notable example, two Jews, Andrew Goodman and Michael Schwerner, were murdered alongside James Cheney, an African American, in Mississippi in 1964 for their efforts to register African Americans to vote. This tragedy was the theme of a popular 1988 film, *Mississippi Burning*.

This outreach was closely coupled with a natural instinct to build alliances with other minority communities, leveraging the voice and impact of all involved. Jews marched with Dr. Martin Luther King Jr. in pursuit of racial justice. Dr. King stood with Jews in support of Israel. And there was much to show for these collaborative efforts.

It is against this decades-long backdrop that many Jews felt disappointed after the Hamas invasion of October 7, 2023, that so many one-time partners did not reach out, did not join in condemnation, and did not march in solidarity with the Jewish community. Was it because the Israeli-Palestinian conflict had become "racialized" in the minds of some, casting Palestinians as the beleaguered "community of color" and Israelis, however mistakenly, as the all-powerful supremacists? Or was it perhaps a simple reluctance to choose sides between competing minority communities? Or was it because the Israeli government of the day, led by a right-wing coalition, alienated some otherwise potential allies?

The bottom line was sadness and dismay in the mainstream Jewish community. It ran deep. Yes, there were notable exceptions to the overall silence and indifference from one-time allies, but not nearly enough to overcome a sense of abandonment at a difficult time for the Jewish community.

Is there more that government can do to address antisemitism?

Inasmuch as antisemitism is increasing, existing strategies, by definition, are insufficient, either in conception or implementation or both. To repeat an earlier point, according to the FBI, year after year more than half of all religiously motivated hate crimes in the United States target Jews, who comprise approximately 2% of the population. There is, therefore, a need to consider a centralized, high-level, interdepartmental government response to coordinate, monitor, and evaluate existing policies and consider new ideas and initiatives.

Government leaders must be quick and unequivocal in their condemnation of antisemitism. When warranted, visits to targeted sites and consultations with affected individuals have both symbolic and substantive value. And on such occasions, the specificity of antisemitism, as opposed to more generalized references to hatred and bigotry, needs to be emphasized as a threat both to Jews and to core American values.

Freedom of speech is a sacrosanct, constitutionally protected right in the United States. But when it is potentially used to incite violence, such as "Globalize the intifada," "Resistance by any means necessary," or "Zionists don't deserve to live," does this still fall under the rubric of protected speech?

Ought there to be consequences for those from overseas on student visas in the United States who promote antisemitism on campus and target Jewish students—in violation of hate crimes law or university codes of conduct?

When universities fail to fulfill their obligations to prohibit discrimination, including of Jewish students, under Title VI of the Civil Rights Act of 1964, should government use its power, including of the purse since federal funds flow to many institutions of higher learning, to punish those in violation?

Government could also be actively monitoring overseas attempts to promote antisemitism in the United States, starting with the educational system. Section 117 of the Higher Education Act requires American colleges and universities to report semi-annually to the Department of Education any foreign gift of $250,000 or more. In reality, as ISGAP[44] has pointed out, many institutions do not file these reports, and government follow-up appears episodic at best.

The U.S. Department of State has designated Hamas and Hezbollah foreign terrorist organizations since 1997. Yet their flags have been seen on several American campuses and in the streets, while some protest leaders have publicly declared, "We are Hamas," particularly since October 7, 2023. Should there be consequences for associating with listed terrorist groups?

The Department of State has the responsibility to monitor antisemitism abroad. There may be little it can practically do, other than shine a spotlight to persuade hostile nations like Iran to stop the promotion of antisemitism. But when it comes

44. "Qatar and the Muslim Brotherhood Funding of Higher Education in the United States," *ISGAP*, https://isgap.org/follow-the-money/.

to countries more closely linked to the United States, such as Qatar, are more diplomatic opportunities available?

And Congress, ideally always in bipartisan fashion, can continue to hold hearings when needed on antisemitism that (1) scrutinize university policies and, where appropriate, grades K–12 policies as well; (2) offer a platform to the voices of affected Jewish students; (3) explore funding sources and possible overseas links of antisemitic groups; and (4) press social media platforms on their standards regarding content review and dissemination of antisemitic material.

What has been the experience of antisemitism in Canada, home to the world's fourth largest Jewish community?

This is a robust community that felt very much at home in Canada and participated in virtually every aspect of Canadian life. While some university groups agitated against Israel over the years, by and large the community as a whole looked to the future with confidence.

That changed in 2023–24, when vehemently anti-Israel, pro-Hamas university encampments surfaced. Many Jews on campuses felt vulnerable and threatened. The far left and jihadists forged a red-green alliance, as it is called. Parliament adopted a nonbinding resolution, initiated by the left-wing New Democratic Party, to ban arms sales to Israel in the middle of a Hamas-triggered war. Jews felt less safe in their synagogues and schools. And the School Board in Toronto, Canada's largest city, adopted a highly controversial initiative of the Arab-Canadian Lawyers Association to introduce the concept of "anti-Palestinian racism" in its "Combating Hate and Racism Learning Strategy."

B'nai B'rith Canada reported that 2023 set a record for incidents, 5,791 in total, doubling the previous high in 2021. Moreover, the number of violent incidents tripled from the previous year. Doubtless, the actual numbers are even higher, as experience has shown that some incidents go unreported in many countries.

According to the Canadian Broadcasting Corporation, "The incidents the group [B'nai B'rith] says it recorded include the firebombing of a synagogue and Jewish community centre in Montreal, eggs being thrown at a Holocaust Memorial Monument in Calgary, a Jewish student being assaulted in an antisemitic attack in [British Columbia's] Lower Mainland and a rise in antisemitic graffiti in public places involving messages such as 'Kill the Jews.'" Plus, B'nai B'rith cited the widespread dissemination of Jew-hatred online, including the use of artificial intelligence "to create antisemitic propaganda and materials," and said the vitriolic hate was coming from the far right, far left, and "those acting at the behest of foreign actors."[45]

The Canadian government noted in a 2023 fact sheet, "Despite representing less than 1% of the Canadian population, Jews are the religious group in Canada most likely to be targeted for hate crimes." It added:

> Antisemitism continues to persist in Canada, manifesting itself through:
> - Vandalism and graffiti
> - Circulation of hate propaganda
> - Intolerant and racist language in places like Twitter, in comments sections, web forums and blogs
> - Bomb threats to Jewish schools and community centers
> - Intimidation of Jewish university students; and
> - The use of the Boycott, Divestment and Sanctions (BDS) movement to delegitimize the State of Israel.[46]

45. Peter Zimonjic, "Number of Antisemitic Incidents Reached Record High in 2023, Says B'nai Brith Canada Audit," *CBC News*, May 6, 2024, https://www.cbc.ca/news/politics/bnai-brith-antisemitic-report-record-high-1.7195197.
46. Government of Canada, "Factsheet—Antisemitism in Canada," October 7, 2022, https://www.canada.ca/en/canadian-heritage/corporate/transparency/open-government/standing-committee/ahmed-hussen-pch-contract-cmac/antisemitism-canada.html.

Announcing a new special advisor on Jewish community relations and antisemitism in July 2024, Prime Minister Justin Trudeau said, "We stand with Jewish Canadians—today and every day. And we will do whatever it takes to fight antisemitism and hate, which is unfortunately too prevalent in our communities. With Mr. Housefather's appointment, we're continuing to make sure Jewish Canadians' voices are heard, protecting Jewish Canadian communities, and making Canada more inclusive for everyone."[47] The new special advisor, Anthony Housefather, said, "There has been no time in my lifetime when Jewish Canadians have felt as threatened as they do today. While we cannot make antisemitism disappear, all levels of government, universities, and police can take concrete steps to make Jewish Canadians feel safer in this country."[48]

Meanwhile, the leader of the Conservative Party opposition in the Canadian Parliament, Pierre Poilievre, posted on X in July 2024, "We cannot close our eyes to the disgusting acts of antisemitism that are happening in our country everyday."[49]

Parliament, once virtually united in support of the Canada-Israel link, has witnessed a growing divide since October 7, 2023, with the center-right overwhelmingly siding with Israel and the center-left and far left more critical.

The legislative body as a whole made a serious mistake in 2023 that attracted global attention. At the invitation of the Speaker, Anthony Hota, an elderly Ukrainian Canadian,

47. Prime Minister of Canada Justin Trudeau, "Prime Minister Announces New Special Advisor on Jewish Community Relations and Antisemitism," July 5, 2024, https://www.pm.gc.ca/en/news/news-releases/2024/07/05/prime-minister-announces-new-special-advisor-jewish-community.
48. Holly Cabrera, "MP Housefather Appointed to New Role Fighting Antisemitism," *CBC News*, July 5, 2024, https://www.cbc.ca/news/politics/anthony-housefather-special-adviser-antisemitism-jewish-1.7255458.
49. @PierrePoilievre, X, July 2, 2024, https://x.com/PierrePoilievre/status/1808137205317025922?lang=en.

Yaroslav Hunka, was introduced in Parliament as a "war hero" and received a standing ovation from all present. It turned out, however, that he had served in a Nazi SS unit. The Speaker subsequently resigned after the truth emerged.

On a different note, Parliament held hearings in May 2024 on campus antisemitism, at which the leaders of four of Canada's most prominent universities acknowledged that it is a "significant problem" and noted that balancing the right of free speech with the need for campus safety for all is an ongoing dilemma.[50]

And, in another challenge for the Canadian Jewish community that has perhaps become emblematic of the worsening situation, media coverage focused on two children in Toronto who, according to their mother, Adi Cohen, had been the victims of "repeated bullying and antisemitic threats" that began before October 7, 2023, and intensified after. This prompted a community-wide effort to accompany the children to school as an act of solidarity and protection.[51]

As in the neighboring United States, in Canada Jewish optimism relies on the belief that resilient liberal democratic values will eventually triumph and restore the status quo ante, while the pessimists point to a changing political landscape, seismic demographic shifts, and the immense power of social media as pulling in the opposite direction.

The experience of Australia's Jewish community, the world's ninth largest, is quite similar to Canada's. Until recently, Jews overwhelmingly felt secure and confident in one of the great liberal democracies, but concern has grown in Australia as

50. "Standing Committee on Justice and Human Rights," *House of Commons Canada*, May 27, 2024, https://www.ourcommons.ca/Content/Committee/441/JUST/Evidence/EV13127317/JUSTEV106-E.PDF.

51. "'Community Support Walk' Held for Bullied Jewish Student at Toronto School," *National Post*, May 17, 2024, https://nationalpost.com/news/community-support-walk-held-for-bullied-jewish-student-at-toronto-school.

antisemitism has skyrocketed.[52] According to the Executive Council of Australian Jewry, 2,062 anti-Jewish incidents (excluding on social media) took place between October 2023 and September 2024, compared to 495 the year before.[53]

How has antisemitism affected Jewish communities in Latin America?

Jews first settled in Latin America in the 16th century, fleeing the Catholic Inquisitions in Spain and Portugal. They were followed by successive waves of immigrants, especially in the late 19th and 20th centuries, including those who managed to arrive either before or after the Second World War. While the majority were Ashkenazi Jews from Central and Eastern Europe, a sizable number came from Sephardic communities in the Iberian Peninsula, Balkans, and Middle East.

Today the total Jewish population in Latin America is estimated at 400,000 to 450,000, the largest communities being in Argentina, Brazil, and Mexico, and smaller ones in almost every other country in the region. While it is impossible to generalize about this vast space, it is fair to say that antisemitism rarely took a violent form. Rather, when it surfaced, it tended to be in the religious and social realms—by and large, though, without inhibiting the growth and development of Jewish community life.

In the postwar era, there have been three main areas of concern. First, in the years immediately following the Second World War, and often with the help of the "ratlines" (in German,

52. Ellie Grant, "Incidents of Antisemitism in Australia Skyrocket in the Wake of War in Gaza," *Jewish Chronicle*, May 31, 2024, https://www.thejc.com/news/world/australian-antisemitism-skyrockets-in-the-wake-of-war-in-gaza-plcvkuqg.
53. Zev Stub, "Anti-Jewish Attacks in Australia Quadrupled after October 7, Report Finds," *Times of Israel*, December 1, 2024, https://www.timesofisrael.com/anti-jewish-attacks-in-australia-quadrupled-after-october-7-report-finds/.

Rattenlinien), including the assistance of Catholic bishop Alois Hudal, an Austrian-born Nazi sympathizer, a number of Nazis resettled in Latin America, notably in Argentina, Bolivia, Brazil, Chile, and Paraguay. They included the infamous Adolf Eichmann, the chief functionary for the Nazi Final Solution. Israeli intelligence found him in 1960, living in Argentina under the name Ricardo Klement. They seized and took Eichmann to Israel clandestinely, as the Argentine authorities would have opposed his extradition. They put him on trial and, in the only judicial case in Israel's history where a death sentence was imposed, executed him in 1962. Meanwhile, Josef Mengele, the Nazi doctor who performed ghoulish medical experiments on Jewish inmates in Auschwitz, reportedly lived out his postwar life in Argentina, Paraguay, and Brazil, where he died in 1979. Others established pro-Nazi German colonies or networks in Brazil, Chile, and elsewhere.

Second, some Latin American nations have experienced wild political gyrations, whether between left and right or between dictatorship and democracy, or both. Those twists and turns were problematic for many, including Jews.

Earlier, it was the right-wing repression in Argentina, Chile, and Uruguay in which a number of Jews were targeted or forced into exile. More recently, in Venezuela, Nicaragua, Chile, and Colombia, there have been left-wing forces profoundly hostile to Israel and its supporters, which include overwhelming majorities of the local Jewish communities (and, it should be noted, sizable evangelical populations in many Latin American countries). Plus, these self-defined left-wing governments that brand "capitalists" or "the wealthy" as "enemies of the state" give Jews good reason for concern, whether or not they are successful capitalists or well to do.

In Venezuela, the Jewish community of 25,000 has dwindled to 5,000 to 6,000 in the span of 20 years due to the country's economic collapse. At the same time, the country has strengthened alliances with Iran and its proxies, including Hezbollah. Even so, the Venezuelan chief rabbi, Isaac Cohen, told the *Times of*

Israel in 2021 that for the Venezuelan people, as opposed to any particular regime, "there is no such thing as an antisemitic culture."[54]

In Chile, the Jewish community increasingly faces a two-pronged challenge. The first is a government which has moved sharply to the left since Gabriel Boric took office, in 2022, as president and became one of Israel's most implacable and outspoken foes. Moreover, Chile is home to what is described as the largest Palestinian diaspora outside the Middle East. Despite the fact that it is largely Christian and fourth generation, it has become increasingly radicalized on Middle East issues, while enjoying significant political, financial, and electoral impact nationwide.

And third, even as violence against Latin American Jews is rare, especially compared to rates in Europe and the Middle East, a few deadly events have cast a long shadow on the communities.

As noted earlier, on July 18, 1994, the AMIA headquarters, the nerve center of Jewish life in Buenos Aires, was destroyed by a bomb. Eighty-five people were murdered, 300 wounded. It was the deadliest attack against a Jewish target since the Holocaust and perhaps the worst act of terrorism in modern Latin American history. In the subsequent government investigations, which took years and in some ways are still ongoing three decades later, it was established that Iran was responsible for organizing the attack, while its affiliate, Hezbollah, carried it out. Two years earlier, the Israeli embassy in Buenos Aires was the target of a terrorist attack from the same sources. The death toll was 29; another 100 were injured.

The day after the car bombing at the AMIA building, July 19, 1994, there was a midair explosion on a domestic flight from

54. Orge Castellano, "Venezuela's Tight-Knit Jewish Community Is Still Mourning Its Surfside Victims," *Times of Israel*, October 18, 2021, https://www.timesofisrael.com/venezuelas-tight-knit-jewish-community-is-still-mourning-its-surfside-victims/.

Colon to Panama City, Panama. All 21 people on board, including 12 Jewish businessmen who were regular passengers on this route, were killed. After extensive investigations by Panamanian authorities, assisted by the United States and Israel, Hezbollah was held responsible.[55]

On a more positive note, in mid-July 2024, for the first time in the history of Mexico, a Jew and a woman, Claudia Sheinbaum, was elected the country's president. While she has not been connected to the vibrant Mexican Jewish community, her election shatters another social barrier, or glass ceiling, in the region. And the libertarian president of Argentina, Javier Milei, though not Jewish, has spoken often and very publicly about the influence of the Jewish faith on his life and outlook. As the *New York Times* reported in July 2024, he "regularly studies the Torah, attends Shabbat dinner and has said that perhaps his most important adviser is his rabbi."[56]

55. *Times of Israel*, "US Offers $5M Reward for Info on 1994 Panama Plane Bombing Blamed on Hezbollah," October 30, 2024, https://www.timesofisrael.com/us-offers-5m-reward-for-info-on-1994-panama-plane-bombing-blamed-on-hezbollah/.
56. Jack Nicas and Daniel Politi, "The Catholic President Who's 'Almost' Jewish," *New York Times*, July 18, 2024, https://www.nytimes.com/2024/07/18/world/americas/argentina-milei-judaism.html.

10

COMBATING ANTISEMITISM

Since the Roman exile, Jews have been grappling with how to respond to antisemitism. Different schools of thought and approaches have emerged: religious, secular, socialist, nationalist. As antisemitism once again is on the rise, there is considerable discussion, both within and outside the Jewish world, about ways to counter it and protect Jewish communities. What is the role of government? Beyond government, any strategy to combat antisemitism must also take into account the role of other key sectors, including, notably, education. Are there examples of best practices in combating Jew-hatred? What are the key takeaways in confronting antisemitism?

What are the various responses from within the Jewish community about how best to combat antisemitism?

After the Second World War, the mainstreaming of American Jews accelerated, ushering in what might be termed a golden age.

Perhaps it was the wartime experience. Americans of many backgrounds found themselves together in boot camps, in the foxholes, on the battlefields. They came to know one another as never before. Stereotypes of various groups were shattered. They learned to trust each other. Their lives depended on it. And they witnessed valor and sacrifice that knew no boundaries of race, faith, or ethnicity. More than 500,000 American Jews were in uniform during the war—in all the branches, every theater of combat, at almost every rank. And many more at home helped the war effort, from the Manhattan Project to the aircraft factories' assembly lines.

Maybe it was also the realization that Nazi Germany was the antithesis of everything America aspired to be as a society—a reminder that America needed to work even harder to fulfill its promise for all. For the next several decades, step by step, the barriers to full Jewish participation in American life, like the walls of Jericho, came tumbling down.

Judaism became elevated alongside the Catholic and Protestant faiths as the theological troika of a country that placed a premium on the role of religion. This was epitomized in the title of a much-discussed book, *Protestant-Catholic-Jew: An Essay in American Religious Sociology*, by Drew University professor Will Herberg,[1] published in 1955.

Jews not only gained fuller entry into the vaunted spaces of American culture but began in many ways to help define that culture through literature, music, art, and, most widely, the world of Hollywood film and television.

Jewish organizations were active in advocating for a more open, welcoming America for Jews and, no less, for other groups previously disadvantaged or marginalized. Essentially, the Jewish strategy was that an inclusive America for all was morally the right policy to pursue—and, needless to say, the best bet for Jews. And it worked.

Antisemitism never disappeared entirely, but it declined and became largely taboo in mainstream society. Both the visible and invisible barriers to full participation began vanishing. Jews were increasingly emerging as elected officials, cultural icons, neighbors, and, yes, potential spouses, which had not always been the case.

1. Will Herberg, *Protestant-Catholic-Jew: An Essay in American Religious Sociology* (Doubleday, 1955).

Reinforcing these positive trends was growing awareness of the Holocaust—and the immense tragedy that had befallen the Jewish people under the Nazis. The NBC television network popularized the story through a widely viewed mini-series in 1978. Elie Wiesel wrote best-selling books. Survivors began to tell their harrowing accounts in schools and houses of worship. Museums were built, including on the National Mall.

And decisive majorities of Americans consistently viewed Israel favorably, identifying with it as a fellow democracy, plucky underdog, or wellspring of both Judaism and Christianity. This only added to the ever-growing sense of the American Jewish coming of age—and of a love affair with America unlike any other diaspora experience in Jewish history.

Truly, the years after the Second World War started to change everything in America. A new awakening was taking root. America became more open and embracing. Minorities were becoming mainstreamed. Alliances across communities were formed. The Holocaust opened hearts. Why wouldn't it simply continue forever? What could possibly disrupt it?

But then came the reminder that history had not ended, the golden age might not last forever, complacency could never replace vigilance, and an "automatic pilot" strategy would no longer work for American Jewry. More was needed, but what?

Signs of change were in the air well before October 7, 2023, as explained elsewhere in the book. But what followed that worst day in Jewish history since the Holocaust was something few American Jews saw coming.

After the initial shock, the overriding question was what to do in response. The October 6 playbook of the Jewish community—which counted on widespread goodwill, intergroup alliances, the lessons of the Holocaust, reason, broad bipartisan support, and a consensus definition of antisemitism—had clearly become inadequate.

Some Jews took off the gloves, believing only actions with consequences had a chance of success. They told their alma maters in no uncertain terms that any tolerance of campus behavior threatening Jewish students or faculty would trigger reputational and financial damage. Meanwhile, a number of Jewish students opted for lawfare, suing their universities for failing to keep them safe.

Several prominent law firms and corporations announced they would do due diligence on job applicants to ensure they were not post–October 7 campus lawbreakers, antisemites, or terrorism cheerleaders. A few Jewish organizations took to social media to call out those people, by name and job title, expressing hatred of Jews, militating for genocide against the Jewish people, and voicing animus for America.

And while some Jews and Jewish groups opted to focus specifically on the danger of rising antisemitism, others framed it more broadly, suggesting that those marching in support of a designated terrorist organization like Hamas or Hezbollah, or desecrating the American flag, or paralyzing universities, posed a larger threat to liberal democracy, and not just to the Jewish community. As one illustration, in August 2024, a group of anti-Israel Columbia University students issued a call for the "total eradication" of Western civilization.[2] These Jewish voices, therefore, were making the case that what was at stake went far beyond American Jews. As the late rabbi Lord Jonathan Sacks said, "The hate that begins with Jews never ends with Jews. Antisemitism is the world's most reliable early warning sign of a major threat to freedom, humanity and the dignity of difference."[3]

In sum, after October 7 many American Jews were waking up to new, perhaps previously unimaginable realities—after

2. Matthew Sedacca, "Columbia University's Radical Anti-Israel Group Seeks 'Total Eradication of Western Civilization,'" *New York Post*, August 17, 2024, https://nypost.com/2024/08/17/us-news/columbia-universitys-anti-israel-group-seeking-total-eradication-of-western-civilization/.
3. @rabbisacks, The Rabbi Sacks Legacy, Twitter, October 23, 2023, https://x.com/rabbisacks/status/1716420041833381958.

a halcyon era that encompassed the entire lives of all but a few—and which, in turn, required new thinking, initiatives, and strategies to ensure their secure place in society.[4]

Meanwhile, there has been ever increasing attention in the Jewish world, as a result of the surge in antisemitism, to physical security for Jews and Jewish institutions. Perhaps the most advanced model in this realm has been the Community Security Trust, which was founded by British Jews in 1994 as a charitable group. It has a large professional staff monitoring hundreds of Jewish communal facilities throughout the country, a well-trained volunteer corps, and sophisticated technical capabilities. Moreover, it maintains close, cooperative ties with British government and law enforcement authorities and is highly regarded for its credibility and effectiveness.

Given the long history of antisemitism and its durability, is it realistic to think that it can be cured? Is there a potential "Pfizer vaccine" on the horizon?

Alas, there is no potential "Pfizer vaccine" on the horizon. Insofar as antisemitism is often referred to as the longest hatred, spanning thousands of years, it would be unrealistic to expect a sudden, magical cure.

But there was a belief in the post–World War II period that, even if it could not be totally vanquished, at least antisemitism might be marginalized and rendered socially taboo, starting with the United States. And for quite some time, that belief showed impressive, and steady, progress. The anti-antisemitism strategy was built on several pillars.

The unparalleled devastation of World War II for Jews and, more generally, democratic societies underscored the deep

4. See Bret Stephens, "The Year American Jews Woke Up," *New York Times*, October 4, 2024, https://www.nytimes.com/2024/10/04/opinion/israel-jews-antisemitism.html?smid=nytcore-ios-share&referringSource=articleShare&sgrp=c-cb.

dangers of radicalism and extremism. And the gas chambers of Auschwitz-Birkenau took antisemitism to a horrific new place. So, too, did the postwar period with the spread of Communism and its permanent threat to basic human freedoms, not to mention its own endemic antisemitism.

Thus, strengthening liberal democratic values—and fulfilling their promise for all—was the surest path, if not to ending antisemitism forever then reducing it to a minor irritant at worst.

Holocaust education became a key element in the strategy, especially in schools and popular culture. The more people grasped the abyss into which antisemitism could lead, the more they heard the harrowing, firsthand accounts of survivors and rescuers, and the more they understood the Holocaust through books, movies, testimonies, and museums, the more likely, it was believed, they would become sentinels in the struggle against it.

Further, Jews jumped in with both feet as societies opened up, and they increasingly shifted their focus of involvement from particular Jewish concerns to the broader world in which they lived—and they largely found acceptance, or so they thought. The interaction would accelerate full integration. Moreover, as discussed earlier, Jews believed that building coalitions with other racial, religious, and ethnic minorities would further strengthen their foothold and break down any remaining barriers of ignorance, stereotypes, or mystery that could fuel bigotry.

And finally, as Jews felt increasingly comfortable, not as guests but as stakeholders in liberal democracies, they put more trust in institutions they felt would have their backs: education, the media, government offices, nongovernmental organizations, the judiciary, evolving social norms.

Jews, whether in the United States, Australia, Canada, or some other Western nation, had come tantalizingly close, or so they felt, to putting in the rearview mirror any major sleep-interrupting concerns about antisemitism. Until October 7, 2023.

In reality, some saw the gathering clouds long before, especially in Europe, and never let their guard down. Others, however, were caught by surprise.

Could it really be that "identifiable" Jews were now at risk on streets simply for being Jews? That subway riders could be told to get off if they were Zionists? That Jewish students at respected universities could be barricaded in a library in fear of their lives, or told to go home and study online for their own safety? That presidents of some of the most prestigious schools in the United States could become tongue-tied when asked how they would respond to calls for genocide against Jews on their campuses? That some Jewish children had to be escorted to and from school by large groups of adults because other children threatened them as Jews? That Jewish-owned businesses could be attacked for being, well, Jewish-owned businesses? That synagogues, houses of worship, could be targeted for political reasons? That Jews expressing identification with Israel, the ancestral Jewish homeland and an American ally, could face danger for peaceful assembly? That Jews could be told to "go back to Poland" or that "Hitler should have finished the job"? Or, perhaps most ominous, that some of the very institutions in which Jews had placed such faith and trust could downplay, ignore, or trivialize Jewish vulnerability?

No, there is no cure around the corner, notwithstanding all the efforts made. And yet while Jews deal with the new realities, hoping they are just a passing moment in time, their faith remains anchored in liberal democracies that regain their footing and staunchly defend core principles. That is, except for those Jews who, in the spirit of Theodor Herzl, the father of modern Zionism at the end of the 19th century, believe antisemitism is simply too deeply embedded in Western civilization and seek a new life in Israel.

Much emphasis was placed on Holocaust education in schools and popular culture as a way of combating antisemitism. Has this proved effective?

Up to a point, yes, but it faces increasing challenges. When first introduced decades ago, the goals were clear. Teach the Holocaust because it was a tragic event unique in the annals of human history and needed to be studied. And, by doing so, educate new generations against antisemitism and about warning signs of any possible recurrence.

The process was quite straightforward. Recount the history of the Holocaust in a module, include powerful readings (*The Diary of Anne Frank*, *Night*, *Maus*, *If This Is a Man*, etc.); take a field trip, when possible, to a museum or monument; and invite a survivor, liberator, or rescuer into a classroom to interact with the children. The effect would almost inevitably be greater awareness of and sensitivity to the slippery slope of antisemitism that can begin with demonization and end with genocide.

And that is what happened in many schools, in the United States, where more than 20 states mandated Holocaust education, and in other Western countries, such as France, Germany, and Poland, where it was also obligatory. In a number of cases, the results were impressive. One notable example was a highly acclaimed documentary film, *Paper Clips*, released in 2004. It told the story of a middle school in Whitwell, Tennessee, that tried to convey the magnitude of the Jewish death toll by having the pupils collect 6 million paper clips.

In Germany, some schools undertook history projects to learn about the Jews who once lived in their towns and were either driven out or deported and murdered, and then they invited a surviving family member to return for a visit from their current home, perhaps in Israel or America. In Poland there were instances, as a result of Holocaust education, of young people adopting an abandoned Jewish cemetery, as there were no surviving Jews in the area to do so. Such examples abounded over the past several decades.

But with the passage of time, other factors began to complicate the picture. First, the history itself has become more distant—nearly a century old now—and therefore harder to convey in a contemporary context. Second, the survivors, liberators, and rescuers have been aging and passing on. Fewer and fewer are available to make personal visits to tell their stories in schools and interact with the children. Third, in some places "Holocaust fatigue" has set in, essentially asking if there is, let's call it, a statute of limitations on talking about a subject that is chronologically, at least, receding in the rearview mirror. Fourth, American and European societies have been undergoing rapid demographic change, with large numbers of newcomers arriving from nations having little to no connection with World War II and the Holocaust.

In the classrooms, this has occasionally translated into resistance to Holocaust education and its emphasis on Jewish suffering in Europe. Such a reaction has been reported, for example, in heavily immigrant neighborhoods in France, where some teachers have faced a backlash from children claiming the Holocaust never happened or was only meant to generate sympathy for undeserving Jews or to justify the "illegal" creation of Israel. A much-discussed book on these challenges, *Les Territoires perdus de la République* (*The Lost Territories of the Republic*), authored by Barbara Lefevre, herself a schoolteacher, was published in France in 2002.

Fifth, in the case of the United States, other social phenomena have also been at work, including greater attention to the histories of multiple victim communities. For educators, this has created new frontiers but also posed difficult questions about traditional ways of teaching the Holocaust. Should all stories of genocide, ethnic cleansing, crimes against humanity, persecution, and exploitation be taught? What if they are disputed? By whom and by what criteria should they be selected? Should the stories be taught together or separately? How much emphasis should each receive? And how can children be expected to retain the material with so much information about victimization and tragedy being directed at them?

Sixth, Jewish history did not start in 1933 with the rise of Adolf Hitler or end in 1945 with his defeat, even as 6 million Jews, including 1.5 million children, were murdered in that 12-year period. Hence the question of how to teach about the Holocaust while placing it in a larger historical context—the Jews did not suddenly appear in 1933 and disappear in 1945, nor, for that matter, did Jew-hatred—has no simple response.

Seventh, a few local U.S. school districts have banned some Holocaust-related books because the contents were deemed inappropriate for children. Yet educating about what actually happened, including to children like Anne Frank, cannot be sanitized or cherry-picked and still remain true to the historical record.

And a final challenge is keeping up with the ways young people obtain, process, and retain information in a world where so many things have become more visual, bite-size, and fleeting, not to mention where fake or twisted information can just as easily be found online as reliable and in-depth information on almost any topic, including the Holocaust.

As *New York Times* columnist Bret Stephens pointed out, "[O]ur universities are failing at the task of educating students in the habits of a free mind. Instead, they are becoming islands of illiberal ideology and factories of moral certitude, more often at war with the values of liberal democracy than in their service."[5]

5. Bret Stephens, "What Does a University Owe Democracy?" *The New York Times*, October 12, 2021, https://www.nytimes.com/2021/10/12/opinion/cancel-culture-college-campus.html/.

Many governments have appointed special envoys against antisemitism and adopted national plans to fight Jew-hatred. Have they made a difference?

Yes, they have made a difference wherever they exist, including the United States, the 27-member European Union, the 57-member Organization for Security and Cooperation in Europe, the 34-member Organization of American States, and, among other nations, Austria, Bulgaria, Canada, Croatia, Estonia, France, Germany, Greece, Israel, Italy, the Netherlands, Spain, and the United Kingdom. In July 2024, Australia appointed a special envoy for the first time.

They have not made enough of a difference, but their very existence sends a message that, on a national level—and, in some cases, on a broader regional level as well—the battle against antisemitism is recognized and has an address.

The combined efforts of these offices, joined by several other government representatives, led to an unprecedented joint statement in November 2023, in the wake of what was described as "the barbaric attack of Hamas terrorists on Israel." The 24 signatories declared:

- We call on governments to assess the needs and provide the necessary security assistance that Jewish communities require at this time of crisis.
- We urge police and law enforcement to be vigilant of threats against Jews and to be aware that Jewish people around the world should not be held responsible for the words and actions of the Israeli or any other government, as illustrated by the non-legally binding International Holocaust Remembrance Alliance Working Definition of Antisemitism.
- We denounce antisemitic acts taking place on some campuses and urge university administrators to condemn them and ensure that their Jewish students, like all other students, have the safety and support needed in these difficult times, to enjoy their right to education.

- We urge civil society—including sports federations, religious communities, the cultural sector and academic circles—not to stand by or stay silent, but rather use their influence to effectively counter antisemitism and promote public acts of solidarity.
- We are distressed about the online upsurge of antisemitic messages, disinformation, hate speech, and terrorist content, which instigate real world hate crimes and threaten the very social cohesion that binds our democratic societies together. We decry the social media platforms that amplify and multiply this content and call on them to act in line with the law and their own terms of service.[6]

That said, there is clearly more to be done. Some offices are led by senior officials with easy access across government ministries. Others are headed by lower-level individuals with limited reach. Some offices are well-funded, able to hire staff and mount legal, political, educational, and civic initiatives. Others are minimally supported. Some offices address not only antisemitism but also related Jewish issues, principally Holocaust remembrance, Holocaust-era property claims, and promotion of communal life. Others have a broader mandate that also encompasses xenophobia, LGBTQ+ rights, racism, Islamophobia, or religious intolerance.

Some offices are largely fig leaves aimed at generating international goodwill but doing quite little on a daily basis. Others fight tooth and nail against antisemitism. One that deserves special mention is the EU coordinator on combating antisemitism and fostering Jewish life. Katharina von Schnurbein has held the post since it was created in 2015. She and her team have pressed for both EU-wide action and individual national

6. European Commission, "Joint Statement of Special Envoys and Coordinators Combating Antisemitism," November 6, 2023, https://ec.europa.eu/newsroom/just/newsletter-archives/48763.

strategies among the 27 member states to battle antisemitism and strengthen Jewish life.

It is also important to note that the mandate for the U.S. special envoy to monitor and combat antisemitism was created in 2004 in response to rising antisemitism outside the borders of America. This contrasts with other special envoy offices around the world, which were established to address antisemitism within national borders.

What is the role of a nation's leaders with respect to antisemitism?

There are three basic responses on the leadership level: fanning the flames of antisemitism, confronting it head-on, or downplaying or ignoring it. In the first category, there are several examples in recent history.

When Pope John Paul II visited Syria in 2001, he was greeted by President Bashar al-Assad, who, speaking to the world's media, said: "They [the Jews] try to kill the principle of religions with the same mentality they betrayed Jesus Christ and the same way they tried to betray and kill the Prophet Mohammad." While the pontiff, for whatever reason, did not react in the moment, the Israeli president later responded by calling Assad's words "careless, racist, antisemitic."[7]

During his two terms of office, from 1981 to 2003 and 2018 to 2020, Prime Minister Mahathir Mohamad of Malaysia was accused on multiple occasions of promoting antisemitism. Indeed, his bigotry was revealed as early as 1970, when he wrote an essay titled "The Malay Identity," in which he exclaimed. "The Jews are not only hooked-nosed . . . but understand money instinctively. . . . Jewish stinginess and financial wizardry gained them the economic control of Europe and

7. *Irish Times*, "Israeli President Slams Assad as Anti-Semitic," May 6, 2001, https://www.irishtimes.com/news/israeli-president-slams-assad-as-anti-semitic-1.382928.

provoked antisemitism which waxed and waned throughout Europe through the ages."[8] In 1984, he prevented a scheduled visit of the New York Philharmonic to Kuala Lumpur because the program included a piece by a Swiss Jewish composer, Ernest Bloch, inspired by a Hebrew melody. And in subsequent years, he invoked many of the classic antisemitic tropes about Jews and control of the media, Jews and financial thievery, and Jews and plots to undermine his country. Incidentally, this was a striking example of antisemitism without Jews. There is no Jewish community in Malaysia, but, to Mahathir, Jews pose a global threat, irrespective of whether they are physically present in a country—and despite the fact that Jews, in total, comprise 0.2% of the world population, or one in every 500 people on the planet.

In 2010, in a particularly noteworthy development, longtime Cuban leader Fidel Castro, a staunch Communist, publicly accused the president of Iran, Mahmoud Ahmadinejad, of antisemitism for, among other reasons, denying the Holocaust. Castro told *The Atlantic* magazine, "The Jews have lived an existence that is much harder than ours. There is nothing that compares to the Holocaust. . . . I don't think anyone has been slandered more than the Jews. I would say much more than the Muslims. They have been slandered much more than the Muslims because they are blamed and slandered for everything. No one blames the Muslims for anything." In the same interview, Castro recalled his childhood: "He reminisced about being a young boy and overhearing classmates saying Jews killed Jesus Christ. 'I didn't know what a Jew was. I knew of a bird that was called a "Jew," and so for me the Jews were those birds. This is how ignorant the entire population was.' "[9]

8. Simon Wiesenthal Center, "In Malaysia, When in Doubt, Blame the Jews," July 22, 2011, https://www.wiesenthal.com/about/news/in-malaysia-when-in-doubt.html.
9. Jeffrey Goldberg, "Castro: 'No One Has Been Slandered More Than the Jews,'" *The Atlantic*, September 7, 2010, https://www.theatlan

Then there is the case of Jeremy Corbyn, leader of Britain's venerable Labour Party from 2015 to 2020 and candidate for prime minister in the 2019 national election.

Corbyn was frequently accused of antisemitism during his tenure, as well as countenancing antisemitism in the party's ranks. Britain's Equality and Human Rights Commission issued a blistering report of that period in 2020: "The investigation was prompted by growing public concern about antisemitism in the Labour Party and followed official complaints received by us. . . . [O]ur investigation found significant failings in the way the Labour Party has handled antisemitism complaints over the last four years. We found specific examples of harassment, discrimination and political interference in our evidence, but equally of concern was a lack of leadership within the Labour Party on these issues, which is hard to reconcile with its stated commitment to a zero-tolerance approach to antisemitism."[10]

Again, it needs to be stressed that the leader of the party under investigation by this politically neutral body was vying for occupancy of 10 Downing Street and was the runner-up in the 2019 election. The report illustrated the constructive role that such a commission can play in a democratic society. After its release, Corbyn did step down, to be replaced by Keir Starmer, who pledged a "zero-tolerance approach to antisemitism and racism." In 2024, Starmer became Britain's prime minister.

In 2024, Venezuelan president Nicolas Maduro, in an election many believe he manipulated, tried to divert attention away from himself and point the finger at Zionism (in other words,

tic.com/international/archive/2010/09/castro-no-one-has-been-slandered-more-than-the-jews/62566/.

10. Equality and Human Rights Commission, "Investigation into Antisemitism in the Labour Party," October 2020, https://www.equalityhumanrights.com/sites/default/files/investigation-into-antisemitism-in-the-labour-party.pdf.

Jews). He said Venezuela's "extremist right" is "financed" and "supported by international Zionism," claiming that "all the communication power of Zionism, which controls all social networks, the satellites, and all the power, is behind this *coup d'état*."[11]

By contrast, there are examples of a country's leaders standing clearly and unambiguously against antisemitism. Does it help? No guarantee, but at the very least it sends the right message to a nation, all the more so if reinforced by actions that back up the words and have some teeth.

After the rape of a 12-year-old Jewish girl in June 2024, which was reportedly accompanied by antisemitic slurs by the three perpetrators, French president Emmanuel Macron minced no words in speaking of the "scourge of antisemitism" plaguing France and urged all schools to devote time to a dialogue about racism and antisemitism. Whether such school discussions take place, including how antisemitism and racism are juxtaposed and addressed, and with what results, remains to be seen, but, again, it reflects a recognition that condemnations of antisemitism alone are woefully inadequate to address the growing threats around the world.

In the face of rapidly rising antisemitism in the United States, President Joe Biden not only forcefully condemned it but also, in 2023, issued the comprehensive U.S. National Strategy to Counter Antisemitism, the first of its kind in American history. In a statement at the launch of the groundbreaking initiative, Biden announced that "it represents the most ambitious and comprehensive U.S. government-led effort to fight antisemitism in American history."[12]

11. Michael Starr, "Maduro: 'International Zionism' behind Civil Unrest in Venezuela," *Jerusalem Post*, August 6, 2024, https://www.jpost.com/western_wall/article-813522.
12. Joseph R. Biden, "Statement on the United States National Strategy to Counter Antisemitism," American Presidency Project, May 25, 2023, https://www.presidency.ucsb.edu/documents/statement-the-united-states-national-strategy-counter-antisemitism.

During Austria's rotating presidency of the European Union in 2018, Chancellor Sebastian Kurz successfully pressed for EU member states to adopt national strategies to combat antisemitism, based on the key dimensions of education, security, law enforcement, integration, documentation, and civil society.

Elsewhere in this book, reference was made to the initiative of the 35-nation International Holocaust Remembrance Alliance, formalized in 2016, to create a standardized definition of antisemitism, including seeking to confront the complex issue of when criticism of Israel spills over into antisemitism. After all, in order to combat antisemitism, some common understanding of what it is (and is not) is needed.

And as a final example of leadership, the UN General Assembly adopted a resolution in 2005, however late in coming, designating January 27, the day in 1945 that Soviet troops liberated Auschwitz-Birkenau, as International Holocaust Remembrance Day. UN commemorations, as well as events in some countries, have taken place since. In the resolution, any attempt at Holocaust denial was strongly condemned.

At the same time, the UN does not have enforcement power and, being such a highly politicized institution, has not always been able to ensure that the original measure would be used as intended by its sponsors. Nonetheless, it offers an example of recognizing the need to go beyond ritualistic condemnations of antisemitism and, in this case, mobilize education and remembrance as ongoing tools to fight it.

As for the third category of leadership response, let's call it the middle ground, this clearly falls short. In 1995, Father Henryk Jankowski, a parish priest in Gdansk, Poland, delivered a fiery sermon that included an attack on Jews. He asserted, "The Star of David is implicated in the swastika as well as in the hammer and sickle."[13]

13. *New York Times*, "Polish Jews Ask Walesa to Disavow Priest," June 17, 1995, https://www.nytimes.com/1995/06/17/world/polish-jews-ask-walesa-to-disavow-priest.html.

While these words were not new for him, what elevated the mass to a global news story was the presence in the church that day of Polish president Lech Wałęsa—and his failure to react either during the service or for the next nine days, until he finally denounced antisemitism, but without any reference to the offender in this case.

In a subsequent meeting with an AJC delegation in San Francisco during the 50th anniversary celebration of the UN founding, Wałęsa defended his long silence by asserting that anything else would have only brought more attention to Jankowski's bigotry. By contrast, the AJC group argued that, by staying silent for as long as he did, he sent the wrong message to his nation of 35 million people. As one Jewish participant in the meeting said, "Two totally different interpretations. No meeting of the minds." Did this story suggest that Wałęsa himself was sympathetic to antisemitism? Not necessarily, but it certainly raised questions for many.

In 2001, as antisemitism erupted in France, home to Europe's largest Jewish community, and as rabbis told religious Jews that taking off a kippah or hiding it under a baseball cap was now permitted for safety reasons, AJC met with President Jacques Chirac in his office. The aim was to alert the French head of state to the growing threat and enlist his help. His response: "I know my country better than you. There is no antisemitism in France."

Chirac was not an antisemite. Indeed, as noted, he had been the first French leader to acknowledge that Vichy collaboration with the Nazis, including in the roundup and deportation of Jews, was part and parcel of French history and could no longer be denied. Yet he was unwilling to acknowledge what had become painfully obvious—that French Jews were fearful for their safety due to intimidation and threats from the country's growing Arab and Muslim population, which dwarfed the Jewish community by a ratio of 10 to 1. In a later meeting with Foreign Minister Hubert Vedrine, in November 2001 in New York, the same group again tried to raise alarm bells, but once more without success. The chief diplomat's reply: "There is no antisemitism in France. Instead, there is hooliganism and also the regrettable importation of the Arab-Israeli conflict onto French soil."[14]

This inability, or unwillingness, to see the rising menace of antisemitism, which after all was not a new or foreign disease in France, delayed the awareness of its magnitude. As a consequence, the state failed to reach out to an increasingly anxious community wondering if its place in France was still assured, as well as the opportunity to formulate a timely national strategy while there was still a chance to nip it in the bud.

In Hungary, President Viktor Orbán has been accused of antisemitism, particularly depicting his political nemesis, the Hungarian-born financier George Soros, in ways that evoke antisemitic tropes—distorted features, money bags, devious plots to sabotage the country—whenever there is an election, not to mention trying to idealize Hungary's less-than-perfect record in the Holocaust.

Orbán's defenders argue that Hungary is home to the largest Jewish community in Central Europe, and that Orbán is one of Israel's staunchest allies in the European Union and at the UN. So, which is he, or is he cunningly both? Certainly each side believes the facts are with them.

As a final example of this middle space, there was the neo-Nazi march in Charlottesville, Virginia, in 2017, when repeated chants of "Jews will not replace us" were heard. President Donald Trump's first reaction was "We condemn in the strongest possible terms this egregious display of hatred, bigotry and violence on many sides, on many sides." Shortly afterward he spoke again: "You had some very bad people in that group, but you also had people that were very fine people,

14. Meeting with American Jewish Committee delegation, Hotel Sofitel, New York, November 2001.

on both sides."[15] That led Speaker of the House Paul Ryan, a fellow Republican, to comment, "It sounded like a moral equivocation or, at the very least, moral ambiguity when we need extreme moral clarity."[16]

Some concluded that Trump was an antisemite by appearing to take a two-handed approach, even as he later sought to dispute that interpretation of his remarks.

Others hastily pointed out that he has always had good friends in the Jewish community, is a grandfather to three Jewish grandchildren, and was one of Israel's best friends ever in the White House.

For those who are genuinely concerned about antisemitism, whatever its source, the response must be quick and unequivocal, and it needs to mobilize the power of government to stand unflinchingly against such hatred. Anything less sends mixed messages to the general public and the organs of state and, however unintentionally, offers wiggle room to potential perpetrators.

What is the role of educational institutions in combating antisemitism?

It is extremely important. In the first instance, it depends on whether a school makes crystal-clear that it takes any potential incident of antisemitism seriously. As experience has shown, too often in recent years antisemitism has been neglected, minimized, or even rationalized, whether in K–12 or university settings.

15. Philip Bump, "What Trump Said with His 'Very Fine People' Comments vs. What He Meant," *Washington Post*, June 28, 2024, https://www.washingtonpost.com/politics/2024/06/28/what-trump-said-with-his-very-fine-people-comments-vs-what-he-meant/.
16. Lauren Fox, "Paul Ryan: Trump 'Messed Up' Charlottesville Response," CNN, August 22, 2017, https://edition.cnn.com/2017/08/21/politics/paul-ryan-town-hall/index.html.

Since Jews are widely viewed as White, and therefore presumed to be "privileged" and "successful," their experiences with antisemitism in the classroom, hallway, gym, dormitory, quad, or online can be met with skepticism or cynicism by administrators, or, if they relate to Israel, to lengthy debates about what is protected speech and what is not.

The sense among some Jews is that, too often, there is a hierarchy of concerns when it comes to targets of bigotry, with Jews at the bottom of the list, if they're even on it. These Jews believe that school administrators are on the lookout for acts of racism, homophobia, transphobia, xenophobia, or misogyny, as they should be, but let their guard down when it comes to anti-Jewish acts, which seem to need, some would assert, a higher threshold of proof and extended periods of investigation.

Ideally, of course, every school and university setting would foster a sense of community, mutual respect, and safety for all—and not just in platitudes but in performance. That should always be the aspirational goal. But, in practice, it is not always the case.

Perhaps the clearest statement after October 7, 2023, about the danger of antisemitism and a school's responsibility to combat it came from the president of the University of Florida, Ben Sasse. A week after the Hamas invasion, he said in a television interview, "You got so many universities around the country [that] speak about every topic under the sun, Halloween costumes and microaggressions. But somehow in a moment of the most grave, grotesque attacks on Jewish people since the Holocaust, they all of a sudden say there's too much complexity to say anything."[17] Separately, in a letter sent to Jewish students the same week, Sasse wrote, "We will protect

17. Kelly Garrity, "Senator-Turned-University-President Disses Fellow Educators for Silence," *Politico*, October 15, 2023, https://www.politico.com/news/2023/10/15/ben-sasse-university-president-israel-hamas-00121627.

our Jewish students from violence. If anti-Israel protests come, we will absolutely be ready to act if anyone dares to escalate beyond peaceful protest. Speech is protected—violence and vandalism are not."[18]

Should schools have a broader curriculum against hate of any kind or specifically target Jew-hatred?

Both. On the one hand, children throughout their education should learn appreciation for one another, for other cultures, for differences in beliefs and lifestyles, and for a variety of points of view. That's essential for any diverse society and for global citizenship. And in schools in particularly heterogeneous communities, where there can literally be dozens of nationalities and backgrounds under one roof, creating mutual understanding and respect is vital for harmonious interaction and strengthening the ties that bind a nation together.

On the other hand, like racism, antisemitism has a long history, an unmistakable specificity, including the ever-present and malevolent conspiracy theories targeting Jews, and a heavy human toll that dates back centuries—and continues to have contemporary repercussions.

Thus, understanding the legacy of racism, including slavery, on African Americans then and now is, and must continue to be, an integral part of any school curriculum. It cannot merely be subsumed under a broader discussion on mistreatment of people or social inequalities.

So, too, with antisemitism. The Holocaust was the culmination of centuries of antisemitism and continues to be felt in daily life; Jews still face Holocaust-related themes and echoes in the 21st century.

18. Andrew Caplan, "UF President Ben Sasse Condemns Hamas Attacks, Ensures Student Safety after Stampede Vigil," *Gainesville Sun*, October 12, 2023, https://www.gainesville.com/story/news/local/2023/10/12/ufs-ben-sasse-pens-letter-to-jewish-students-warns-of-protests/71154956007/.

Moreover, the Holocaust has universal messages which are timeless, including for a nation's schools. As time passes, these messages warrant even greater attention, perhaps, than in the past.

First, democracy is fragile. The German Weimar Republic, 1918–33, was a freewheeling democracy. It did not survive. Rather, with lightning speed, it gave way to a totalitarian regime, whose crimes were unparalleled in the annals of human history.

Second, Germany was arguably the most educated nation on earth, with a rich cultural tradition of music, art, and literature. Yet neither its education nor its culture prevented the Holocaust, nor called into question the murder of 1.5 million Jewish children, nor blunted the ultimate German responsibility for as many as 60 million deaths in World War II.

In other words, education without empathy—and culture without compassion—will not safeguard societies and the sanctity of human life.

And third, a failure of imagination can prove fatal. Hitler never hid his intentions. To the contrary, he shouted them from the rooftops. But too many chose not to believe him. And when he embarked on the slippery slope from dehumanization of the Jewish people to its annihilation, some chose to avert their eyes, hide behind professed ignorance, assume he had a "good" reason, or claim helplessness.

Teaching in a thoughtfully constructed manner about antisemitism—and its culmination in the Holocaust—can help young people understand the need to watch for early warning signs of something gone seriously amiss, speak up before it is too late, and understand the world's eternal need for champions of moral courage.

Is online antisemitism a major issue and, if so, what can be done about it?

Yes. Government envoys on antisemitism have been meeting regularly to discuss what can be done, including consultations with big tech companies. The Inter-Parliamentary Task Force to Combat Online Antisemitism was created by an international group of concerned legislators in 2020. And surveys by the EU's Fundamental Rights Agency, AJC, and other groups have documented time and again the large numbers of Jews, across many countries, who report seeing or even experiencing online antisemitism, including harassment and cyberbullying.

Moreover, the Center for Countering Digital Hate has actively monitored antisemitism, including Holocaust denial, and racist caricatures on social media platforms. According to the Center, in November 2023, 85% of such posts which were reported to X (formerly Twitter) were still up a week later. In addition, 84% of the offensive posts reported on Facebook, Instagram, TikTok, X, and YouTube reported in 2021 were not taken down by the platforms.[19]

These are, of course, complex issues. Some argue that freedom of speech protections must be fully respected, and that any restrictions, other than addressing outright incitement, would curtail those fundamental rights. Often cited are the words of U.S. Supreme Court justice Louis Brandeis, incidentally the first American Jew to sit on the highest court in the land, in the 1927 case *Whitney v. California*: "If there be time to expose through discussion, the falsehoods and fallacies, to avert the evil by the processes of education, the remedy to be applied is more speech, not enforced silence."[20]

On the other hand, the internet and social media have become principal purveyors of hatred, racism, and antisemitism, and have at times led to radicalization and acts of violence.

19. Center for Countering Digital Hate, "Understanding Antisemitism on Social Media," February 23, 2024, https://counterhate.com/blog/understanding-antisemitism-on-social-media/.
20. First Amendment Watch, "Brandeis Concurring with Holmes in Whitney v. California, 1927," January 27, 2018, https://firstamendmentwatch.org/history-speaks-brandeis-concurring-holmes-whitney-v-california-1927/.

Thus the persistent questions revolve around (1) whether or not there should be any limits to online free speech; (2) whether tech companies should be expected to do more to regulate themselves or be trusted to do so without outside monitoring; (3) how transparent these companies must be in revealing to the public their standards, content review, and algorithmic practices; and (4) the appropriate role of government in addressing the many challenges in this sphere.

The Anti-Defamation League has summarized three points to pursue both for government and social media platforms:

1. Increase platform accountability for their role in the prevalence, virality and impact of online hate.
2. Require platforms to share information about their products and policies.
3. Protect users and support victims of online harassment.[21]

Since democratic nations do not have a single definition of freedom of speech, approaches will inevitably vary from country to country. What is unmistakably clear, however, is that, in the 21st century, any discussion about strategies for combating antisemitism must include, centrally, online antisemitism. If the internet is the principal source for information on any issue today, which can also result in intentional misinformation or disinformation, and if social media platforms are the major tools of communication for billions of people worldwide, then ever-increasing attention must be paid to their profound societal consequences.

21. Anti-Defamation League, "Disrupt Online Hate and Harassment," accessed April 22, 2025, https://www.adl.org/what-we-do/disrupt-online-hate-harassment.

Are there positive examples of action against antisemitism?

As discussed earlier, in the Second World War there were shining examples. They were too few to save 6 million victims of the Holocaust, but they demonstrated what a belief in shared humanity—and the courage to act on it—could accomplish.

Their common denominator was that they did not see Jews as somehow the "other," the "alien," the "stranger," but rather simply as fellow human beings.

And, ultimately, returning to the earlier question of whether there could ever be a "Pfizer vaccine" to inoculate against antisemitism, or perhaps even intolerance more broadly, the admittedly utopian answer lies in seeking to educate in homes, classrooms, houses of worship, the political arena, the worlds of sports and culture, and our public spaces—and not just in one lesson plan, one sermon, one speech, one gesture, but consistently and in real-life behavior—genuine respect for one another.

Not tolerance. That sets the bar too low. The aim should be not tolerance for one another but rather appreciation for those of different backgrounds. In other words, affirming one's own identity should not have to come at the expense of denigrating or denying someone else's.

Those Second World War rescuers put themselves on the line to protect fellow human beings and affirm the kind of world in which they wanted to live.

As Dr. Martin Luther King Jr. said in 1962, "We must learn to live together as brothers or we will die together as fools." And as the Hebrew Bible states, "God created humankind in God's image." No hierarchy. Universal equality. All the major religions have a variation of the Golden Rule—"Love thy neighbor as thyself," in the Christian tradition—embedded in their teachings. The age-old challenge has been to put these noble visions into daily practice.

One community that did so was in the city of Billings, Montana. In 1993, some White supremacists and admirers of the Ku Klux Klan moved into town. In December, during the Jewish holiday of Hanukkah, a cinder block was thrown through the window of a small child's bedroom, where a holiday menorah was displayed. Luckily, the child, Isaac, was in another room at the time. But the incident, following other threats to the tiny Jewish community, galvanized the city into action.

Led by the executive director of the Montana Association of Churches, the publisher of the *Billings Gazette* newspaper, and the chief of the Billings Police Department, together with Isaac's mother, Tammie Schnitzer, the city made available paper menorahs and encouraged residents of all faiths to display them prominently. The message to the haters: The Jews were no longer few in number. They now had thousands of allies. The minority had become the majority. The tables had been turned on the antisemites. In the end, those extremists vanished.

The police chief early on reacted to the hate mongers in Billings: "Silence is acceptance. These people are testing us. And if we do nothing, there's going to be more trouble. Billings should stand up and say, 'Harass one of us and you harass us all.'"[22]

Maybe the millennia-long search for the end of antisemitism is, in reality, as straightforward as that: communities of goodwill everywhere banding together and saying loudly to the world "Harass one of us and you harass us all."

At the end of the day, what are the four most important things to remember about confronting antisemitism?

First, it requires a swivel-headed approach. Antisemitism derives from multiple sources. It is not limited to the far right

22. Edwin Dobb, "When Anti-Semitism Showed Up, This Whole Town Responded," *Reader's Digest*, February 7, 2023, https://www.rd.com/article/town-stands-up-anti-semitism/.

or far left. It comes from both. It is rooted in radical Islam as well. And it can also appear in other guises. Antisemitism reinvents itself as needed, just as it contradicts itself when needed, to stay "in step" with the times.

Those who point the finger in only one direction are seeking to politicize antisemitism. That is neither serious nor helpful. Indeed, a member of Congress, Rashida Tlaib, tweeted just after the Jersey City tragedy in 2019, "White supremacy kills." When the murderous perpetrators turned out to be self-declared Black Hebrews, she deleted the tweet and lost interest in the identity of the assailants.

Second, never underestimate the durability, elasticity, irrationality, ingenuity, or lethality of antisemitism.

As has been said, it may be the world's oldest social pathology, dating back literally thousands of years. Countless numbers of Jews have been murdered—and millions more have been relentlessly persecuted, ghettoized, exiled, forcibly converted, and otherwise victimized—in the name of antisemitism.

Just because Jews in today's world may appear successful to outsiders, that is not a guarantor of security. Jews in Germany in the 1920s also seemed mainstreamed, or so they thought, yet within a decade they were the targets of a genocidal Nazi regime that outmaneuvered and replaced a liberal democratic government.

Third, antisemitism cannot be separated from the overall health of society. If antisemitism rises and, as a result, Jews feel a growing sense of vulnerability and threat, then, history has amply shown, it represents a clear and present danger for liberal democracy as a whole. The ultimate targets are likely to include other minority groups, the tapestry of pluralism, the belief in the inherent dignity of each individual, and the very quest for human freedom and equality.

And fourth, antisemitism is not a Jewish problem for Jews to solve. It is a non-Jewish problem, millennia in the making, for non-Jews to solve, if, that is, there is the will and determination to do so.

Meanwhile, as has been the story throughout recorded history, and notwithstanding the endless minefields, the majority of Jews will continue to embrace their faith, affirm their identity with pride, take comfort in the outsized contributions of the Jewish people to the moral foundation and intellectual advancement of Western civilization, and look to the future with undiminished hope.

RECOMMENDED READING

American Jewish Committee. "Translate Hate." Accessed April 22, 2025. https://www.ajc.org/translatehate#uncovering-antisemitism.

Baddiel, David. *Jews Don't Count*. Harper Collins, 2021.

Carroll, James. *Constantine's Sword: The Church and the Jews*. Houghton Mifflin, 2002.

Cohn, Norman. *Warrant for Genocide: The Myth of the Jewish World Conspiracy and the Protocols of the Elders of Zion*. Serif, 2006.

Dawidowicz, Lucy. *The War against the Jews: 1933–1945*. Bantam, 1991.

Laqueur, Walter. *The Changing Face of Anti-Semitism: From Ancient Times to the Present Day*. Oxford University Press, 2008.

Lipstadt, Deborah. *Antisemitism: Here and Now*. Schocken Books, 2018.

Lipstadt, Deborah. *Denial: Holocaust on Trial*. Harper Collins, 2016.

Meddeb, Abdelwahab, and Benjamin Stora, eds. *A History of Jewish-Muslim Relations: From the Origins to the Present Day*. Princeton University Press, 2013.

Nirenberg, David. *Anti-Judaism: The Western Tradition*. W. W. Norton, 2013.

Rich, Dave. *Everyday Hate: How Antisemitism Is Built into Our World—And How You Can Change It*. Biteback, 2023.

Samuels, Maurice. *Alfred Dreyfus: The Man at the Center of the Affair (Jewish Lives)*. Yale University Press, 2024.

Small, Charles A. *Global Antisemitism: A Crisis of Modernity*. Martinus Nijhoff, 2013.

Tibi, Bassam. *Islamism and Islam*. Yale University Press, 2012.

Weiss, Bari. *How to Fight Anti-Semitism*. Crown, 2019.

Wiesel, Elie. *Night*. Penguin Books, 2008.

Wistrich, Robert S. *Antisemitism: The Longest Hatred*. Schocken Books, 1991.

Wistrich, Robert S. *A Lethal Obsession: Anti-Semitism from Antiquity to the Global Jihad*. Random House, 2010.

Wyman, David. *The Abandonment of the Jews: America and the Holocaust, 1941–1945*. New Press, 2007.

INDEX

For the benefit of digital users, indexed terms that span two pages (e.g., 52–53) may, on occasion, appear on only one of those pages.